Against High-Caste Polygamy

AMERICAN ACADEMY OF RELIGION

RELIGION IN TRANSLATION

SERIES EDITOR
John Nemec, University of Virginia
A Publication Series of
The American Academy of Religion
and
Oxford University Press

PRELUDE TO THE MODERNIST CRISIS
The "Firmin" Articles of Alfred Loisy
Edited, with an Introduction by C. J. T. Talar
Translated by Christine Thirlway

DEBATING THE DASAM GRANTH
Robin Rinehart

THE FADING LIGHT OF ADVAITA ĀCĀRYA
Three Hagiographies
Rebecca J. Manring

THE UBIQUITOUS ŚIVA
Somānanda's Śivadṛṣṭi and His Tantric Interlocutors
John Nemec

PLACE AND DIALECTIC
Two Essays by Nishida Kitarō
Translated by John W.M. Krummel and Shigenori Nagatomo

THE PRISON NARRATIVES OF JEANNE GUYON
Ronney Mourad and Dianne Guenin-Lelle

DISORIENTING DHARMA
Ethics and the Aesthetics of Suffering in the Mahābhārata
Emily T. Hudson

THE TRANSMISSION OF SIN
Augustine and the Pre-Augustinian Sources
Pier Franco Beatrice
Translated by Adam Kamesar

FROM MOTHER TO SON
The Selected letter of Marie de l'Incarnation to Claude Martin
Translated and with Introduction and Notes by Mary Dunn

DRINKING FROM LOVE'S CUP
Surrender and Sacrifice in the Vārs *of Bhai Gurdas*
Selections and Translations with Introduction and Commentary by Rahuldeep Singh Gill

THE AMERICA'S FIRST THEOLOGIES
Early Sources of Post-Contact Indigenous Religion
Edited and translated by Garry Sparks, with Sergio Romero and Frauke Sachse

GODS, HEROES, AND ANCESTORS
An Interreligious Encounter in Eighteenth-Century Vietnam
Anh Q. Tran

POETRY AS PRAYER IN THE SANSKRIT HYMNS OF KASHMIR
Hamsa Stainton

THE UBIQUITOUS ŚIVA VOLUME II
Somānanda's Śivadṛṣṭi and His Tantric Interlocutors
John Nemec

FIRST WORDS, LAST WORDS
New Theories for Reading Old Texts in Sixteenth-Century India
Yigal Bronner and Lawrence McCrea

THE LUMINOUS WAY TO THE EAST
Texts and History of the First Encounter of Christianity with China
Matteo Nicolini-Zani

RELIGIOUS READING AND EVERYDAY LIVES IN DEVOTIONAL HINDUISM
Emilia Bachrach

JEWISH PIETY IN ISLAMIC JERUSALEM
The Lamentations Commentary of Salmon ben Yeruhim
Jessica Andruss

AGAINST HIGH-CASTE POLYGAMY
An Annotated Translation
Ishvarchandra Vidyasagar, Translated by Brian A. Hatcher

Against High-Caste Polygamy

A Colonial-Era Appeal to Abolish Kulinism in Bengal
An Annotated Translation

ISHVARCHANDRA VIDYASAGAR,
TRANSLATED BY BRIAN A. HATCHER

OXFORD
UNIVERSITY PRESS

OXFORD
UNIVERSITY PRESS

Oxford University Press is a department of the University of Oxford. It furthers the University's objective of excellence in research, scholarship, and education by publishing worldwide. Oxford is a registered trade mark of Oxford University Press in the UK and certain other countries.

Published in the United States of America by Oxford University Press
198 Madison Avenue, New York, NY 10016, United States of America.

Library of Congress Cataloging-in-Publication Data
Names: Vidyasagar, Ishvarchandra, 1820–1891, author. |
Hatcher, Brian A. (Brian Allison), translator.
Title: Against high-caste Polygamy : A Colonial-Era Appeal to Abolish Kulinism in Bengal / an annotated translation by Brian A. Hatcher.
Other titles: Bahubibāha rahita haoẏā ucita ki na. English.
Description: 1. | New York : Oxford University Press, 2023. |
Series: AAR religion in translation |
Includes bibliographical references and index. |
Includes Quotqtions in Sanskrit and Bengali, romanized.
Identifiers: LCCN 2023006082 (print) | LCCN 2023006083 (ebook) |
ISBN 9780197675908 (hardback) | ISBN 9780197675915 (epub)
Subjects: LCSH: Non-monogamous relationship—India. | Non-monogamous relationship—India—West Bengal. | Kulins—India—West Bengal—Marriage customs and rites. | Widows—Legal status, laws, etc.—India. | Widows—Legal status, laws, etc.—India—West Bengal. | Polygamy—Law and legislation—India. | Polygamy—Religious aspects—Hinduism.
Classification: LCC HQ980.5.I4 B5313 2023 (print) | LCC HQ980.5.I4 (ebook) | DDC 306.84/23095414—dc23/eng/20230302
LC record available at https://lccn.loc.gov/2023006082
LC ebook record available at https://lccn.loc.gov/2023006083

DOI: 10.1093/oso/9780197675908.001.0001

Printed by Integrated Books International, United States of America

In loving memory of Ann and George

. . . parce qu'elle y a sa place réservée et immuable comme une mosaïque.

Marcel Proust

Contents

Preface ix
Note on the Text and Translation xi

Introduction 1

Against High-Caste Polygamy: The English Translation 45
Author's Notice 45
Against High-Caste Polygamy 48
Conclusion 87
Appendices 89
Supplement One 93
Supplement Two 96
Conclusion to the Second Supplement 110

Supporting Evidence 113
Notes 127
Glossary: English to Sanskrit/Bengali 151
Glossary: Sanskrit/Bengali to English 155
Bibliography 159
Index 167

Preface

Having previously translated Ishvarchandra Vidyasagar's epochal work promoting Hindu widow marriage, I had long contemplated the idea of tackling his other major intervention on the issue of high-caste polygamy. It was the occasion of his 200th birth anniversary in 2019–2020 that got me started, with crucial inspiration arriving in the form of an invitation to deliver a keynote address for the Asiatic Society of Bengal in September 2019. It is only appropriate that I begin by thanking Satyabrata Chakrabarty, general secretary of the Asiatic Society, for the invitation to speak. My plan at the time was to return to Kolkata in the spring of 2020 to enjoy the conclusion of year-long celebrations marking Vidyasagar's birth, but the global pandemic changed everything. During the subsequent long months of lockdown, it was the work of translation that gave me both solace and a sense of purpose.

Work on this book has benefitted from the assistance and encouragement of many friends and colleagues, notably Jyoti Atwal, Arun Bandyopadhyay, Milinda Banerjee, Sharbani Banerjee, Abhijit Bhattacharya, Sumit Chakrabarti, Aishika Chakraborty, Deepra Dandekar, Kamalika Mukherjee, Tapan Paul, Sarah Pinto, Parimala V. Rao, Rajat Sanyal, Subir Sarkar, and Bart Scott. I want to offer special thanks to Malavika Karlekar and Mandar Mukherjee for sharing materials from their family histories and from their own research into the lives of Kulin women in colonial Bengal. I am grateful as well for invitations I received to speak about the text, not least from Mahitosh Mandal and Priyanka Das in the Department of English at Presidency University; Koral Dasgupta of TMYS.org; Shuvatri Dasgupta and Alok Oak in the Centre for Research in the Arts, Social Sciences and Humanities at the University of Cambridge; and Swati Guha, director of the Institute of Language Studies and Research in Kolkata. I also would like to thank Semanti Ghosh for offering me the opportunity to present some of my ideas in *Anandabazar Patrika*. Needless to say, none of the aforementioned individuals and institutions should be held accountable for what I offer here.

John Nemec was kind enough to consider *Against High-Caste Polygamy* for inclusion in AAR's *Religion in Translation* Series. I was delighted when the book was eventually recommended to Cynthia Read at Oxford University

Press. Like so many others, Cynthia played an important role in shaping my academic career, and I wish to congratulate her on her tenure as executive editor. Moving forward, the project was carefully stewarded by Theo Calderara, Alex Rouch, Steve Wiggins, and Madison Zickgraf. My thanks to Katherine Ulrich for the index. I would like to thank Hemalatha Arumugam for managing production of the volume.

Amid all the pain and loss occasioned by the COVID-19 pandemic, my spirits and my work were sustained by all these friends, colleagues, and institutions. Even though the translation arrives too late for the 200th anniversary celebrations, I hope it may nonetheless kindle renewed interest in the complex and contested legacy of a remarkable individual.

Note on the Text and Translation

Against High-Caste Polygamy offers a complete, annotated translation of Ishvarchandra Vidyasagar's first book arguing against the practice of high-caste Kulin marriage in Bengal. The translation is based on the text of the first edition of *Bahuvivaha rahita haoya uchita ki na etadvishayaka vichara*, published by the Sanskrit Press in 1871 (Samvat 1928)—henceforth simply *Bahuvivaha*.[1] I have relied on the version of the text as found in the second volume of Gopal Haldar's *Vidyasagar-rachanasamgraha*, as well as on a digitized version of the 1871 first edition available online.[2]

Later that same year Vidyasagar published a second edition of the text, also from the Sanskrit Press (see Illustration 2). The second edition poses some curious problems. For one thing, the text of the second edition is shorter than that of the first edition.[3] What the later edition omits is the second of two Supplements (*krorapatra*) and the brief Conclusion (*upasamhara*) as found in the first edition. I construe the role of the Conclusion in the first edition as something like a Conclusion to the Second Supplement, rather than to the work as a whole; readers will see that Vidyasagar had already provided a Conclusion prior to the Appendices. As readers will also see, the Second Supplement takes up criticism of two of Vidyasagar's close associates, Taranath Tarkavacaspati and Dwarkanath Vidyabhushan. My suspicion is—given Vidyasagar's tense and contentious relationship with the former—that he may have chosen to omit this material in the second edition in order to avoid the appearance of being uncharitable.[4] In any case, what the first edition reveals is a fluid moment when Vidyasagar both presented his original proposal to the public and also incorporated some of the earliest responses to it in the original work. This is what makes the first edition so interesting to translate.

To my knowledge there has been only one other scholarly translation of *Bahuvivaha* into a European language, which is the 2014 French translation of France Bhattacharya. That translation is not widely known; more importantly Bhattacharya chooses to omit important portions of the first edition, not least the Appendices and Supplements. The present translation is intended to make the entirety of the first edition available to English-language readers.

It bears noting at the outset that this is not the only work Vidyasagar composed on the topic of Kulin polygamy. In 1873 he published a second book under the same title, to which he merely added the subtitle, "Book Two" (*dvitiya pustaka*). If I choose not to translate that second book, it is for three reasons. To begin with, the first of the two books (translated here) coheres as a stand-alone volume, right from the Author's Notice to its final Appendices and Supplements; it does not gesture toward, nor depend upon, Book Two. Second, as readers will discover, the first book displays several characteristics that make it highly significant from a political, moral, and historical perspective. These I address in the Introduction. The same cannot be said for Book Two. The latter certainly showcases Vidyasagar's gift for irony, but it remains narrow in its focus, seeking to refute in turn the views of five pundits who opposed Vidyasagar's views. This brings us to the third reason for not translating Book Two: with its extensive quotation from, and review of, scriptural passages—not to mention its occasional *ad hominem* arguments—Book Two remains far less accessible to a non-specialist reader.

By contrast, *Bahuvivaha*, or as I translate it, *Against High-Caste Polygamy*, may be read with great profit by non-specialist readers. It also has a variety of gifts to offer specialists, not least scholars of Dharmashastra, historians of Anglo-Indian law, and scholars interested in religion, gender, caste, and social reform in the colonial era. But since my overall goal is to help the text speak to non-specialist readers, I have done away with Sanskrit diacritical marks in all but a few cases. Specialists should have no trouble identifying the respective Sanskrit or Bengali originals. In a similar vein, I have chosen not to include transliterated versions of the Sanskrit texts cited by Vidyasagar. Most of these he translated into Bengali for the benefit of his readers, and I translate his Bengali versions wherever possible. Where he does not provide a Bengali translation of his own, I have provided my own or quoted from an available scholarly translation. As for the Sanskrit passages themselves, many are drawn from texts like *Manu-smriti* that are widely accessible in Sanskrit and English translation.[5] In any case, general readers are likely to be less concerned about issues of textual provenance than about the interpretive issues at the heart of Vidyasagar's argument.

In the interest of enhancing overall readability, I have on occasion translated more intentionally toward English usage, rather than seeking to retain literal accuracy. For instance, where Vidyasagar writes "this land" I have preferred "our land"; I believe that whether he refers to Bengal specifically or India more generally, it is clear he addresses a public with shared sensibilities. In some cases I have been a bit more aggressive, not least by making some minor structural revisions to the text. In one instance, this has involved adding explanatory rubrics to the titles of each of the seven sections of the main text, which are just numbered "objections" in the original. In other places, I enumerate successive points made by Vidyasagar within lengthy passages in the hope of revealing the overall structure of his claims. In rare instances, I have added a paragraph break to assist with readability. All of these more aggressive emendations are indicated in the accompanying notes.

When considering the text, readers should bear in mind that Vidyasagar was a Sanskrit scholar writing amid the ebb and flow of public opinion and official policy. He tended to work rapidly and could not always be bothered to provide detailed textual citations. Often he provides no more than the name of an author such as Manu or the title of a text like the *Udvahatattva*; in such cases I have introduced more substantive references. In the interest of economy, I have omitted any of his original footnotes that merely duplicate information he has already provided within the text. All footnotes are Vidyasagar's; all endnotes are my own.

Beyond this, I have risked one substantial revision to the original text. There are times when Vidyasagar interrupts the flow of his argument by inserting large blocks of evidence; this might include a genealogical list, statistical data on polygamous marriages, or the names of co-signatories on petitions. For the general reader these interruptions can be jarring and tend to distract attention from the flow of his argument. I have therefore decided to relocate such evidence to a section of my own creation, entitled Supporting Evidence; this can be found following the main text. Any material relocated here has been identified within the body of the main text by a bracketed insertion (e.g., [*2.1]) that serves to direct readers to the appropriate section in the Supporting Evidence. My intention is not to suggest that this evidence is of no importance; to the contrary, it is vitally important, and I comment on the significance of the empirical data in the Introduction. However, I believe readers primarily interested in assessing Vidyasagar's review of arguments for and against Kulin polygamy may easily skip over this information without any loss of meaning; at the same time it all remains easily accessible in the Supporting Evidence.

When it came to providing a title for this translation, my goal was to avoid a cumbersome literal translation such as, "An examination into whether or not polygamy should be abolished." That said, the one virtue of the original title is that it reminds us that the present work originated in a moment when the nature and validity of Kulin practice were open for debate. The phrase "whether or not" in the original title might make it appear as if Vidyasagar hoped to provide an even-handed examination (*vichara*) of the matter. That is not the case. Instead, he makes a compelling argument for government intervention to abolish a practice he considers both degraded and degrading. He does not ask whether polygamy should be banned; he pleads for it to be banned.[6] The title, *Against High-Caste Polygamy*, aims to make Vidyasagar's position clear from the outset. If I have taken the liberty of adding the words "high-caste" it is simply to underscore a point made by Vidyasagar himself: this is not a wholesale indictment of polygamy. Instead, *Bahuvivaha* offers a focused analysis and forceful repudiation of Kulin polygamy among Brahmins and Kayasthas in the Hindu communities of Bengal.[7]

Even if Vidyasagar's opinion is clear, I encourage readers to bear in mind the structuring conceit of *vichara*, or examination, since it reminds us how Vidyasagar went about his work. In *Bahuvivaha* he proceeds in pundit-like fashion to raise and then answer a series of objections commonly made by opponents of efforts to abolish polygamy. This dimension of the text constitutes one more reason *Bahuvivaha* merits our attention. No less than in his earlier two tracts on Hindu widow marriage—known in brief as *Vidhava-vivaha*—in *Bahuvivaha* Vidyasagar offers a vivid illustration of the way a traditionally trained Sanskrit scholar repurposed the argumentative tools of classical Hinduism to promote reflection on a question of modern social change.[8]

However, the tools employed by Vidyasagar in *Bahuvivaha* go beyond the merely exegetical and hermeneutical. *Bahuvivaha* is a different sort of work than *Vidhava-vivaha*, and one of my goals in translating the text is to invite readers to take the time to appreciate what is distinctive here. The context, tone, and overall intent of *Bahuvivaha* speak to a different moment in colonial history, in the author's life, and in the framing of appeals to the colonial government. If *Vidhava-vivaha* sought to expand the options for Hindu widows to realize the possibilities of married life, *Bahuvivaha* seeks to abolish a system of marriage practices that in Vidyasagar's view offered no more than marriage in name alone. To make his point he engages in a wide range of strategies aimed to convince readers of the legitimacy of his argument. His investigative, exegetical, and rhetorical skills are displayed at their finest.

Introduction

> Our friends turn away, God turns away; our fathers and our brothers, too—even the heartless ones we call our husbands.
>
> —*Kulin-mahila-vilap* ["The Lament of the Kulin Woman"], Hemchandra Bandyopadhyay

To say that polygamy is a loaded term is an understatement. The United States alone harbors a troubling history of attempts to condemn the practice by equating it with barbarism and slavery. For instance, in 1862 Abraham Lincoln signed the Morrill Anti-Bigamy Act, which not only outlawed polygamy but struck a blow against the legal incorporation of Mormonism in Utah. His fellow Republicans—unable to find any real grounds in biblical Christianity for opposing Mormon marriage—simply likened it to "pagan" religious practice. Once polygamy was racialized as uncivilized and even "Asian," Mormons became the others against which a vision of white, Protestant America could be promulgated. Amid such rhetoric and legislation, the women involved in polygamous marriages went from being pitied as innocent victims to being framed as degenerate co-conspirators.[1]

Curiously, while anti-polygamy discourse in the United States pictured plural wives as willing participants in "Hindoo" error, when we look at contemporaneous debates around polygamy in nineteenth-century India, it is the woman-as-victim who occupies a central place. Far from lending her support to a socially deviant form of life, the Hindu woman married to a polygamous husband was regularly portrayed as a powerless and enfeebled prisoner. Her emancipation would perforce require the intervention of some noble friend, the celebrated *abala-bandhu*, or "friend of the weak." The most celebrated of such friends was Ishvarchandra Vidyasagar (1820–1891; see Illustration 1).[2] Enshrined in biography and public memory as an "ocean of compassion" (*karuna-sagar*), Vidyasagar is both renowned and revered for his efforts on behalf of child-brides, widows, and—as we find in *Against*

Against High-Caste Polygamy. Ishvarchandra Vidyasagar, Translated by Brian A. Hatcher, Oxford University Press.
 DOI: 10.1093/oso/9780197675908.003.0001

Illustration 1 Bust of Ishvarchandra Vidyasagar; photo by Brian A. Hatcher

High-Caste Polygamy—women trapped in marriages to men with as many as five, ten, or twenty other wives. As readers will learn, Kulin wives often led lives of loneliness, ostracism, and deprivation; many rarely saw, and scarcely knew, their husbands.

No less than in the United States at this time, reformist projects like Vidyasagar's campaign to abolish high-caste polygamy were embedded in and framed by notions of civilization and progress. However, we find in Vidyasagar no simple acquiescence with hegemonic colonialist conjurings of "oriental paganism." Vidyasagar's campaign does not turn on an indictment of "Hindoo" inferiority, but in fact strives to define and recover true Hindu custom and practice, or *dharma*. This project depends not upon the othering of polygamy or polygamists per se; in fact, contexts and conditions for polygamy were recognized across communities in India, and elements of the practice were codified in Hindu law. Vidyasagar's project was not about the demonizing of Hindu custom but about asserting a particular kind of authority to correct it in the name of social improvement; his authority drew on a distinct blend of high-caste, Brahmanical learning and privilege; access to colonial-era developments in administration, education, and public-sphere debate; and finally, his direct experience of the colonial state's prior willingness to reform Indian social life. The complexities of such a project are evident; they take on even greater weight when one sees—as in the text translated here—evidence of the resistance of other Hindus to Vidyasagar's particular vision, not least the reluctance of the Bengali public to support pleas for further British legislative intervention. Clearly no straightforward parallel can be made with the American case; the anti-polygamy campaign in Bengal reveals itself as its own congeries of social, political, and religious forces. When one recognizes the further contextual frameworks of caste, community, gender, and patriarchy—not to mention the idiosyncratic character of Vidyasagar himself—one can appreciate that no less than in the United States, the limitations and aporias here are many.

Pursuing Reform in the Wake of Rebellion

Vidyasagar published the first of two books contesting high-caste polygamy in 1871, just fifteen years after his triumphant role in securing passage of the Hindu Widow's Remarriage Act (Act XV).[3] Both campaigns sought to intervene in Hindu customary life through a review of relevant literature on *dharma*. As such, it might be tempting to look for continuity between the two endeavors. However, in the decade and a half since passage of Act XV, India had witnessed considerable disruption, not least the violence, chaos, and political transformations associated with the Rebellion of 1857. Regardless of what historians might say about the causes of that conflict, in the wake of the Rebellion many British administrators became convinced it had been triggered by the East India Company's aggressive intervention in the religious life of Indians.[4] Almost overnight, official zeal waned for reformist intervention in religious and customary matters; caution became the word of the day.[5] At the same time, Indians themselves began to turn against the idea of seeking government assistance to promote social change. Even if the rhetoric of improvement, reform, and general welfare still suffused public discourse, Indian intellectuals now felt a greater need to shape the nature and character of reform. Thinking in particular about the case of high-caste (or Kulin) polygamy, the editors of one Bengali daily commented in 1864, "We would not uphold the custom, all that we say is let not the Government act injudiciously in interfering, but let the more enlightened of our countrymen rise and determine to put a stop to this pernicious habit."[6]

This comment helps us appreciate that by the 1860s India had crossed a kind of watershed. In retrospect, the age of robust reform prior to 1857 appears to have been a short-lived time of collaboration between Britons and Indians on a range of social issues, chiefly centered on the "women's question." To the fore were such issues as the banning of widow immolation, the prohibition of child marriage, and the promotion of widow marriage.[7] Vidyasagar was a product of this age of reform and one of its most celebrated exemplars. Educated in the Calcutta Government Sanskrit College, where he came to admire the legacy of British patrons like Horace Hayman Wilson, he would in time take up the reforming mantle of Rammohun Roy. The example of Rammohun's leading role in gaining government support for the abolition of widow immolation in 1829 surely struck him as a viable model by which to pursue the improvement of Indian society. His subsequent campaign on behalf of Hindu widow marriage and eventual passage of the Hindu Widow's Remarriage Act in 1856 could be seen as both a continuation of Rammohun's efforts and the very zenith of the age of reform.

This makes it all the more poignant to learn that by the time he drafted *Against High-Caste Polygamy*, Vidyasagar looked back on the era of Bentinck and lamented, "Those days are gone!"[8] The comment is important for at least two reasons. On the one hand, his remark was issued amid an extended debate with fellow Indians about the viability of continuing to request government assistance on matters of Indian social change. Many of his contemporaries were in harmony with the sentiments of the editor quoted above, and they felt confident that the steady spread of education would soon lead to the disappearance of unwanted customs. Vidyasagar disagreed. The success of Bentinck and Rammohun remained for him a kind of inspiration. On the other hand, Vidyasagar's lament over the passing of the age of reform can be read as proof of his almost quixotic belief that the British would once again deliver on their promise to promote the welfare of Indian people.[9] In this respect, his lament registers the almost desperate hope that fuels *Against High-Caste Polygamy*. And, of course, the ultimate failure of the anti-polygamy campaign to issue into any legislative action demonstrates how misplaced Vidyasagar's hope was. Stepping back, if there are grounds for reading the text today, they rest both on the opportunity to understand the distinctiveness of Vidyasagar's approach and on the chance to fathom something about him as a frustrated, but unbowed, proponent of change.[10]

Following the 1858 transfer of power from the East India Company to the British Crown, India entered the era of high colonial rule, a full-blown age of empire that led to the wholesale transformation of India's economy, the flaring of European racism, and—in due course—the first expressions of Indian culturalist and nationalist self-assertion.[11] Beginning in the 1860s and 1870s, there was a corresponding rise in print-based, public-sphere organizing by a range of Indian actors eager to promote such goals as the protection of Hinduism or the celebration of Aryan-Vedic culture.[12] One galvanizing development, in the very moment Vidyasagar was preparing his proposal to ban polygamy, was public debate around the legislative initiative that would be known as the Brahmo Marriage Act (Act III of 1872). Advanced by the progressive wing of the Brahmo Samaj, this new legislation offered the option of a civil marriage to parties not claiming membership in the Hindu, Muslim, Jewish, Christian, Jain, Parsi, Buddhist, or Sikh communities. The final Act also prohibited child marriage and polygamy, while giving further sanction to widow marriage. There was considerable contention and petitioning around this issue, even among the divided Brahmo community itself. The initiative was passed into law, and one might wonder whether passage of Act III put a kind of seal over British desire to intervene further in such matters.[13]

For many readers the year 1872 will also resonate as the year the British completed the first Indian Census. Along with changes in legislative initiatives, the introduction of the census reminds us of how the imperial state was expanding its arsenal of tools for mapping, measuring, and ultimately governing India. Publication of *Against High-Caste Polygamy* happened just one year before publication of new census data, a fact I find noteworthy, as I will demonstrate below. Suffice it to say, in this text Vidyasagar demonstrates that he too had come to appreciate the utility of presenting empirical data as a tool for shaping public opinion.[14] In this respect, *Against High-Caste Polygamy* reveals clear affinities with an age that was beginning to harness the potential—for colonizer and colonized alike—of new epistemologies framed by such modern disciplines as history, sociology, and statistical science.[15]

For Vidyasagar, the years since 1857 had been eventful on a personal level as well. Toward the end of 1858, at the age of thirty-eight, he resigned from his position as principal of the Sanskrit College; he would never hold another official position. Nonetheless, his energies continued unabated in a wide range of other areas, from writing and publishing, to new journalistic endeavors, as well as a leadership role at the Metropolitan Institution, which affiliated with the University of Calcutta in 1864. One must marvel that amid such extensive and time-consuming endeavors he also managed to volunteer considerable energy and income to famine and malaria relief, to take up an intensive interest in promoting and practicing homeopathic medicine, to provide financial support for widow marriages, and to see his own daughters married.[16] The social, familial, and economic strain wrought by his efforts to promote widow marriage alone was enormous. He often faced resistance from local communities, not to mention his own family members; among others, his wife was distraught when he consented to their son's decision to marry a widow.[17]

The stresses and disappointments were continuous and considerable, and his general health had never been robust; he struggled over the years with chronic and debilitating ailments like dysentery. To make matters worse, in 1866, while escorting a visiting educational reformer to various sites around Calcutta, he was seriously injured in a carriage accident—an event some biographers have seen as the root cause of the conditions that would eventually lead to his death.[18] Then, in February of 1871, he received news that his father, who had been living in Varanasi, had suffered a change in health. Vidyasagar made the long trip to Varanasi and remained there until his father recovered his health. No sooner had he returned to Calcutta than his mother passed away. That was in April. Stricken with grief and struggling with his own poor health, Vidyasagar sought a change of air in the quieter environs of Kashipur (Cossipore) on the Hooghly River north of Calcutta. While staying there he performed the necessary postmortem rituals for his mother and committed himself to a full year of mourning, denying himself many pleasures and living on just a single meal a day of rice and vegetables.[19]

This is the place and the moment in which Vidyasagar compiled *Against High-Caste Polygamy*; readers will note that the Author's Notice was signed from Kashipur in the summer of 1871. If I say the text was compiled, it is because for all that this is an original work with a clear authorial stamp, it nonetheless bears the hallmarks of being cobbled together from a variety of materials, and apparently in a kind of desperate haste. Notable in his day for the care he took to footnote sources, Vidyasagar at one point confesses to his inability to provide proper citations for some of the key genealogical material

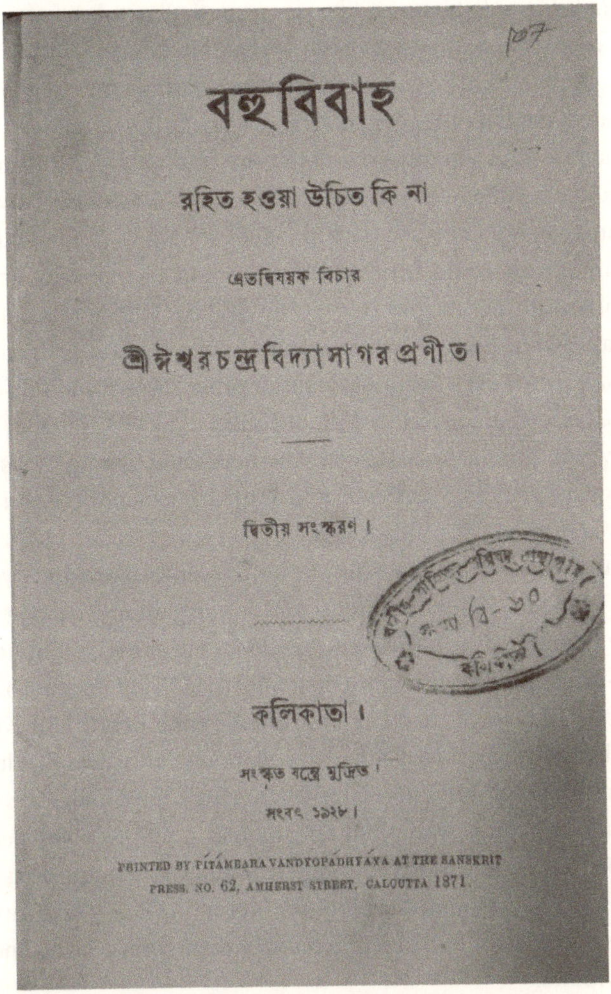

বহুবিবাহ

রহিত হওয়া উচিত কি না

এতদ্বিষয়ক বিচার

শ্রীঈশ্বরচন্দ্র বিদ্যাসাগর প্রণীত।

দ্বিতীয় সংস্করণ।

কলিকাতা।

সংস্কৃত যন্ত্রে মুদ্রিত।

সংবৎ ১৯২৮।

PRINTED BY PITAMBARA VANDYOPADHYAYA AT THE SANSKRIT PRESS, NO. 62, AMHERST STREET, CALCUTTA 1871.

Illustration 2 Title-page of the second edition of *Bahuvivaha* (1871); image courtesy of the Centre for Studies in Social Sciences, Calcutta

he drew upon. And the curious fashion in which the two Supplements and an additional Conclusion are appended to the text seem to suggest a process that resisted closure. The fact that the Second Edition would end up being shorter confirms that the creation of the original text had been something of a makeshift affair.

Vidyasagar and the Problem of Polygamy

Against High-Caste Polygamy addresses a particular subset of polygamous marriage as practiced among the highest castes in Bengal. This form of high-caste polygamy came to be known in English as Kulinism, from the term used to designate a person of high clan rank (in Sanskrit, *kulina*; see Illustration 3). Kulinism rests on a highly articulated and historically entrenched system of status and rank that—as readers will see from Vidyasagar's text—served to structure hypergamous marriage alliances among Brahmin and Kayastha caste communities. Kulinism could thus be said to represent an elite and highly marked social category in use among these two communities.[20] This means that *Against High-Caste Polygamy* is not a treatise against polygamy in general, nor is it even an indictment of other forms of Hindu polygamy as practiced elsewhere in South Asia. It comes to us instead from a charged moment when Kulinism in Bengal was becoming synonymous with the extremes of casteism in South Asia and something of a *cause célèbre* among progressive reformers like Vidyasagar.

Vidyasagar was born into a Kulin Brahmin family of the Bandyopadhyay surname. While his family did not practice polygamous marriages, he was intimately acquainted with the phenomenon. One of his childhood teachers was a Self-Broken Kulin with more than one wife.[21] There is reason to believe that as a boy Vidyasagar had been appalled by the practice of Kulin marriage, not least by the kinds of ritual and economic pressures that led certain Bengali Brahmin and Kayastha families to marry their daughters to highly ranked Kulin husbands who often already had multiple wives. As we shall see, Self-Broken Kulins like Vidyasagar's teacher were notorious for their willingness to take on multiple alliances, accepting more and more brides even as they grew older and older. Inevitably many young wives ended up as destitute widows.

Against High-Caste Polygamy attests to Vidyasagar's unflinching repudiation of this system. His sympathies were drawn to the many young girls and women who were trapped in wretched or abusive domestic situations; to those who—though married in name—never saw their husbands, let alone enjoyed anything like domestic happiness; to those young women whose elderly husbands inevitably died, leaving them widowed, abandoned, and impoverished; and to those desperate wives and widows who ended up being trafficked for sex. Vidyasagar does not shy away from highlighting the predatory behavior of greedy family members and the kinds of procurers who preyed on abandoned Kulin wives and widows. Readers of *Against High-Caste Polygamy* should also bear in mind how often Kulin women turned to suicide as their only escape from a life of certain misery.[22]

To say this is to remind readers that while a work like *Against High-Caste Polygamy* belongs in the general category of texts on Hindu social reform, it is not a text concerned with advancing a wholesale reformation within Hinduism. The focus here is on Kulinism. Vidyasagar rarely even refers to Hinduism *tout court*; his eyes remain fixed on the scriptural injunctions, customary practices, historical claims, and social conditions associated with Kulin marriage. The very narrowness of Vidyasagar's focus in this regard could be said to illustrate the limits of his own elitist vision of things: what concerns him are high-caste marriage practices. Not only does he not address marriage customs or gender roles found among low-caste communities, he is in some respects blind to the differences between high- and low-caste customary norms.[23] His vision belongs to an elite, Brahmanical, and essentially patriarchal moral universe. This has led some to argue that he was in fact ill-suited for—if not disinterested in—the pursuit of real, structural change in Hindu social life. The point is difficult to contest; Vidyasagar's positionality as a Brahmin pundit with immense enunciative power in traditional settings, as well as within the new colonial public sphere, outfitted him for only a limited course of action in relation to a limited range of women.[24]

Some might even suggest it is unwise to take the designation "reformer" too seriously when thinking about a figure like Vidyasagar. After all, to read the Conclusion of Book Two of his work on widow marriage is to hear the anxious pleas of a modern Brahmanical patriarch who is reluctant to grant complete autonomy to women.[25] In this respect, the obverse side of promoting the Hindu widow's right to marry was securing a kind of guarantee that she would not be able to live life on her own terms. This applied both to her sexuality and to her access to property, since one of the consequences of the Hindu Widows Remarriages Act (Act XV of 1856) was that remarried widows lost any claim to their deceased husband's property.[26] This is but another reminder of the contradictions of liberal reform, which in the end actually helped usher in new modalities of Hindu patriarchy.[27] Thus rather than crediting Vidyasagar with the reform of modern Hinduism, one could argue he played an important role in the consolidation of new, legally sanctioned—and yet not always improved—social roles for Hindu women.

I say "not always improved" in order to reserve a small space to acknowledge that in popular imagination as well as in some strands of feminist history, Vidyasagar is still celebrated as one of the earliest reformers—second only to Rammohun Roy—to draw public attention to the fraught status of women in Hindu society. Such praise is not entirely misplaced, even if it must be balanced against the ambiguities and failures mentioned above. The methods adopted by reformers like Vidyasagar, and the legal resolutions they sought, may not stand up to the tests we place on the protection of gender, sexuality, and personal life today. And yet, if figures like Rammohun and Vidyasagar are still celebrated, it is because of their basic commitment to resolving some of the manifest challenges faced by Hindu women. One might even credit Vidyasagar with promoting the recognition of Hindu women as human beings, moral agents, and valued members of society. He dared to point out—as few others had—that the nominally high ritual status of a Kulin woman did not necessarily translate into a life of either comfort or dignity.[28]

A parallel for thinking about Vidyasagar's approach to the reform of women's lives may be found in his own bourgeois pedagogy as enshrined in the vernacular schoolbooks he created. Today both the language and the values of books like *Varnaparichay* and *Nitibodha* tend to strike us as elitist and paternalistic; and yet few would challenge Vidyasagar's pioneering role in transforming, and expanding, the landscape of Bengali education. Perhaps the same may be said for his campaigns in relation to issues like child marriage, widow marriage, and polygamy. What merits our admiration, and our continued scholarly attention, is the fact of his having identified these issues as points of concern for both himself and for Bengali society more generally. We might take note of the fact that he was never one to shy away from proposing solutions, even if those solutions (whether or not they were realized in law or practice) may seem questionable or ill-considered to us today. To put this somewhat differently, what we can still admire today in Vidyasagar is his fundamental ethical commitment, even if this is limited or undercut by elements of his own Brahmanical heritage, male voice, or unsuccessful legislative proposals.

On the History and Practice of Kulinism

The discourse and practice of Kulinism in colonial Bengal is best viewed as the outgrowth of transformations reaching back nearly a millennium. While recovering this history is made difficult by the intermingling of mythic, legal, genealogical, and historical materials, I would like to sketch the broad shape of these developments. This will help readers appreciate the strictures and deprivations placed upon Kulin women in Vidyasagar's day, the terms by which he sought to mount his critique, and the level of resistance he and other reformers faced when setting out to put an end to the system.

While the roots of Kulin ideology can be traced to the postclassical era in Bengal, the largest corpus of textual evidence for Kulinism comes to us from only the past five hundred years or so. Most of this evidence is found in Brahmanical legal texts and high-caste genealogies. Bringing this literature into view and unpacking its symbolic and normative dimensions is an enormous task. One of the first comprehensive modern attempts was made by N. N. Basu in his early twentieth-century study of Bengali history, which drew on a wide range of genealogical literature from premodern Bengal.[29] A second important contribution was made in this direction by Ronald Inden in his 1976 *Marriage and Rank in Bengali Culture*. In response to the romantic nationalism of Basu, Inden sought to provide an account of both the cultural logic and the historical changes that had contributed to the rise of Bengali Kulinism.[30]

Inden demonstrated that the modern Kulin system developed through a series of stages, commencing with the rule of a mythical king named Vena. According to ancient texts like the Mahabharata, Vena was an evil ruler. One of his sins was to force his subjects to enter into marriages without regard for orthodox restrictions on marriage alliances and social class, or *varna* (which I translate as "class" rather than "caste"). Faced with the threat of class confusion (*varna-samkara*)—a major concern for orthodox Hinduism at least since the time of Manu and the Bhagavad-Gita—some Brahmins chose to kill Vena. They in turn produced a new ruler named Prithu, who then charged the Brahmins with re-establishing social order. When the Brahmins saw the chaotic state of *varna* mixing, they realized they were unable to restore the original four-class system of Brahmins, Kshatriyas, Vaishyas, and Shudras. When it came to Bengal, the best the Brahmins could do was to identify two broad class groups: Brahmins and Shudras. In this mythic account we find an etiology for the recognized fact that Bengali Hindu society effectively knows only these two broad classes, even if each is internally complicated by the further distinction between clean (*sat*) and unclean (*asat*) Shudras, each of whom provide ritual services to differently ranked Brahmin groups. The highest-ranking ritual pair of Brahmins and Shudras came to be known as Kulins. Thus the Kulin system enshrines a system of social ranking applicable to both Brahmins and clean Shudras, who are known in Bengal as Kayasthas.[31]

The actual articulation of Bengal's characteristic Kulin system depended on the alleged arrival of an in-migrating group of Brahmins from north India. This is said to have occurred following the era of Prithu, during the reign of a king named Adisura. Adisura is said to have been troubled by the lack of Vedic prowess among the Brahmins already residing in Bengal. And so tradition states that around 942 CE Adisura invited five Brahmins and five Shudras from Kanauj (Kanyakubja) in the fabled heartland of Brahminical culture.[32] The arrival of these Brahmins was essential for Adisura's plan to restore the legitimacy of his realm by restoring the practice of proper marriage alliances.[33] As for the previously existing Brahmin communities of Bengal, they came to be known as the Seven Hundred. And as Vidyasagar reminds us, they were looked down on by the descendants of Adisura's Brahmins. Sharing food or forming marriage alliances with the Seven Hundred was cause for social ostracism.[34]

As for the newcomers, they and their descendants were settled in a series of villages and became the "seed males" for Bengal's Kulin clans.[35] As readers will learn, the surnames (*gai*) adopted by these Brahmin families reflect the names of the eight villages (*grama*) where they settled: Bandya, Chatta, Mukhaiti, Ghoshal, Putitunda, Ganguli, Kanjilal, and Kundagrami. So, for instance, one of the original five Brahmins was Bhattanarayana. His son Varaha settled in the village of Bandyaghati, and his descendents carry the Bandya surname (*gai*). Vidyasagar was born into just such a family, his surname being Bandyopadhyay ("teacher of the Bandyas").

The defining moment in the articulation of Kulinism in Bengal came under the reign of Vallala Sena (r. 1158–79). By this point, there were said to be fifty-six sons of the original five Brahmins. Meanwhile, the socio-economic situation in Bengal had also been complicated by the fact other groups had begun to encroach upon the ritual and material entitlements granted by Adisura to the original Brahmin families. Vallala Sena's response was to set about evaluating Brahmins in terms of their clan status, or *kaulinya*. Proper establishment of Kulin rank would ensure the proper regulation of marriage alliances and the appropriate exchange of property.

In short, Vallala predicated Kulin status on Brahmanical conduct (*achara*).[36] The way he went about testing the conduct of Bengal's Brahmins can be seen from a vignette shared by Vidyasagar. He tells us that on the day when the new Kulin ranks were to be announced, Vallala invited the Brahmins to come to his court upon the completion of their daily rituals. Since a ruler's favor and patronage was highly coveted, it is easy to imagine that some Brahmins hastened to the court, expecting to bask in the munificence of the king. However, it turned out otherwise. In Vallala's estimation, the earliest arrivals had to be the most lax in terms ritual performance, while those who arrived after them were clearly more punctilious about worship. And so Vallala granted the highest grade of conduct to the latecomers.[37] Needless to say, this story backs up the claim that the highest Kulins were those who possessed all nine distinguishing attributes (*guna*) of *kaulinya*, or clan status. These attributes were said to be: conduct, humility, learning, fame, pilgrimage, faith, exchange, austerity, and generosity.

This is the moment we can begin to speak of Kulin rank as a special kind of status. In relation to the highest-ranked, or Mukhya Kulins, the others were given a descending range of ritual statuses: Shrotriyas, Vamshajas, and Aris.[38] For a newcomer to this material, the distinctions and terminology can be overwhelming, not least because further distinctions would arise even within groups like the Shrotriyas (as readers will see). Suffice it to say that in announcing a rule to distinguish between Kulins and other high-caste groups, Vallala set in place a system aimed at restricting the practice of marriage (i.e., the exchange of daughters) among graded clans.[39] Henceforth, the highest-grade Kulins would be allowed to accept daughters from lower-ranked groups like the Shrotriyas, but the high-ranking Kulins would be prohibited from giving their daughters to Shrotriyas.[40]

Vallala's scheme alerts us to the practice of hypergamy, and with hypergamy our attention shifts from the normative character of Brahmanical habitus to the ritualized practice of marriage. Within Vallala's nine-fold scheme, this is encapsulated in the concept of exchange (*avritti*). And it is with exchange that we come to the "essence" of Kulinism.[41] By most accounts it was during the reign of Vallala's son Lakshman Sena, that the principle of correct exchange in marriage gained precedence over all other matters of ritual prestige. In other words, "From this time onward Kulinism ceased to be based on personal qualification. It became hereditary."[42]

Vidyasagar notes in *Against High-Caste Polygamy* that "The chief mark of a Kulin is to give daughters to good Kulin homes and to receive daughters from good Kulin homes."[43] The colonial-era ethnologist H. H. Risley commented on the nexus between exchange and social rank, remarking that marriage outside the rule of Kulin exchange led to a loss of rank, while conversely the marriage of a young woman (*kanya*) into a Kulin family "conferred a sort of reflected honor" on the woman's entire family. From this idea developed what Risley called the "singular and artificial institution" known as Kulinism. He went on to say that it had "deranged" the "natural balance of the sexes" and precipitated intense competition for husbands among Kulin families.[44]

As it happened, Vallala Sena and his son Lakshmana Sena were the last great Hindu kings to rule over Bengal. After 1200 CE, the Sena dynasty gave way to new Muslim polities. And in this changing political landscape, high-caste groups needed new avenues for financial security. Some took official positions under the new rulers; some married into high-ranking Muslim families. However, from the vantage point of clan status, the practice of associating with non-Hindus (known in Sanskrit as *yavana* or *mleccha*) raised concerns. Attention turned again to the regulation of high-caste marriages. And if the material welfare of high-caste communities remained an issue, then this gave new salience to the question of rank. By virtue of possessing *kaulinya*, Kulin grooms found that they represented a valuable commodity. Ronald Inden reviewed a range of genealogical texts from this period and concluded that a newfound emphasis on marriage gifts had "marvelous effects" on the material wellbeing of Kulin families.[45] In a market context, poorer Kulin families with eligible grooms saw the benefits of marrying those grooms to multiple wives, each of whom brought new wealth to the family.[46] This combination of clan pride and concern for profit would remain a central feature of Kulinism down to Vidyasagar's day.

Another consequence of the passing away of centralized Hindu kingship in Bengal after 1200 CE was the proliferation of a range of smaller Hindu rulers, none of whom actually possessed the authority to enforce regulations around Brahmin and Kayastha marriage. Instead, what developed was the institution of regional councils (*samaja*). These served the purpose of advancing and protecting the prerogatives of various classes and their subcastes. These councils took guidance from a group known broadly as genealogists, or *ghatakas*.[47] In time the genealogists—with their digests of clan lore and marriage regulations—would become the arbiters of *kaulinya*.[48]

Some two centuries after Vallala Sena, a particularly renowned genealogist (*ghataka*) by the name of Devivara is said to have determined that the Kulin families of Bengal were guilty of various ritual faults (*dosha*). Rather than simply relegating all these families to the lower status of Vamshaja—which would have outright destroyed Kulin rank—Devivara chose to promulgate a new classification of rank based precisely on the evidence of such faults. According to his system, families who retained Kulin status were arranged in thirty-six assemblages, or *mela*.[49] Membership in an assemblage was determined by the presence of certain ritual faults.[50] Henceforth, each assemblage would operate as an endogamous group, with families in any given assemblage arranging marriages in a reciprocal fashion. This put an end to an earlier ideal of generalized or "mutual" (*sarvadvari*) marriage exchange among Kulins. Readers will see that Vidyasagar actually traces the real degradation of Kulinism to this moment, which marked the closing of *sarvadvari* marriage. The pain induced by the "shackles of Melism" (to use the coinage of more recent commentators) was still evident well into the late twentieth century.[51]

To appreciate the pressures wrought by Devivara's "shackles," it helps to offer a hypothetical example. Suppose one assemblage (*mela*) was composed of Mukhaiti, Chatta, and Bandya families. And suppose that at a given moment there was only a single eligible groom among the Mukhaitis. Now what if, in addition, there happened to be ten marriageable women among the Chatta and Bandya families? In essence, the Mukhaiti family would be obliged to marry all ten women to the single eligible groom.[52] As if this were not enough, many high-grade Kulins had by this time lost their rank through improper marriage alliances. They came to be known as Broken Kulins (*bhanga kulin*; also "Self-Broken," *svakrita-bhanga*). The rise in Broken Kulin families led to a concomitant decrease in the number of available high-grade grooms. Under such circumstances and amid such ritual prescriptions, polygamy was inevitable. This led the colonial ethnologist Risley to remark archly that Kulin hypergamy did not mean "marriage in a higher rank" as much as it meant "too much marriage."[53]

Illustration 3 Kulin Brahman, Eastern Bengal; image courtesy of the British Library

We are fortunate to have a compelling account of the life of a Kulin bride from Vidyasagar's own day, as found in the self-narrative of Nistarini Debi. Nistarini Debi was a Kulin woman from Hooghly District who was born in 1832. She was married sometime in her teens and seems to have become a widow already by the time she turned twenty. Much later in life, destitute and confined to an *ashram* in Varanasi (where many widows were dispatched by their families), she dictated a frank account of the harsh realities of her life in a Kulin Brahmin family.[54]

Since one of my goals in translating *Against High-Caste Polygamy* is to call attention to what I will refer to as Vidyasagar's ethic of recognition, I find it significant that Malavika Karlekar comments on the widespread blindness among nineteenth-century Kulin families when it came to the straitened lives of their daughters, sisters, and wives.[55] Vidyasagar's desire to bring Kulin women into view reflects his awareness of this blindness. He knew all too well that few of these women ever lived in their husbands' homes. Instead, they remained under the watchful eye of their natal kin. While their fathers could satisfy themselves that they had arranged a ritually sanctioned marriage, the brides rarely shared domestic life with their partners. As Karlekar notes, given the foregrounding of the "commercial and transactional" dimensions of Kulin marriage, little thought was given to the ordinary joys of conjugal marriage, child-bearing, or the raising of a family.[56]

Accounts like Nistarini Debi's also remind us of the systemic hold of Kulin customs. That structural logic is nicely summarized by Aishika Chakraborty, who notes that within a hypergamous system, marriage is the chief mechanism for upward mobility. If a mid-rank Shrotriya or lower-ranking Vamshaja family has sufficient resources, they may purchase a high-ranking Kulin son-in-law and enjoy a rise in ritual prestige. By contrast, women from high-ranking Kulin families cannot marry down without their families suffering socially. If their families have no material means, high-ranking women might therefore remain unmarried. Meanwhile men from Kulin ranks were free to marry women from lower ranks and were often induced to do so by the wealth lower-ranking families were willing to sacrifice for a concomitant gain in honor.[57]

Most notorious in this regard were the aforementioned Broken Kulins, who had lost their clan rank through a failure to abide by the norms of marriage exchange.[58] As Chakraborty puts it, Broken Kulins turned marriage into an "occupation," being ever ready to sell their ritual status to women from any rank, Kulin, Shrotriya, or Vamshaja.[59] In Nistarini Debi's case, various exigencies had led her father to marry her to a Broken Kulin. Her new husband came from an impoverished family, which helps explains why he had already by this time married more than thirty women.[60] As it turned out, he only visited his wife's home on two occasions, and in both cases money was the inducement. Nistarini Debi's story helps account for the disgust Vidyasagar felt toward his own Broken Kulin teacher.

What emerges is a pattern in which fathers negotiated their daughters' marriages like business deals.[61] Nor were the grooms any different. Kulin grooms seem to have thought of their wives as symbolic and material assets and little else. The material factor was far from insignificant. Kulin husbands moved regularly from one village to another, wherever they might have a wife, collecting gifts from their various in-laws, before moving on to the next village. Meanwhile their brides passed their lonely lives in the homes of maternal uncles. They were often viewed as little more than another mouth to feed and often became objects of resentment. Their basic lot in life was one of ostracism, if not outright neglect and abuse.

An Ethics of Recognition

I like to think of Vidyasagar's approach to the problem of Kulin polygamy as being driven by an ethics of recognition. Elsewhere I have argued that this ethic of recognition can be seen operating in a wide range of his writings, from overtly reformist works like *Hindu Widow Marriage* to books intended for use in school curricula, such as *Shakuntala*.[62] Despite the very different character of such works, in each of them Vidyasagar can be seen to foreground the need for recognition. Whether asking Bengalis to confront the consequences of the high-caste prohibition on widow marriage, or inviting readers to feel the pain of Shakuntala's rejection by a husband who does not recognize her, Vidyasagar highlights the need to see things as they really are. Drawing on his unique skills as a pundit, storyteller, and school-book author, he seems committed to pressing one fundamental demand: the need to recognize the plight of Hindu women, and widows in particular.[63] Nowhere is this demand stated more directly than in the lines with which he concludes the second book of *Hindu Widow Marriage*:

> Alas, people of India! For how much longer will you lay prostrate on a bed of delusion? Open your eyes just once so you can see how this blessed land of India is carried away by an evil tide of prostitution and abortion. You need only ask why.[64]

If in Kalidasa's drama Dushyanta is unable to recognize his own wife, Shakuntala, in *Hindu Widow Marriage* Vidyasagar suggests that the Bengali public is similarly cursed not to see the plight of its own daughters, sisters, wives, and widows. And yet, unlike in the story of Shakuntala, Vidyasagar suggests that lifting the curse of non-recognition depends on no secret token, no *deus ex machina*. All his fellow Bengalis need to do is open their eyes to the prevailing social situation. The words quoted above, coming as they do at the end of a dense exercise in scriptural exegesis, suddenly make what had appeared like an abstruse and legalistic exercise seem not only straightforward, but attainable. Bengalis need only open their eyes and ears.[65]

While it is taken as axiomatic that Vidyasagar's concern for women and widows was grounded in his *sui generis* compassion and pity, I believe it is important to shift our attention away from the satisfying comforts of quasi-hagiography to do the necessary work of unpacking his life's work in relation to the kind of moral vision that guided it.[66] In other words, we are not simply talking about one man's incredible pity. Vidyasagar's efforts in the areas of education, reform, and philanthropy all point to a consistent ethical project. We might even say that his ethical project seeks (to borrow Rosemary Hennesey's terms) to "translate the collective, lived experience of social injustice into ways of knowing that are psychologically, politically, and structurally transformative."[67]

That the simple act of recognition is the key to a transformed way of knowing is evident even in Vidyasagar's translation of Shakespeare's "Comedy of Errors" (*Bhrantivilasa*). There the entire text is an extended play on mistaken identities and on the consequences that follow from the failure of recognition. The same concern colors Vidyasagar's posthumously published autobiography. In that text, he explores the consequences that flow from people failing to recognize others (as when his grandfather Ramjay roams through Birsingha disguised in the garb of a sannyasi) as well as the redemptive potential of simple acts of recognition (as when a poor widow, noticing Vidyasagar's father is hungry and penniless, revives him with food and drink).[68] The consistency with which the theme of (mis)recognition recurs in Vidyasagar's writings supports the idea that his ethics, his pedagogy, and his social work are all aimed at helping people see one another.[69]

That said, it cannot be denied that Vidyasagar's ethic of recognition remained a limited one. By this I mean to say that the Bengali woman for whom Vidyasagar sought to earn greater recognition remained for all intents and purposes a shastrically defined social category. For all that he wanted Hindu wives and widows to experience domestic happiness and security, he also seems never to have confronted the conditions of limited autonomy granted to women within the structures of Hindu law. Here one cannot help thinking of his thundering silence on an issue like a widow's inheritance rights. While under the legal regime prevailing in Bengal (informed by the *Dayabhaga* interpretation of Hindu law) a widow was entitled to a share in her deceased husband's property, with the passage of Act XV of 1856, that right was forfeited. As Section 2 of Act XV made perfectly clear, "All rights and interests which any Widow may by law have in her deceased husband's estate, either by way of maintenance or by inheritance, shall, upon her second marriage, cease and determine as if she had then died."[70]

The language here is stark and the consequences for the widow were (and remain) enormous: passage of Act XV represented her legal death as far as prior property rights. What is truly remarkable is that while passage of this legislation owed much to Vidyasagar's *Hindu Widow Marriage*, the latter text never once addresses the issue of a widow's property rights. That text has a great deal to say about the rights to inheritance enjoyed by various legally recognized sons (natural, adopted, etc.), but it has nothing to say about what would become of the widow's property rights were the legislation to be passed. Even looking at documents from official debates over the legislation, we find no evidence of Vidyasagar raising the issue. It is a startling illustration of the limits of his shastrically guided vision.[71]

This is a reminder that justice requires more than just the healing of emotional wounds or the resolution of immediate personal concerns around health and safety. The problem of social misrecognition is not simply that it damages what we might call an individual's subjective integrity; nor is it merely about the restoration of some ideal of domestic harmony or conjugal happiness. Fundamentally, misrecognition of widows denied them what Nancy Fraser refers to as "the status of full partners in social interaction." As Fraser puts it, "misrecognition is wrong because it constitutes a form of institutionalized subordination," and as such it is a "serious violation of justice."[72] The ongoing deprivations, abuses, and injustices that have haunted Hindu widows even into the postcolonial era should remind us that while the reform ethic of Vidyasagar remains notable for its stress on moral recognition, its advocate remained blinkered by his steady reliance on shastric norms.

As such, we must grant the validity of post-orientalist critiques that find fault with Vidyasagar's project in works like *Vidhava-vivaha* and *Bahuvivaha*, not least for falling prey to the colonialist fiction of a single Hindu legal code grounded in the *dharmashastra*. Scholars informed by the insights of Edward Said, such as Lata Mani, have argued that the adoption by reformers like Rammohun Roy and Vidyasagar of scripturalist modes of Hindu reform only worked to re-entrench the prerogatives of high-caste patriarchy.[73] In light of this critique, and bearing in mind the ultimate failure of the anti-polygamy campaign to instigate any legislative enactment, one could be forgiven for thinking there is no need to spend time reflecting on a work like *Bahuvivaha*. However, such a decision would be misguided. If nothing else, as Asok

Sen brilliantly illustrated decades ago, even the failures and frustrations of Vidyasagar's reform efforts remain powerfully instructive. Studying them helps bring greater clarity to our understanding of the very contradictions at the heart of liberal reform projects in the colonial era.[74] Even if *Bahuvivaha* proved to be a failure at the legislative level, it nonetheless has a great deal to teach us about the practice (and abuses) of Kulin polygamy in Bengal, about the vision and methods of colonial-era reform, and about both the genius and the limitations of one remarkable figure.

Petitioning for Change

Vidyasagar was not the first to question the abuses of Kulinism in Bengal. The issue had in fact been raised for critical scrutiny already by Rammohun Roy in the second decade of the nineteenth century, and we are told the topic was actively discussed among Rammohun's earliest followers.[75] Like Vidyasagar, Rammohun was a Kulin Brahmin and like Vidyasagar, he had his own personal experience of the custom.[76] In 1820, while advancing well-known objections to the concremation of widows (*sahamarana*, or "Suttee"), he highlighted the plight of the Kulin bride in terms that clearly foreshadow Vidyasagar's prose. He wrote, "How many Kulin Brahmins are there who marry ten or fifteen wives for the sake of money, that never see the greater number of them after the day of marriage, and visit others only three or four times in the course of their life."[77] Likewise, in his *Brief Remarks regarding Modern Encroachments on the Ancient Rights of Females, according to the Hindu Law of Inheritance*, Rammohun reviewed some of the same passages from the shastras that would be important for Vidyasagar, while like him also concluding there was no scriptural warrant for the custom as then practiced in Bengal.

Two decades later the matter resurfaced in an essay published in the journal *Vidyadarshan*, most likely written by one of Vidyasagar's contemporaries and close associates, Akshay Kumar Datta.[78] Datta was known to be committed to the rational examination of religious rituals and customs, and in this essay he trained such analysis on a practice he deemed to be a great enemy (*mahashatru*) of modern civilization in Bengal. Akshay identified Hindu polygamy, in particular, with a technical concept drawn from the shastras that would later be discussed by Vidyasagar: *adhivedana*, or supersession. As Datta pointed out, premodern legal digests such as the influential

Mitakshara—which gained increased currency as Hindu law under the British law—allowed for the supersession of a previous wife through subsequent marriage, but also stipulated that the husband who took an additional wife would have to arrange to give to his first wife one third of his property.[79] For Akshay, the fact that this was no longer standard practice was one way to illustrate the errors of contemporary Kulinism.

While notably progressive for his day, Datta was not alone in raising such concerns. Other voices joined in the call for change. By mid-century an active reading public had begun to emerge in cities like Calcutta, informed and invigorated by a robust vernacular press, and eager to debate topics of general concern; this is true from the earliest debates around widow immolation in the 1820s to debates in the 1830s and 1840s over missionary activities, educational programs, and other issues of general welfare. It seems clear that by the 1840s polygamy was generating a similar level of discussion. In fact, a letter to the editors of *Vidyadarshan* that appeared in the issue immediately following Akshay's essay drew a fascinating correlation between the "waves" of emotion generated by the topic and the growing "movement" (the same word, *andolan*, in both cases) that was beginning to take shape around opposition to Kulinism.[80] Both the emotions and the movement would gain steam as time went on.

These public expressions of concern with Kulinism were soon translated into other media, not least modern Bengali drama, which was then enjoying its infancy. A cursory review of Bengali publications from the 1850s reveals several dramatic works that sought to highlight the predicament of Kulin women. One notable author was Ramnarayan Tarkaratna, who published a well-received play entitled *Kulin Kulasarvasva* ("The Paragon of Rank among the Kulins") in 1854.[81] Just three years later Ramnarayan's play premiered in Calcutta, and the next year Vidyasagar himself attended a performance.[82] Progressive dramas like this had an important role to play in shaping the sentiments of the emerging public sphere, which was then exploring new tastes in everything from literature and art to education and social mores. In fact, Ramnarayan had been inspired to compose his work after reading a notice placed in a Bengali journal. In that notice, a wealthy landholder (*zamindar*) from north Bengal called for the composition of a drama to explore how the plight of Kulin women might be traced to the system initiated in Bengal by the Hindu ruler Vallala Sena.[83] Ramnarayan's adoption of a quasi-historical lens in his own drama work reminds us of the growing awareness among educated Bengalis that historical analysis could be employed to query current affairs and to advance a vision of change.

During this period Bengalis also began drafting petitions to the government requesting intervention on the issue of Kulin polygamy. Summaries of these petitions, counter-petitions, and responses from the government are commonplace in the literature on social reform.[84] Rather than summarizing these petitions, it might be more useful to adopt a wider lens that allows us to appreciate how the *andolan* of growing opposition to Kulin polygamy began to gain momentum at the very moment Vidyasagar was deeply immersed in the other great social reform cause of his lifetime: the question of Hindu widow marriage. In 1855, even as Vidyasagar published his two works on *Vidhava-vivaha*, the Friends Harmony Association (or *Banduvarga Samavaya Sabha*), under the leadership of Kishorichand Mitra, appealed to the Legislative Council seeking a ban on Kulin marriage practices. Later Vidyasagar would refer to this petition in the opening of the Author's Notice to *Against High-Caste Polygamy*. There he credits that appeal with being the first real initiative taken against the practice. Curiously he does not mention that in December of 1855, he had invited the Maharaja of Burdwan and other prominent figures to join him in another petition. That petition carried some 25,000 signatures.[85] An oft-quoted line from the petition reads, "The Coolins marry solely for money and with no intention to fulfil any of the duties which marriage involves."[86]

By 1857 the government had received hundreds of petitions, both pro and con.[87] Speaking from the Legislative Council, the Lieutenant Governor J. P. Grant promised to introduce a new Bill addressing the question; he indicated he was working on a Draft Bill with help from Rammohun Roy's son, the barrister Ramaprasad Roy.[88] As it happened, this was the very moment when the Indian Rebellion broke out; all work came to a halt. It would not be until the early 1860s that new petitions would be drafted. By that time Ramaprasad Roy had passed away and in any case the times were changing, as we have seen. As if in recognition of opportunities lost, in 1863 one Calcutta resident submitted an appeal to the government, noting ruefully that, "Some years ago a similar Petition was laid before the old Legislative Council, but, owing to the horrors of the Sepoy insurrection . . . it was not made the subject of consideration."[89]

Things did not look promising. Writing nearly ten years later, Vidyasagar would sum up the situation this way:

> Real confidence was engendered that the Legislative Council would enact a law banning polygamy. However, fate dealt our unfortunate land a blow when the Rebellion broke out. The Government turned all its attention to quelling the Rebellion. There was no longer occasion for them to focus on banning polygamy.
>
> And so this great undertaking came to nought.[90]

Even so Vidyasagar found a glimmer of light in the darkness. In *Against High-Caste Polygamy*, he reminds his readers that in 1862–63 Devnarayan Singh, Raja of Varanasi, had served as one of the Indian members of the Legislative Council. At that time the Raja had drawn up his own Draft Bill to present to the government, but his term on the Council expired before his Draft Bill could be taken up. When Vidyasagar applied himself to the task in 1871, he appears to have considered the Raja's Draft Bill an adequate statement of the matter. Hence, readers will see that he included the entire English-language text of the Draft Bill as an Appendix to *Against High-Caste Polygamy*. And in an effort to forestall concerns over negative fallout that might be anticipated from the passage of new legislation, Vidyasagar even suggested that had the Raja's original Bill been passed at the time, India might not have witnessed the kinds of social and political unrest the British were now so fearful of.[91]

Raja Devnarayan Singh's Draft Bill having come to nought, the next salvos against Kulinism were fired in 1866, prompted by a counter-petition to the government filed by Raja Radhakanta Deb, already well known for his opposition to British interference in Hindu social and religious life.[92] Radhakanta's petition was submitted in January of that year and Vidyasagar responded the very next month with a new petition containing over ten times as many signatories. In the petition Vidyasagar expressed disappointment that the Legislative Council had failed to move in response to earlier pleas and added that it now seemed as if the Rebellion "overshadowed" all else. Seeking to diffuse British anxieties, the petitioners stressed that India had by this time entered into a "new era of peace, progress and prosperity." As such, they continued, it was high time for government to take action to alleviate the "pains, cruelties and attendant crimes" of Kulinism.[93]

The next month Vidyasagar followed up this petition with a personal visit to Lieutenant Governor Cecil Beadon. Joining him for the visit were Justice Dwarkanath Mitter (appointed to the High Court after Ramaprasad Roy's death) and Kristodas Pal, celebrated editor of the *Hindoo Patriot*. It is an index of Vidyasagar's stature and public persona that he could boast direct access to a figure like the lieutenant governor (access he had enjoyed since the 1850s); he clearly had no difficulty finding others with equal gravitas to join him in pressing his case.

The moment did seem to be propitious, not least since more and more petitions were flooding in by this time.[94] Lieutenant Governor Beadon registered the importance of the matter and apparently expressed his support for some kind of government action. He is quoted as having given his personal assurance that he would use his "best endeavors" to see that something was done.[95] Sadly, it took only a few months for Beadon's enthusiasm to wane. In August of 1866 he suggested that the question of a ban on Kulin polygamy merited further consideration; buying time, he announced the formation of a committee to include four Indian members, one of whom was to be Vidyasagar. And with this we reach a crucial turning point in the narrative, a moment that highlights both the sense of expectancy informing a work like *Against High-Caste Polygamy* and the undercurrent of frustration generated by dealing with a government increasingly reluctant to act.

The work of Beadon's new committee illustrates all this clearly. During the autumn and early winter of 1866, the committee carried out its review, examining the question of Kulinism in terms of its history, shastric warrants, and present-day abuses. When it came to formulating a conclusion, the members of the committee agreed that Kulinism had no proper sanction in the shastras; they also noted the revulsion felt by many Bengalis for the practice. However, when it came to recommending a declaratory law against polygamy, the majority of the committee stopped short. Three of the Indian members were willing to believe that the practice would diminish with time and the progressive advance of modern education.[96] Other members argued that the injunctions of the shastras themselves posed a problem, insofar as ancient lawgivers like Manu appeared to have stipulated the validity (in certain cases) of a husband taking a second wife. The majority of the committee members felt there could be no way for the government to outlaw polygamy and yet maintain the government's official commitment not to interfere with Hindu personal laws as enshrined in the shastras. And yet a compromise solution seemed equally untenable: What kind of moral authority could the government claim if it were to ban polygamy, and then (in order to accommodate Manu's conditions) allow it in certain cases?

It is easy to imagine Vidyasagar's frustration as he listened to the arguments of his fellow committee members.[97] Having to sit on an official committee that looked as if it had been convened to foreclose on his hopes for legislation must have been doubly irking. In the end he registered his disappointment by stating simply, "I do not concur in the conclusion come to by the other gentlemen of the Committee."[98] He faulted certain prominent members of the Committee like Joykrishna Mukherjee for having changed his views regarding the necessity for legislation.[99] Vidyasagar also directly challenged the claim that a declaratory law would interfere with the freedom of Hindus when it came to marriage, stating simply: "I am of opinion [*sic*] that a Declaratory Law might be passed without interfering with that liberty which Hindoos by now possess in the matter of marriage."[100]

To appreciate his reasoning, it helps to reflect on the emphasis he places on the distinction between required (*nitya*), contingent (*naimittika*), and voluntary (*kamya*) duties in Hindu law. As Vidyasagar notes, all Hindu householders are required to fulfill the dictates of Dharma; to do this they must marry, since a wife is essential both for the performance of duty and for the birth of sons, who are required to perform a father's last rites.[101] Any marriage beyond that required for a householder to perform his duties would thus have to be either contingent or voluntary. In the former case, the need for a second marriage might arise if particular conditions made it necessary, such as the barrenness of a wife. Vidyasagar felt that any law appropriately attentive to the reality of contingencies would be able to accommodate the possibility of a man needing to marry more than once.

In fact, the Draft Bill prepared by Raja Devnarayana Singh (mentioned above) takes this kind of contingency into account. Its second clause stipulates that any man who wished to contract a second marriage would first be required to submit a written application "setting forth the grounds on which he claims to be allowed to remarry." This application would then be evaluated by a local committee authorized to inquire into the legitimacy of the grounds alleged by the applicant. If the grounds were deemed to be valid, then another marriage would be allowed even while the first wife remained living.[102] Vidyasagar believed that provision for this kind of administrative oversight would be sufficient to redress any apparent contradiction between the state issuing a general interdiction of plural marriages and the necessity of second marriages under certain conditions.

As for voluntary marriages, Vidyasagar acknowledges that the shastras contain injunctions to this effect, but also argues that the mere existence of such injunctions is not enough to justify the practice of Kulin polygamy. It may be true that Manu permits a twice-born man to marry more than once, but Manu also requires any marriage after the first to be arranged outside a man's social class (*varna*). As such, a Brahmin who wished to marry a second time would be allowed to do so only if he married a woman from the Kshatriya, Vaishya, or Shudra classes. Necessarily this would rule out the possibility of further marriages to Brahmin women and therefore would be in accord with the proposed ban on plural marriages among Kulin Brahmins.

The force of this argument notwithstanding, Vidyasagar acknowledged that Manu also seems to allow for the practice of voluntary polygamy. This is where Vidyasagar ran into the very problem foreseen by other members of Beadon's committee. They worried any declaratory law instituting a blanket ban on polygamy would contravene this dimension of the shastras. But Vidyasagar had a further trump card to play, in the form of the doctrine of the four eons, or *yugas*.[103] According to Hindu cosmology and time-reckoning, human beings are currently living in the eon known as Kali Yuga. This is the fourth, and most degraded, of the four eons and is thought to be a time when the health of Dharma is precarious and the religious abilities of humans are diminished. Many of the practices enjoined for earlier eons were in fact decreed by Hindu lawmakers to be no longer permissible during the Kali Yuga. Among these was the practice of marrying outside of one's class. Hence Vidyasagar's trump card: While Manu's provision for voluntary polygamous marriage may have applied in earlier eons, it could not apply now, during the Kali Yuga. So confident was Vidyasagar that this settled the matter, that at one point he concludes, "there is no need to say anything more on this score."[104]

This terse comment suggests that by 1871 Vidyasagar had grown impatient with the flip-flopping of his fellow Bengalis and the British government. His frustration is especially noticeable in the second Supplement appended to the first edition translated here. Here he attempts to refute the opinions of two respected Sanskrit scholars with whom he had enjoyed a close working relationship over the years, Taranath Tarkavacaspati and Dwarkanath Vidyabhushan. The second Supplement provides a fitting finale to his passionate, if despairing, plea for a declaratory law consistent with Hindu Dharma.[105]

The sheer scale of what Vidyasagar hopes to achieve bears noting. Far from being merely a review of the origins and degradation of Kulinism, *Against High-Caste Polygamy* is nothing less than an appeal for a new legal ruling (*nutan vyavastha*) that seeks to reform the system promulgated by King Vallala Sena and Devivara Ghatak. As Vidyasagar puts it, "The first time around, when Vallala Sena saw weakness among the Brahmins, he established

Kulin rank . . . When Devivara saw that weakness had once again befallen the Kulins, he established the assemblages. Today . . .we will need a new ruling (*nutan vyavastha*)."[106] It might be easy to read over this claim without actually recognizing what it implies. Here we have Vidyasagar embracing—or perhaps we should say enacting—the role not merely of Sanskrit scholar or social reformer, but almost of shastric lawmaker.

Beyond Textualism

Having just pictured Vidyasagar in the role of Hindu lawmaker, I want to complicate matters here by making the case that *Against High-Caste Polygamy* is not best understood—or at least should not only be understood—as a work of shastric exegesis. In this respect it actually differs markedly from its predecessor, *Hindu Widow Marriage*. The latter work reveals many of the intellectual habits and argumentative tools its author owed to premodern traditions of legal exegesis. In fact, elsewhere I have argued that in *Hindu Widow Marriage* Vidyasagar looks like a medieval *nibandha-kara*, or digest writer.[107] This is just another way of saying that *Hindu Widow Marriage* is indebted to, and structured by, fundamental practices of shastric analysis and argumentation.[108] *Against High-Caste Polygamy* is quite different in this regard. Vidyasagar may still indulge in a good deal of shastric exegesis; he may even advance a new ruling, or *vyavastha*; but in *Against High-Caste Polygamy* he makes his overall case using a more diverse set of tools.

Where a text like *Hindu Widow Marriage* proceeds by reviewing hundreds of scriptural passages drawn from the Vedas, Smritis, Puranas, and Nibandhas, *Against High-Caste Polygamy* combines the tools of exegesis and hermeneutics with other techniques, such as descriptive narration, critical historiography, sociological inquiry, and even an appeal to what we might today call "hard data." One immediate difference this makes for the reader is that whereas the experiences of actual Hindu widows are almost lost amid the legal sources reviewed in *Hindu Widow Marriage*, in *Against High-Caste Polygamy* the presence and plight of Kulin women are front and center. Here one encounters compelling stories about Kulin wives, vivid illustrations of family life in Bengal, and empirical data that serves to illustrate the pathology and consequences of Kulin customs. This is what makes reading *Against High-Caste Polygamy* so moving and so rewarding.

Once we appreciate this, we are prepared to revisit some long-standing assumptions about the character of Vidyasagar's reformist writings. Above all, we might wish to rethink claims about his overwhelming indebtedness to shastric reasoning. Clearly the dense textual exegesis of *Hindu Widow Marriage* had marked a departure from the proto-sociological approach of his 1850 work "The Evils of Child Marriage" (*Balyavivaher dosha*).[109] Asok Sen was right to say that *Hindu Widow Marriage* represented a "significant contrast" in this regard.[110] However, in *Against High-Caste Polygamy* Vidyasagar reprises some of the very methods that proved effective in "The Evils of Child Marriage." He may still engage in some necessary scriptural work in the present text, but it would be wrong to think of *Against High-Caste Polygamy* as merely a clone of the tract on widow marriage.[111]

In *Against High-Caste Polygamy*, Vidyasagar demonstrates a real penchant for enriching the results of scriptural exegesis with evidence drawn from direct experience and even from what we might call social research.[112] And while he never informs his readers precisely why he chose to compose the text in the way he did, its structure does provide a kind of clue. *Against High-Caste Polygamy* is framed around Vidyasagar's answers to a number of objections that had been raised around the question of abolishing Kulin polygamy. Since these objections range from specialist claims about Hindu law to more general observations about the state of social life in Bengal, Vidyasagar clearly feels the need to employ a range of methods to address them.

In total there are seven objections that Vidyasagar addresses in the main body of the text. Of these, only two or three actually require him to delve into issues like the content of the shastras, the nature of Dharma, or the appropriate way to address claims about the various injunctions, prohibitions, and entitlements associated with Hindu marriage. That leaves several other objections to answer. And as readers will discover, in his replies to these other objections, Vidyasagar takes up such methods as historical-critical analysis, social research, and the amassing of empirical data. The pandit's toolbox has clearly expanded.

To appreciate this change in overall strategy, it helps to imagine the public for whom Vidyasagar was now writing. To a greater degree than most of his pundit contemporaries (and most of his adversaries), he understood there were likely to be very few readers who would feel prepared to enter into—let alone could claim to master—the analysis of legal texts and scriptural injunctions. It was far more likely that his readers would respond to compelling stories about the suffering of Kulin brides, to an overview of the historical developments that explained the rise and transformation of Bengali Kulinism, and to the provision of concrete data regarding the prevalence of Kulin marriage practices. Belying his image as mere scripturalist, Vidyasagar proves himself more than able to provide on all these counts.[113]

One point he stresses is that readers ought to gain accurate knowledge of things before they could be expected to make any decision about the validity of Kulin customs and practices. At one point he advises his readers, "It is typically not a good idea to comment on matters about which one has no special knowledge. And one cannot gain special knowledge about something without careful investigation."[114] In view of his frustrations with the work of Beadon's committee, one might well think of *Against High-Caste Polygamy* as Vidyasagar's unofficial report on the origin, spread, and persistence of Kulin polygamy. It is as if, stepping outside the confines of his committee role, he chose to communicate what he took to be the kinds of "special knowledge" that both Bengalis and the British government would need in order to assess the viability of Kulinism. And he is confident that once his readers were equipped with such knowledge, they would reach the only possible conclusion: "Anyone with eyes and ears and a heart will admit that the custom of polygamy is the cause of immeasurable harm."[115]

With this remark we are reminded that Vidyasagar's goal is to prompt a moment of ethical recognition. The urgency of the moral problem is made evident in the opening lines,

> Women are weaker than men and completely subservient to them on account of social regulations. Because of this weakness and subservience, they live cowering and humiliated before men. The sovereign and powerful class of men does as it pleases, committing outrage and injustice; being utterly without means, women bear it all throughout their lives. This is the condition of women in almost every region of the earth. But nowhere else does one find women in the kind of condition one finds in this unfortunate land, all due to the excessive sway of the cruelty, selfishness, and thoughtlessness of its men.[116]

It is worth noting how closely these opening lines echo the tone of the 1850 tract against child marriage. In that earlier text Vidyasagar had spoken movingly of the fragility of young lives, both male and female, not to mention of the developmental challenges posed when young boys and girls are required to marry before they had fully matured, either socially or sexually. That early work demonstrated Vidyasagar's incipient awareness of the deleterious role played by constraining practices around gender, sexuality, and family.[117] The point is, we hear these same chords struck in the opening lines of *Against High-Caste Polygamy*, which highlight the force of masculinist and patriarchal social structures. Here we see Vidyasagar holding men accountable for their abuse of social position—for the "outrage and injustice" they routinely commit. Men are said to be susceptible to the vice of selfishness; they prove unable to subordinate their passions to higher standards of morality. Such moral weakness accounts for the evils of polygamy, which for Vidyasagar is marked by the voluntary, let us say willful, accumulation of multiple marriage alliances. Of course *Against High-Caste Polygamy* has a legal argument to make; but its goal is also to unveil the horrors associated with Kulin social practices and to rectify the moral failings that support them.[118] To do this, Vidyasagar understands that far more than scriptural exegesis will be required. He must examine history and myth, he will need to employ original sociological analysis, and he will need to bring forth compelling data if he is to cement his case. These become some of the defining features of this remarkable work, putting paid any claim that it is just another scholarly exercise in proof-texting.

Putting History to Work

When thinking about Vidyasagar's recourse to historical analysis, it helps to situate the text in its late nineteenth-century context. As Sudipta Kaviraj long ago observed, one of the ways late-colonial Indian intellectuals began to advance new claims about the dignity and integrity of Indian culture in the face of colonial discourse was by crafting histories that they could claim as their own. British colonial historiography had famously denied to Indians the possession of any indigenous history, claiming this distinction solely for Europe. Kaviraj explored the way an author like Bankimchandra Chatterjee (a younger contemporary of Vidyasagar) responded to such European exceptionalism in a colonial context. For Bankim, as Kaviraj famously argued, the answer was to be found in "imaginary history," which we may think of as something like the novelization of a wide range of myths, ballads, and popular legends.[119] Even if, as Kaviraj points out, such imaginary histories could not finally reject or transcend the fact of alien rule, they demonstrated how history as discursive tool and literary register could be harnessed to creative ends by Indian intellectuals.[120] We may situate Vidyasagar in the same temporal and epistemic context, which is to say the moment when Bengali authors began to pair their growing fluency in European modes of historical analysis with an innovative embrace of indigenous narrative traditions. Such traditions could be used to tell new stories that would celebrate such crucial matters as region (*desh*), people (*jati*), and the nation (*rashtra*) itself.

We know that early in his career Vidyasagar had been commissioned to translate into Bengali the kinds of British historical narratives that were taught to East India Company servants and to the first generations of educated young men in Bengal. Himself the product of a colonial-era educational institution (the Calcutta Government Sanskrit College)—that he subsequently went on to guide as principal—he had imbibed and refined the skill of positivist history-writing in the European mode. Even if his early work based on English historical accounts such as *Bangalar Itihasa* (1852) may have been derivative in nature, his ability to publish critical editions of Sanskrit texts, and his application of modern critical tools to shastric debates around widow marriage, both speak to his facility with the canons of historical method.[121]

Indeed, it is Vidyasagar's ability to account for the rise, transformation, and present-day condition of Kulinism in Bengal that makes *Against High-Caste Polygamy* more than a polemical text. Earlier we noted how Vidyasagar relied on the genre of Kulin genealogical texts or "lineage histories" (*vamshavali*) to make his case. Here we can expand on this point to say that by turning to such texts, Vidyasagar anticipated a major development among late-colonial Bengali intellectuals, who would increasingly look for ways to craft historical narratives independent of hegemonic British sources. This is an important point to emphasize, because Vidyasagar is not often included in scholarly discussions around the development of historical discourse in the late colonial moment.[122] However, *Against High-Caste Polygamy* reveals that he was in the vanguard of Bengali efforts to employ local source materials (both written and oral) to fashion new histories about the region, the people, and their customs.

At one point, Vidyasagar tells his readers that the historical data he relied on to frame his account of the rise of Kulinism had been gathered from sources he had found thanks to the assistance of a particular genealogist (*ghataka*) from Vikrampur, who was by that time already deceased. On the one hand, Vidyasagar issues a kind of apology for being unable to provide more information about these sources; on the other hand, he clearly felt empowered to offer this genealogical data as a contribution toward what we might call his own critical history of Kulinism. In his hands this history looked all the way back to transformations begun by the medieval Bengali ruler Vallala Sena and then traced how the original Kulin system degraded over time. As Vidyasagar told it, this process of decline had proceeded to such an extent that by the nineteenth century the Kulins themselves were unable to realize the vitiated character of the system they defended.[123]

Here we see that through his pioneering recourse to an overlooked genre of genealogy, informed by the spirit of positivist historical analysis, Vidyasagar was able to compose a compelling argument against the claims of orthodox apologists for Kulinism. Put simply, Vidyasagar contended that the entire matter needed to be understood as history; there was no need to invoke God in any of this.[124] As he puts it so forcefully:

> [T]he system of Kulin rank established by Vallala prior to the creation of the assemblages has been lost. Those who today boast of being Kulin have actually for a long time been Vamshaja. If one follows the rules of Kulin custom, there is not the least difference between those who are reckoned Vamshajas and those proud Kulins of today.
>
> And so it can be shown that for a long time the system of Kulin rank among the Brahmins of Rarh has been vitiated. It is impossible to find anyone today who can be counted a Kulin according to the rules of the Kulin system. And if this is the case, since the Kulins are completely inauthentic, then one cannot accept as reasonable the objection that banning the custom of polygamy would lead to the loss of caste or destruction of Dharma among the Kulins.[125]

Interestingly, in the wake of Vidyasagar, other Bengali intellectuals would begin to explore similar possibilities for using genealogical texts to craft new histories for their caste communities, if not for India itself. For instance, three or four years after the publication of *Against High-Caste Polygamy*, Lalmohan Vidyanidhi produced his influential *Sambandhanirnaya*, which was subtitled in English, *A Social History of the Principal Hindu Castes in Bengal*. In this book Lalmohan tackled the colonial-era Shibboleth that Indians had no history; and he did this by using the same sort of premodern genealogical texts as Vidyasagar had. In fact, comparing Lalmohan's text with Vidyasagar's, one discovers that Lalmohan actually quotes genealogical material verbatim from *Against High-Caste Polygamy*, treating the latter as an authoritative source. Even though Lalmohan only obliquely acknowledges this fact in a single isolated footnote, several of the Sanskrit genealogical sources he offers as evidence had first been adduced by Vidyasagar.[126] That fact has not hitherto been noted, whereas the apparent novelty of Lalmohan's research is often singled out for comment.[127] Recognizing Lalmohan's minor debt to Vidyasagar serves to add further complexity to the latter's intellectual legacy.

Imaginative Sociology

Along with crafting an explanatory historical framework to account for the degeneration of Kulinism, Vidyasagar also appealed to what I am tempted to call "imaginative sociology" as a tool for demonstrating the ravages wrought by Kulin marriages in his own day.[128] In offering this coinage (with a respectful nod toward Kaviraj) I wish to stress two things in particular: First, it should be remembered that in 1871 we are still at a moment that predates the rise of the discipline of sociology in India, at least as it would come to be practiced by notable late-colonial proponents such as Benoy Kumar Sarkar; in fact, we are even still in advance of the rise of the Positivist School in Bengal, which would in short order begin to draw many leading Bengalis into its intellectual orbit.[129] All of this inclines me to designate Vidyasagar's approach here—as it had already been in "The Evils of Child Marriage"—proto-sociological. Second, I want to make an explicit parallel to Kaviraj's discussion of "imaginative history," insofar as coinages like these are meant to alert us to the creative ways in which new disciplinary perspectives could be employed by innovative thinkers who were eager to address the problems of their day. Vidyasagar's imaginative sociology belongs, in other words, to the same generative moment—and relies on similar creative instincts—as Bankim's imaginative history.[130]

Putting things this way reminds us that Vidyasagar's approach to Kulinism in Bengal is not merely the work of a social reformer, but is shaped as well by his gifts for observation, narrative, and language. While he is not known for creating vast narrative canvases or for framing complex character studies, Vidyasagar nonetheless possessed considerable skills as an informal ethnographer and storyteller. These skills are at their best when yoked to the task of communicating the social and emotional costs of practices like Kulinism. It turns out that the same literary tools he deployed so effectively when telling the stories of Shakuntala or Sita could be put to equally good use for sketching the horrors of Kulinism.

Consider the story he tells, when addressing the First Objection, of a certain Kulin Brahmin who through either his carelessness or callousness allows his daughters to be lured away by a shady procurer and presumably forced to work as prostitutes.[131] As Vidyasagar tells it, there eventually came a time when the father had to find a way to get the two girls married. But how? Who would be willing to accept them as brides? It turns out that the best the father could do was to find a six-year-old Kulin boy, who agreed to marry the girls on the promise of lavish gifts. Vidyasagar tells us that no sooner had the marriage been finalized, than the new groom disappeared and the girls were returned to the man who had originally lured them away for illicit ends.

This is what I mean by imaginative sociology. There is no way to know if this story corresponds to actual events, observed by Vidyasagar directly or reported to him secondhand. But it scarcely matters; what does matter are the social context, the moral failure of the father, the greed of the groom's family, and the powerlessness of the girls. We find a similar sort of evocative protosociology at one point in Vidyasagar's answer to the Third Objection, when he illustrates how marriage has become a "business" (*vyavasaya*) among the Broken Kulins. Unleashing his narrative skills, he envisions a young girl, technically married, but abandoned by her Broken Kulin husband and forced to live with her own parents. As must have often happened, the young girl became pregnant, even though her husband had not been seen in the village for ages. Vidyasagar asks his readers to imagine the anxiety experienced by the girl's family; and to imagine the lengths to which such a family might go to in order to account for the girl's pregnancy. As he puts it, the best solution in such cases was for the girl's family to resort to a ruse that would be plausible enough to throw the neighbors off the scent. In such a case, for instance, a pregnancy might be "explained" by a subterfuge in which the women of the family dropped suggestive remarks to their neighbors while going about their various errands in the village. From these stray comments the neighbors would be led to think that the Kulin son-in-law had paid his bride a brief overnight visit—unobserved by others in the village, but long enough to explain the pregnancy. Suspicion would be allayed and life could proceed as before. The way Vidyasagar accounts for the virtue of such a ruse makes it seem as if this was far from fiction. He remarks that for a poor rural family, there were two obvious benefits to such a deception: it was cost-free and it required no recourse to abortion.

Again, we cannot know the veracity of all this—but it clearly conveys something like the truth. The same can be said about a stray comment Vidyasagar records as coming from the mouth of a particularly shameless Kulin, married many times over. When someone asked him how it was possible to visit all his wives, he replied without the slightest embarrassment, "I go where I get a 'visit.'" The comment is curious enough that Vidyasagar appends an explanatory footnote, in which he tells his readers that the English term "visit" is commonly used in colloquial Bengali to refer to the fee received by a doctor when making a house call. In one stroke the crude calculus of the Kulin is underscored. The old man has confessed to living off the *douceur*—as it was known in the colonial-era literature—a Kulin husband could expect to receive from any family whose daughter he consented to marry. Here is an incisive sociological and lexicographical observation offered by a man who had ample firsthand experience of high-caste family life in colonial Bengali.

Watching as Vidyasagar yokes sociological observation to inventive storytelling should encourage us to appreciate that his achievements in the realms of Bengali literature were not entirely isolated from his reform-based work. His storytelling and his gifts for observation work in tandem. And yet in this case he is not merely retelling of the stories of mythic heroines like Shakuntala and Sita; in *Against High-Caste Polygamy* the stories bear a clear relation to actual people and to the kinds of events and tragedies he observed.

There is, in fact, one lengthy vignette in the Third Objection that appears to draw directly on Vidyasagar's own experiences growing up in the village of Birsingha. I refer to the story of a certain Mr. Bhattacharya (*Bhattacharya mahashaya*). The title seems unnecessarily generic and that may be our first clue that it represents an anonymized way to refer to a particular Kulin who was well known to Vidyasagar. What we subsequently learn of Mr. Bhattacharya is as follows. One day we are told that an unnamed Brahmin comes home to find his wife sitting with an unknown woman and her daughter. When the Brahmin asks his wife who the women are, she tells him they are the wife and daughter of Mr. Bhattacharya, who lives nearby. The Brahmin then learns that Mr. Bhattacharya has driven these two women from his home and that they had come to the Brahmin's house seeking refuge. What then follows is a moving story of Kulin greed and abuse, not to mention the futile efforts of one kind-hearted Brahmin to intercede. I leave it for readers to discover for themselves.

The point I want to make here is that this particular narrative mirrors what we know about the behavior and family life of young Vidyasagar's former village schoolmaster, Kalikanta Chattopadhyay, himself a Broken Kulin. Sources tell us that Kalikanta behaved in the same way as Mr. Bhattacharya.[132] If there had been a time when Vidyasagar looked up to his teacher, that all appears to have changed when he found himself called upon to intercede on behalf of the women of Kalikanta's family. In the story Vidyasagar provides in *Against High-Caste Polygamy*, there is no resolution to the women's suffering; in the end they are drawn into lives of prostitution. It is a rather lurid ending and Vidyasagar plays it for full moral effect. As he notes, even though these two women were abused, abandoned, and rendered socially invisible, Mr. Bhattacharya's reputation remained unscathed. He suffered no stain on his Kulin status, and there was nothing anyone could say against him. Vidyasagar's point was simple: this kind of behavior would continue as long as Bengalis continued to believe in the myth of Kulin rank.

The story of Mr. Bhattacharya may be compared to another vignette Vidyasagar offers at the close of the Seventh Objection. Here he tells his readers about the time he met a Kulin woman and her daughter. Vidyasagar gives us what purports to be his conversation with them, and whether invented or not, its emotional force is palpable. The two women begged him to do something to address the sad fate of Kulin wives in Bengal. As he puts it, these two knew all too well that their lot had been cast; their lives were already ruined. Even if Vidyasagar were able to win a campaign against high-caste polygamy, it would be too late for them. And yet even so, they pled with him in the name of future generations of women. Through him they even hoped to address an appeal to Queen Victoria, wondering out loud how any woman who claimed to rule over India could allow a custom like Kulinism to persist within her realm. Their plea in turn prompts Vidyasagar to close the scene with a rhetorical flourish of his own, reminiscent of the closing lines of *Hindu Widow Marriage*. He calls out to Fate, asking why such suffering is meted out to innocent women like these.

The appeal is admittedly melodramatic—and of course, it is aimed far less at Queen Victoria than it is at Vidyasagar's fellow Bengalis. In the end, this should remind us of the goal of all this imaginative sociology, which is to compel the Bengali public to confront a reality they daily turn away from. And my point is simply to say that the imaginative sociology of vignettes like these gains its force from Vidyasagar's gifts at storytelling; we can appreciate how skills as a prose stylist work to support his ethic of recognition. We may have no way to determine when direct observation gives way to imaginative narrative, but nonetheless the effect is clearly to promote the kind of "special knowledge" he believed his fellow Bengalis needed if they were to make responsible choices about the problem of Kulin polygamy. This is what I call his imaginative sociology, and it is aimed at readers with "eyes and ears and a heart."

Data Collection

Perhaps one of the most fascinating features of *Against High-Caste Polygamy* is its recourse to what we might call empirical data collection. We see this most clearly in the context of the Fourth Objection. Under this topic, Vidyasagar addresses the claim that there is no need to legislate against polygamy because it is already fast becoming a thing of the past. He clearly rejects this claim, but it is *how* he rejects it that is perhaps most fascinating. Far from simply dismissing the claim out of hand, Vidyasagar turns to what we might today call the persuasive force of "hard data." If some of his opponents hoped to argue that polygamy was on the decline, Vidyasagar provides evidence to show that this is not the case. As he tells his readers, "To avoid pointless debate on this issue, I provide here the names, ages, places of residence and corresponding number of marriages for some present-day Kulins."

One cannot help wondering whether Vidyasagar hit upon this strategy after realizing that there was in fact an established practice of informal record-keeping already in place among Kulin husbands. It turns out that many of these husbands were in the habit of compiling lists or ledgers (*talika*) of their many wives, all in the interests of keeping track of their assets.[133] After all, as mentioned above, this was a business practice for them. In a brilliant twist, Vidyasagar turned the practice of list-making to a contrary purpose. Under the Fourth Objection he provides a list of 133 Kulin husbands then living in the Hooghly District to the west and north of Calcutta just over the Hoogly River. The list (which can be found in Supporting Evidence *4.1) is remarkable for its audacious "outing" of Kulin husbands. There is no semblance of anonymization here; to the contrary, as evident from his comment above, Vidyasagar freely supplies the name of each Kulin, the number of marriages he had concluded, the Kulin's age, and even his place of residence.

Today we may well baulk at the idea of identifying people publicly in this fashion, but of course there were no best practices or standards for research on human subjects in Vidyasagar's day. I think it is safe to assume that he went so far as to include these details both as a way to ensure his data would not be taken as fictitious and to raise the ante on all that was at stake. It seems very likely he hoped to direct a good measure of shame onto these Kulin grooms and their families.

In the original print version of *Bahuvivaha* the list of Kulins from Hooghly District covers five and half octavo pages. Even so, Vidyasagar comments that the list could have been longer had he wished: "I have not shown the names of those individuals who contracted only three to four marriages."[134] It is as if he invites his readers to do some calculations of their own, pushing them to imagine for themselves just how much longer such a list might actually become. And once presented in black and white, what a damning picture it provides. I know from my own informal conversations with people who have read the first book of *Bahuvivaha* that nearly everyone can recall the impression made upon them by this list—both for the concrete data it provides and for the indication it gives of Vidyasagar's willingness to "play hard ball," as it were.

In addition to the genius and sheer temerity driving this presentation of data, we should also be struck by how self-aware Vidyasagar proves to be about the strengths and weaknesses of such an informal survey method. Needless to say, the very length of the list speaks for itself; but at the same time Vidyasagar found it pertinent to reflect on the kinds of factors that could have skewed the data in one direction or the other. I want to suggest that the Vidyasagar we meet in these comments is not the educator and reformer with whom most of us are familiar; we are looking at a less familiar Vidyasagar, one we might even think of as an incipient social scientist or *samajvijnani*.[135] I say this because here, in the very midst of a heartfelt polemical appeal, he gestures toward such key scientific values as accuracy and transparency. At one point he even tells his readers, "I have shown what I have been able to learn through my inquiries. I have not knowingly introduced any error."[136]

Readers will discover that there is actually one point in the Appendices when Vidyasagar engages in something like "error calculation." In that context he informs his readers that the data he collected on polygamous marriages was, by the time of publication, already five years old. He mentions this by way of suggesting that if a reader were to go out now (i.e., in 1871) and conduct another survey of the same population, they would surely find that the numbers had changed. Furthermore, he goes on to advocate caution when handling his data; he recommends the public should avoid jumping to premature conclusions. Why? Because at first glance, he notes, it might appear from the data collected in 1866 as if younger Kulins tended to marry on average fewer times than older Kulins. After all, if one examines the list, it does appear as if the older Kulins have more wives. However, Vidyasagar says, "Not so fast." He reminds his readers that the young Kulin men surveyed in 1866 would have gone on accepting additional wives as the years rolled on. As such it would be a mistake to use the data from 1866 to conclude that polygamy was less popular among the younger generation. If anything, Vidyasagar adds, new data would likely show that by 1871 the number of Kulin marriages among the younger population had significantly increased. Why? Here he puts the matter bluntly, reminding his readers that Kulin men tend to go on marrying right up until the day they die!

Returning to the Fourth Objection, we find that the first lengthy list of Kulins living in Hooghly District is followed by another list, this one a more focused sampling of Kulins from a single village in the same district.[137] In this instance, Vidyasagar provides the names, number of marriages, and ages of sixty-four individuals from this village. Although he does not use this language, when placed in relation to the list covering the entire Hooghly District, this second list may be thought of as offering something like a statistical sample. The force of that sample is clear; it seems as if Vidyasagar expects his readers to extrapolate from this one village in Hooghly District to the entire Rarh region of western Bengal, where high-caste polygamy was most prevalent. What might such an exercise yield? Well, if it turned out that the Kulins of this single village married an average of three times (as his data shows), then extending that rate of marriage across the population of Rarh would yield how many Kulin marriages? One scarcely needs to do the math; the damning implications of the calculus are clear enough.[138]

Even if accurate statistics on Kulin social customs were not available in Vidyasagar's day, he obviously appreciated how powerfully numbers could be used to support his case. In this he seems to have been ahead of late nineteenth-century developments around the collection, tabulation, and presentation of statistical data.[139] This suggests that further attention should be given to the ways in which a text like *Against High-Caste Polygamy* begins to model for Bengali readers the fruits of thinking sociologically.[140] Bear in mind that the first official Census of India would be conducted a year after the publication of Vidyasagar's book. And even if the colonial state had begun gathering demographic and other data as early as the late eighteenth century, it was only in the latter decades of the nineteenth century that public dissemination and debate over such information really began to take off. Vidyasagar published his work on the cusp of a set of profound changes through which the publication and review of data would come to play a role in creating new understandings of citizenship and governance.

As Talal Asad has noted, from the nineteenth century onward, modern statistics have been implicated not merely in the work of representation but also in the work of political intervention. While the role of statistical information in colonial governmentality is now well known, what we see in Vidyasagar's case is an early appropriation of the same tools by a local intellectual to pursue an avowedly political project, one that involved yoking quantitative data to a claim for state intervention. Does this make Vidyasagar a tool of the regulatory work of the colonial state? In his recourse to statistics in *Against High-Caste Polygamy*, do we find evidence for the working of what Asad calls the "strong languages" that have transformed the life of non-Western peoples in the name of progress? If so, does this make Vidyasagar a colonial derivative, or might we also see him as a forerunner of new modes of indigenous knowledge production? Such questions continue to resonate, and I believe the present work represents an important occasion for further critical reflection. But one thing is clear: while today we routinely consume and evaluate all kinds of statistical data, in 1871 this was still something new. Indeed, Vidyasagar appears to have intuited the power of numbers in relation to social and political change at the very moment social statistics was being advanced as a new kind of tool in the West.[141]

Frustration, Failure, and Success

With or without the aid of statistics, it does seem as if by 1871 the abuses of Kulinism were increasingly recognized and bemoaned in the Bengali public sphere.[142] Even a pandit like Taranath Tarkavacaspati, whose views on the matter Vidyasagar challenges in Supplement One, was prepared to admit that Kulinism was a degraded and shameful practice. Furthermore, those whom Vidyasagar somewhat off-handedly lumps in the "new community" of educated, urban elites (which would have included literary luminaries like Bankimchandra Chatterjee) were largely optimistic about the imminent demise of Kulin polygamy, mostly thanks to the spread of education. In large part, the disagreement was really no longer over the scriptural defensibility of Kulin practices; instead it turned on the question of how Bengalis should go about the work of transforming their social life and customs.[143] And on this point, by 1871 the idea of beseeching the government to intercede had clearly lost its appeal.

According to the well-known argument framed by Partha Chatterjee in his essay on the colonial-era "women's question," Indians had by this time begun to think of the sanctity of their religious values as standing in need of protection from the incursions of colonial reason and law.[144] Viewed in this way, the ultimate failure of Vidyasagar's efforts was due less to the soundness of his ethics than it was to his willingness to make his case to the government. Anxieties around the need to sequester religion, gender, and family from the state—not to mention the concomitant growth of anti-colonial sentiment—do not appear to have moved him.

Even so, we should exercise caution when assessing his position. If anything, *Against High-Caste Polygamy* reveals two important facts about him. First, unlike a younger generation of budding nationalists, Vidyasagar did continue to believe that appeals for British legislation were legitimate and necessary. Does this mark him as a collaborator, or indicate the failure of his loyalty to the nation? Or does it index the formation of his own subjectivity during the heyday of colonial reform? Second, unlike those who were increasingly drawn to culturalist positions in the name of defending Hindu Dharma, Vidyasagar's appeals to shastra did not begin or end in conservatism or obscurantism; for him, shastric exegesis was but one of the many tools that could be deployed toward shaping public opinion and influencing official policy. The *dhoti*-clad pandit could summon the resources of both shastra and statistics even as he pursued social transformation with the aid of colonial legislation. Tensions abound. And even if *Against High-Caste Polygamy* failed to achieve its ultimate goal, it provides valuable evidence of the fluid grounds on which religion, gender, and family were debated in the late-colonial era.

I say all this because there have been times, of course, when Vidyasagar has been blamed for either collaborating with or deferring to colonial power. And when viewed against platforms predicated on the outright defense of culture or religion, his proposals can perhaps give the appearance of yielding too much to the authority of the colonial state. However, as I have tried to demonstrate, when *Against High-Caste Polygamy* is read in the context of the early 1870s, it reminds us of the lingering hopes—and the growing frustrations—characteristic of an era in transition.

The tensions I mentioned above can be both stark and confusing. For instance, what are we to make of a key proponent of vernacular education in Bengal like Vidyasagar scoffing at a younger generation of educated youth?[145] Is it not disconcerting to hear one of the most successful authors of schoolbook literature dismiss the arguments of his younger contemporaries as mere "schoolboy talk?"[146] Furthermore, what does it reveal about Vidyasagar's own anxieties around achieving social improvement, when he complains that no sooner do the newly educated leave school than their lofty principles yield to the harsher realities of the day? Is he blaming Bengali youth for their naivete or is he upset that they do not have the courage of their convictions? Furthermore, when does he pause to consider the limitations of his own position? Would he have been prepared to admit that his vision of improvement for Bengal remained problematically dependent upon begging the sanction of colonial authorities?

To raise such questions is one way to return to the issue that I raised at the outset. A significant social, moral, and political divide separates the context of *Against High-Caste Polygamy* from what might otherwise seem like its immediate analogue, a text like *Hindu Widow Marriage*. In the latter, a dense exegetical exercise had proven sufficient to gain government recognition of the need for change and to ensure the passage of a new legislative enactment. In the present text, neither scriptural exegesis nor even the novel presentation of historical and sociological data proved to be enough to inspire legislative action. And this despite the fact that the arguments of *Against High-Caste Polygamy* earned far more approval generally than had those Vidyasagar made in *Hindu Widow Marriage*. Sentiments in opposition to Kulin polygamy were always far stronger than those in support of high-caste widow marriage.

We are thus led to conclude that by 1871 the situation in Bengal had radically changed, perhaps without Vidyasagar either acknowledging or accepting the fact. We might use a courtroom analogy here, and say that both the judge and the jury were new. If the lieutenant-governor was the judge, then there was by this time no way he was going to find in favor of Vidyasagar. The risks to the interests of British rule appeared to be too real. And if we imagine a jury made up of Vidyasagar's peers, they were no longer willing to listen to the kind of appeal he was making. To them not only was the venue wrong but the remedy, if granted, could only represent a kind of self-betrayal.

India had entered a new era. Vidyasagar had fallen out of step with the times, and despite his derision it would be the views of the "new community" that would eventually prove correct. Kulin polygamy was on the wane; by the early twentieth century the topic had largely faded from public view.[147] That said, it would not be until 1955 that polygamy was finally outlawed within the Hindu Marriage Act.[148]

If Vidyasagar had somehow failed to understand the times, we should not make the mistake of missing what remain the distinctive and even innovative elements within *Against High-Caste Polygamy*. The text has much to tell us about the evolving methods of a canny agent of change who, despite his grounding in Sanskrit intellectual habits, explored new tools for investing shastric debate with elements of historical critique, social analysis, and empirical study. Comparing *Against High-Caste Polygamy* to *Hindu Widow Marriage*, one might even say that while the latter text found success in terms of legislative enactment, it ultimately harbored failure in both its rigidly shastric framework and in its inability to redress material and legal deprivations faced by Hindu wives and widows. By contrast, even if *Against High-Caste Polygamy* failed to initiate legislative action, this should not blind us to the success of its vision. In time, Vidyasagar's moral denunciation of Kulinism would become common sense, while his methodological insights would likewise soon become crucial tools for modern social analysis. For all these reasons, *Against High-Caste Polygamy* is a text that speaks to the remarkable, if complicated, legacy of Ishvarchandra Vidyasagar.

Against High-Caste Polygamy: The English Translation

Author's Notice

Because the custom of polygamy is practiced in our land, women suffer tremendously and numerous ills come to plague society. There is no possibility of ending either this suffering or these ills without a law enacted by the Government. This is why the people of our land have occasionally submitted petitions to the Government seeking an end to the custom. The first of these came sixteen years ago, when a petition was presented to the Legislative Council from the Friends Harmony Association at the instigation of Kishorichand Mitra.[1] A petition was also submitted by opponents of such a measure, arguing that polygamy is in accord with the Shastras and claiming that Government intervention constituted a threat to Hindu Dharma. At that time these two petitions were the only initiatives of note.

2 | Two years later, the rulers of Burdwan, Navadwip, Dinajpur, Natore, Dighapati and nearly all the leading figures of the land submitted a petition to the Legislative Council seeking the end of the custom of polygamy.[2] At that time one could say that the people of the land were in agreement on this issue, since petitions came in from all over, supporting the end of the custom, while not a word was heard from any party in opposition.[3] The amount of effort undertaken to prevent this despicable custom by the well-known Ramaprasad Roy, now deceased, and all the work he did with incredible energy, earned him immense praise. Real confidence was engendered that the Legislative Council would enact a law banning polygamy. However, fate dealt our unfortunate land a blow when the Rebellion broke out. The Government turned all its attention to quelling the Rebellion. There was no longer occasion for them to focus on banning polygamy.

Against High-Caste Polygamy. Ishvarchandra Vidyasagar, Translated by Brian A. Hatcher, Oxford University Press.
 DOI: 10.1093/oso/9780197675908.003.0002

3 | And so this great undertaking came to nought. Thereafter the late Raja Devnarayan Singh began to invest incredible energy toward banning polygamy.[4] At the time the noble Raja was a member of the Legislative Council. He resolved to bring this matter before the Council. He remained committed to this, but sadly his appointment on the Council expired before he found an occasion to raise the issue as he had intended.

4 | After another five years efforts were once again made to ban polygamy. At the time, the rulers of places like Burdwan and Navadwip, along with various landholders in the region, several influential individuals, and a number of ordinary people—all being of one mind—submitted a petition to the Lieutenant Governor, Sir Cecil Beadon.[5] The noble Sir Cecil Beadon received the petition enthusiastically and indicated that the Legislative Council would work to enact a law banning polygamy. However, either because of opposition from opponents of the measure, or for some other reason, he abandoned all efforts in this direction.

5 | The last time a petition was submitted to the Government, objections were raised from this and that quarter. It was then that I set out to publish this book, realizing how essential it was to examine all these objections. However, things stalled unexpectedly. I fell quite ill at the time and was confined to bed. I saw no pressing need to bring out the book and in any case did not have the strength to complete it. And so it remained half-finished for some time.

6 | Lately I have heard that the Calcutta-based Society for the Protection of the Eternal Dharma has turned its attention to the banning of polygamy; they would like to see this hideous and cruel custom abolished.[6] In order to ascertain whether banning the custom would bring shame on the Shastras and transgress Dharma, the officers of the Society have sought the opinion of leading scholars of Dharmashastra; they have also made repeated submissions to the Government. I believe they are motivated by the best intentions in taking up this matter, which is so crucial for the welfare of the land. I am now printing and distributing the present work in the hope it may be of assistance to them.[7]

7 | The last time such an effort was made, there were some who claimed that the petition seeking a ban on polygamy had only come about because the Government had indicated its approval of the matter. Some claimed that those who had undertaken to submit the petition were despisers of Hindu Dharma, whose very purpose was to destroy Hindu Dharma. But

when it comes to the Society for the Protection of Hindu Dharma, one can scarcely imagine such a disgraceful motive; the Society was established precisely to protect Hindu Dharma in this land. Only the most ignorant or unsophisticated person could claim that the officers of a society such as this would follow the instructions of the Government and set out to destroy Hindu Dharma. Then again, those who consistently stand in the way of helping this land will stop at nothing. The whole affair has driven them mad and they will use any means to see that the proposal is stopped. Such people are the greatest obstacle to the eradication of social evils in this land.[8] Their natures and characters really are amazing: willing to do nothing themselves, they prevent others from doing anything as well. Long may they live!

8 | Back when Raja Devnarayan Singh considered the need for legislation on this issue, he drafted a manuscript.[9] If his draft manuscript had become law and had been promulgated as a ruling on polygamy among the Hindus of this region, it is impossible to think it would have represented anything other than a blessing for the land and for the society; it certainly would not have caused any trouble or misfortune. The draft manuscript is printed as an Appendix to this book.

9 | In closing, I would beseech the Society for the Protection of Hindu Dharma not to spare any care or effort in taking up this matter. It is no exaggeration to say that our land and our society will be incalculably benefitted if their efforts prove successful. Clearly they would not have undertaken this matter if they did not appreciate this fact. Their heartfelt hatred and revulsion toward polygamy stem from the realization that its continued practice triggers a chain of dire social consequences. Obviously it is the same revulsion and hatred for the practice that drives their efforts to see it banned.

Shri Ishvarchandra Sharma
Kashipur
1st of Shravan | Samvat 1928

Against High-Caste Polygamy

Women are weaker than men and completely subservient to them on account of social regulations. Because of this weakness and subservience, they spend their lives cowering and humiliated before men. The sovereign and powerful class of men does as it pleases, committing outrage and injustice. Being utterly without means, women put up with this throughout their lives. This is the condition of women in almost every region of the earth. But nowhere else does one find women facing the conditions they do in this unfortunate land, all because of the excessive sway of the cruelty, selfishness, and thoughtlessness of our men. Here, whenever men fall under the sway of some awful custom, it is the unfortunate women who face endless misery. And worst of all is the evil wrought today by the custom of polygamy. Because of the ongoing practice of this hideous and cruel custom, there is no limit to the misfortune of women. It breaks your heart to contemplate all the affliction and misery that befalls women because of the sway of this custom. Indeed, the outrages on this score are so many and so unbearable that anyone with even the slightest conscience and sense of right and wrong is bound to become an ardent opponent of the custom; they can desire nothing less than to see the custom abolished immediately by law. In the current state of our land, the only way to ban this all-pervading evil is by Government decree. This is why so many people are energetic about petitioning the Government to ban the truly evil custom of polygamy. At the same time there are those who have raised objections. I intend to provide answers to all these objections to the best of my ability.[10]

First Objection: Polygamy Is in Accord with the Shastras

There are some people who, as soon as you list the evils of polygamy or raise the possibility of banning the custom, reach for their swords. They are convinced that polygamy is in accord with the Shastras and conforms to Dharma. Anyone who displays anger or revulsion on this topic is, according to such people, a Shastra-denying, Dharma-hating non-believer and should be ranked among the lowest of the low. People like these have concluded that were polygamy to be banned it would lead to disrespect for the Shastras and a decay of Dharma. They argue and they debate in the name of the Shastra and Dharma, but they do not fully understand just how far the Shastras actually support the matter; nor do they appreciate the degree of ignoble conduct that arises from the untrammeled behavior of men. In this land, the entirety of Dharma is rooted in the Shastras. Those matters on which there are injunctions in the Shastra are considered to be in conformity with Dharma. Likewise, what is prohibited in the Shastra is considered to be opposed to Dharma. So let us follow out all the injunctions or prohibitions issued by the creators of the Shastras in the matter of marriage; let us examine them to decide whether or not the matter of polygamy is in accord with the Shastras and in conformity with Dharma; and let us determine whether we should fear that banning the custom of polygamy will lead to disrespect for the Shastras and a decay of Dharma.[11]

Daksha has said:

> A twice-born man—that is to say a man from one of the three classes of Brahmin, Kshatriya, or Vaishya—should not live a single day outside of his life-stage. To do so is to fall from caste [*Daksha Samhita* 1.10].[12]

If we follow this Shastra, then it is prohibited for a twice-born man to live outside of a life-stage. In this case, by implication "twice-born" really applies to all four classes: Brahmin, Kshatriya, Vaishya, and Shudra.[13] Thus, in the *Vamana Purana* it is stated:

> These four life-stages are indicated for Brahmins: Student, Householder, Forest Dweller, and Renouncer. The first three are indicated for Kshatriyas; the first two for Vaishyas. For Shudras Householder is the only life-stage; he should practice it contentedly [*Vamana Purana* as cited in the *Udvahatattva*].[14]

Following this ruling, there are a total of four life stages: Student, Householder, Forest Dweller, and Renouncer. In accordance with differences in a man's age and entitlement, it is necessary for him to adopt one or the other of these four life stages. A Brahmin is entitled to all four life stages. A Kshatriya may adopt the three life stages of Student, Householder, and Forest Dweller. For the Vaishya, there are two life stages, Student and Householder. The Shudra is entitled only to the life stage of the Householder. Studentship is said to follow on investiture with the sacred thread, leading to residence at a teacher's home, Vedic study, and lessons in good conduct. After completing studentship a man marries and pursues worldly life, which is the Householder stage. The Forest Dweller stage is said to come after completion of the duties of Householder and consists of resorting to forest life for the purpose of Yogic practice. When the duties of the Forest Dweller are complete, one is said to abandon all concerns in a life of renunciation.

Manu says:

> A twice born man, having taken his guru's permission, and having bathed and performed the ritual of return,* should marry an attractive woman of his own caste [*Manu-smriti* 3.4].

This is the first injunction concerning marriage. In keeping with this injunction, after Vedic study and lessons in good conduct, a man enters the Householder stage by taking a wife.[15]

> Having properly completed the last rites for his first wife, a man should take another wife and re-establish his sacred fires [*Manu-smriti* 5.168].

This is the second injunction concerning marriage. In keeping with this injunction, if a householder should lose his wife, it is necessary for him to take another wife.

> A man should practice supersession, which is to say he should marry again, in those cases where his wife is addicted to drink, wanton, fractious, continually ill, harsh, or wastes his income [*Manu-smriti* 9.80].[16]

> A wife should be superseded in the eighth year if she is barren, in the tenth year if her son dies, in the eleventh year if she bears only daughters, but immediately if she speaks harshly† [*Manu-smriti* 9.81].

This is the third injunction concerning marriage. In keeping with this injunction, if a wife is found to be barren, etc., then even during her lifetime another marriage is necessary.

> For the twice-born, marriage within one's class is enjoined first of all; those who undertake to marry voluntarily should marry into other classes according to order. That is, a Brahmin may marry a Brahmin, Kshatriya, Vaishya, or Shudra; a Kshatriya may marry a Kshatriya, Vaishya or Shudra; a Vaishya may marry a Vaishya or Shudra; and a Shudra may only marry a Shudra [*Manu-smriti* 3.12–13].

* A particular ritual ceremony following on completion of Vedic study and studentship and prior to entering the householder stage.

† She who always uses foul language toward her husband.

This is the fourth injunction concerning marriage. In keeping with this injunction, marriage with a woman of one's own class is the option that is preferred for the three classes of Brahmin, Kshatriya, and Vaishya. But if someone from one of the highest classes marries a woman of his own class, and then, from his own desire, chooses to marry again, he should marry someone from a class beneath his own.

These injunctions suggest three types of marriage: Required, Contingent, and Desired. A marriage according to the first injunction is a Required marriage. If a man fails to marry in this way, he is not entitled to the householder stage. A marriage in accord with the second injunction is also a Required marriage. If it is not performed, a man is outcasted for having fallen from his life stage.[‡] A marriage in accord with the third injunction is a Contingent marriage, since it occurs by reason of a wife's barrenness, etc. A marriage in accordance with the fourth injunction is a Desired marriage. Such a marriage is not necessary as are the Required and Contingent marriages.[17] It is entirely due to a man's desire, which is to say, such a marriage happens only if it is desired and for no other reason. Only the three classes of Brahmins, Kshatriyas, and Vaishyas are entitled to Desired marriages; there is no such entitlement for Shudras.

The purpose of the Householder stage is to procure sons and carry out one's duties. These two things cannot be fulfilled without taking a wife. This is why, in the first injunction, taking a wife is like the doorway that allows entry into the Householder life stage; it is also the essential means for fulfilling the Householder stage. If a man were to lose his wife while carrying out the Householder stage and did not marry again, then being bereft of a wife, he would be outcasted for having fallen out of his life stage. This is why the creators of the Shastras caused the second injunction to apply to Householders who found themselves in this condition, namely to communicate the necessity of taking another wife. If a wife suffers from a fault, such as barrenness or extended illness, then this represents an obstacle to the acquisition of sons or the performance of Dharma. The creators of the Shastras provided an injunction that in such cases, even a man with a wife may marry again. If, after completing a marriage to a woman of the same class—in accordance with the injunctions of the Shastras and so as to pursue the Householder stage—a man of a higher class chooses to marry again, the creators of the Shastras promulgated the fourth injunction, which communicates the entitlement to

‡ Since it arises due to the loss of a wife, this marriage can also be called Contingent.

marriage outside of one's class. When it comes to marriage, there are no further injunctions to be found. And thus, when a wife is living, the creators of the Shastras did not approve of forming marriages within one's class purely out of desire—apart from the conditions just discussed. Basically, due to the existence of the injunction regarding marriage outside of one's class, a man is prohibited from forming another marriage within his class purely out of desire.

The last mentioned injunction is known as Exclusionary.[18] The rule pertaining to Exclusionary injunctions is that since there is an injunction that already applies in this case, a prohibition applies in all other cases. Injunctions are of three types: Originative, Restrictive, and Exclusionary. In cases where it is not possible to act without an injunction, one speaks of an Originative injunction. An example would be, *svargakamo yajeta*, which means "one who desires heaven should perform sacrifice." Without this injunction, people would not perform sacrifices out of a desire to gain heaven, since there is no other way to know that sacrifice leads to heaven. Any injunction that serves to limit a matter is known as Restrictive. An example would be the phrase *samadeshe yajeta*, meaning "one should sacrifice on level ground." We know there is an injunction for people to perform sacrifice. Such a sacrifice could be performed in various places; depending on their preference, people might choose to sacrifice on either level or uneven ground. But the Restrictive injunction, *samadeshe yajeta*, restricts the place of sacrifice to level ground. Any injunction that serves to prohibit action in cases that go beyond the enjoined matter—and in which following the injunction as enjoined would be voluntary—is known as Exclusionary. An example would be, *pancha panchanakha bhakshyah*, which means "the group of five, five-nailed animals may be eaten."[19] People could voluntarily eat as many five-nailed animals as they wished. However, by the injunction *pancha panchanakha bhakshyah*, there is effected a prohibition on eating five-nailed animals other than those in the group of five-nailed animals, such as dogs, etc. In other words, when people set out to eat the meat of five-nailed animals, they should not eat the meat of five-nailed animals other than those in the group of five, five-nailed animals. Furthermore, whether or not to eat the meat of the five-nailed animals in this group is entirely something people may choose. If they wish, they may eat; if not, they do not have to eat. In the same way, a man could voluntarily undertake additional marriages with wives of either the same or different class. However, because there is an injunction that if one voluntarily undertakes another marriage it should be outside of one's class, then there is a prohibition on marrying any women but those outside of one's class. Furthermore, such marriages outside of one's class are also a voluntary matter; a man may or may not choose to do so. The purpose of the fourth injunction is to stipulate that if a man voluntarily chooses to marry, he may not undertake any marriage except one that is outside his class. This injunction cannot be called Originative because such a marriage is only obtained by people voluntarily. One refers to Originative injunctions to indicate matters that cannot be accomplished in any other way. Nor can this marriage injunction be called Restrictive, since this injunction does not stipulate the necessity of marriage outside of one's class. As such, we must necessarily acknowledge that this marriage injunction is Exclusionary [*1.10].[20]

The basic purport of the four-fold injunction on marriage is as follows: The first injunction requires a Householder to marry a woman of his class. The second injunction requires another marriage in one's class should a Householder lose his wife. The third injunction requires another marriage in one's class if a wife is barren, etc. The fourth injunction allows a man who has married to marry again if he desires, provided the next marriage is outside his class; no marriage other than one outside his class is allowed. And since the practice of marriage outside of one's class has been abolished for the Kali Yuga, there can no longer be a place for voluntary marriages.

Thus it is clearly established that not only were the creators of the Shastras not in favor of the sort of voluntary polygamy we see today, they absolutely prohibited it. This means that those who voluntarily enter into plural marriages become outcast on account of performing a prohibited action.[21]

About this, Yajnavalkya says:

> If a man fails to perform what is enjoined, performs what is prohibited, and cannot bring his senses under control, he will fall [*Yajnavalkya-smriti* 3.219].[22]

Some passages in Manu refer to one man having many wives. When they see this, some people say that since we can clearly find in the Shastras places where one man has simultaneously had many wives, it makes no sense to say that the creators of the Shastras were not in favor of the voluntary practice of polygamy. Such people tend to cite Shastras like the following:

> If a man has several wives of the same caste living, he should complete his religious rites with the eldest of them [*Vishnu Samhita* 26.1].[23]

> Manu says that if one of a man's co-wives has a son then all his wives should be considered to have a son [*Manu-smriti* 9.183].[24]
>
> A man married three times who fails to marry a fourth time destroys his clan to the seventh generation; he should perform the penance for foeticide [*Grihastha-ratnakara* as cited in the *Udvahatattva*].[25]

None of these passages show that a man may voluntarily accomplish plural marriages beyond what is stated in the Shastras. In the first passage from Vishnu Samhita, there is mention of one man with many wives; however, there is no reason not to believe that these marriages were made by "supersession." In the second passage from Manu, it is evident that the many marriages mentioned are only due to the barrenness of previous wives. This is why a ruling is given in the case of wives who are without sons. In the third passage, quoted from the *Udvahatattva*, there is instruction on the need to conduct a fourth marriage after three other marriages; but this passage does not pertain to plural marriage. Its context is as follows: if a man who successively marries two wives chooses to marry again, he will then have three marriages; his failure to marry a fourth time will constitute a sin. To remove this sin a custom has now arisen, such that the man desirous of marrying will initially imagine a flowering tree as his wife. In this way he will complete his third marriage to her. Afterward, the next time he marries will be counted as his fourth marriage. In this way there is one passage for both the third and the fourth marriage. Some rule that this passage applies to cases where there are three living wives [*1.14]. If we accept this ruling, then the existing three wives should be considered supersessionary, and the fourth marriage is meant to remove the fault as mentioned in the passage. That is, since the first three wives were barren, etc., three marriages took place over time; since there are now three wives living and since the passage quoted in the *Udvahatattva* stipulates the need to marry a fourth time, another marriage is thus necessary. Beyond all the reasons provided for supersession in the passage from Manu, this passage is said to add the need for removing the aforementioned fault.[26] The point is: since the creators of the Shastra have given an injunction stipulating that voluntary marriages should be outside of one's class; and since through this injunction there is a clear and absolute prohibition on taking marriages within one's class when other wives are still living; and since it is entirely possible to consider all these plural marriages as supersessionary; then there is no way to establish that the creators of the Shastras were in favor of making as many marriages as one wished.

Some say that since we find examples in Purana and Itihasa of certain kings who had multiple wives simultaneously, then it cannot be accepted that a man's having many marriages is not approved by the Shastras. It is true that evidence can be found that kings in earlier ages had many marriages. But not all these marriages were voluntary. The Ramayana states that Raja Dasharatha had many ladies. Even so, it cannot be demonstrated that he conducted all these marriages voluntarily. The Ramayana indicates that he was not privileged to see the face of his son until reaching old age. This certainly suggests that his first wife was determined to be barren. So he married a second time. And when that wife also failed to produce a son, the king married again on the understanding that his wife was barren. In this way he formed many marriages. Finally, in his old age, sons were born to his three queens, Kaushalya, Kaikeyi, and Sumitra. This is why we can easily see that King Dasharatha's many marriages arose from the need to overcome his fear that his wives were barren. And other kings had multiple marriages for the same reason as Dasaratha, or for other reasons approved by the Shastras. There is no doubt about this. Still it can also be seen that other kings married multiple times voluntarily. But such examples do not help demonstrate that polygamy is a matter approved by the Shastras. It would be inappropriate to take the conduct of kings as an example for ordinary people. The kings of India were each by their own entitlements all-powerful. When the people violate the rulings of the Dharmashastra, it is often the king who places them on the right path by dispensing justice. But if kings take to the wrong path, there is no one to return them to the right path. Basically kings are completely independent in all matters. Which is to say, if some king, acting of his own accord and in defiance of the Shastras, voluntarily undertakes multiple marriages, ordinary people should not conclude that following his example and undertaking many marriages is authorized by scripture. Manu states:

> In his power a king is like Agni, Vayu, Surya, Chandra, Yama, Kubera and Varuna. Even if a king is still only a boy, it is not appropriate to think of him like an ordinary mortal. He truly rules as a god on earth in human form [*Manu-smriti* 9.7–9.8].

Kings are not ordinary mortals. The creators of the Shastras reckon them to be mighty divinities. Therefore, just as the behavior of divinities is not to be copied by mortals, neither should the behavior of kings. This is why the creators of the Shastras have ruled that what is unauthorized for ordinary people is not a cause of sin among brilliant rulers.

Basically, the matter of voluntary polygamy is rooted in unrestrained behavior. This hideous and cruel practice is neither approved by the Shastras nor in accord with Dharma. And if it should be banned there would be no possibility of disrespect for the Shastras nor reason to fear the decay of Dharma.

Second Objection: Abolishing Polygamy Will Destroy Dharma

Some people object that if the custom of polygamy is banned, Kulin Brahmins will suffer a loss of caste and the decay of their Dharma. Were this objection justified, it would be completely improper to seek a ban on the custom of polygamy. To determine whether or not this objection is justified, it is necessary to thoroughly review the custom of Kulinism. Hence I will briefly discuss the original ruling that established Kulin rank as well as its status in the present-day.

The Raja Adisura resolved to perform a sacrifice to gain a son. He invited qualified Brahmins to complete the sacrificial session.[27] In those days the Brahmins of our land followed degraded customs and were completely unlearned in the performance of the rites enjoined by the Veda. As such, they were not capable of completing the sacrificial session desired by Adisura. And so, in the year 942 CE, the king—having no other recourse—sent an envoy to beseech the king of Kanyakubja to send him five Brahmins who were learned in the Shastras and of excellent conduct [*2.1].[28] In response, the king of Kanyakubja dispatched five Brahmins belonging to the following five different lineages [*2.2]—

Lineage	Name of Brahmin
1. Shandilya	Bhattanarayana
2. Kashyapa	Daksha
3. Vatsya	Chandara
4. Bharadwaj	Shriharsha
5. Savarna	Vedagarbha

The Brahmins came to the land of Gauda on horseback, along with their wives and servants. They arrived at the gate of the royal palace with their leather sandals and finely sewn clothes, chewing betel leaf.[29] They told the guard, "Inform the king immediately of our arrival." When he heard the news, the king was delighted. However, when the guard told him of their behavior and dress, the king fell to thinking, "I have brought Brahmins from a distant land because the Brahmins of this land follow degraded customs and do not observe the rites. However, from what I have just heard, I have to wonder how excellent their conduct is and how skilled they are in the rites. That being the case, I shall not meet them right away, but will first learn the nature of their conduct. Then I will decide what to do." So resolved, the king instructed the guard, "Inform the Brahmin Lords that I am currently distracted by other duties and cannot meet them right now. Let them take rest at the residence and I will meet them when time allows."

Upon hearing this, the guard left to inform the Brahmins. The Brahmins, thinking the king would welcome them at any moment, were standing there with their hands cupped, making offerings of water. When they heard the king would not be coming, they took the water for blessing and poured it over a nearby wrestler's staff. Such was the power of the Brahmins that no sooner had the water fell onto the staff than the long-desiccated wood came to life, sending forth buds and new flowers.[§] This amazing news was immediately conveyed to the king. He was astounded. Initially, on hearing of their behavior and dress, the king had been upset and was not inclined to trust the Brahmins; now he felt great faith and affection toward them. He presented himself at their door, carrying a scarf, his hands folded respectfully. He fell at their feet in a display of ardent devotion and beseeched their pardon.[**]

Not long after this, on a day chosen for its auspiciousness, the king had the five Brahmins perform the sacrifice for a son. Through the power of the sacrifice the queen became pregnant. In time she gave birth to a son. The king was so greatly pleased that he encouraged the Brahmins to settle in his realm. Finding themselves unable to decline the king's offer, the Brahmins accepted

[§] The people of Vikrampur say that to the south of Vallala Sena's house there is a pond, on the north side of which is a stone landing-stage where a tree still grows. It is an enormous tree known as the Gajari Tree. There is no other tree of its kind in Vikrampur; they are not seen anywhere but on Mount Madhupur in Mymensingh District. Many say that the site of the wrestler's staff is where elephants used to be tethered. [Trans.: I am indebted to Rajat Sanyal, who directed me to colonial-era conversations about the antiquity of this site in Munshiganj District in present-day Bangladesh, and to legends surrounding the Gajari tree—the name of which seems to play on the words for "sprouting" (*gajāno*) and "elephant" (*gaja*). See especially Roychowdhuri, *Adisura o Vallalasena*, 4].

[**] I provide here a faithful account of the way this story is typically told.

the proposal. To each of them the king donated one of five villages as a place to settle down: Panchakoti, Kamakoti, Hirakoti, Kankagram, and Batagram [*2.5].[30]

In time these five men produced fifty-six sons. Bhattanarayana had sixteen, Daksha sixteen, Shriharsha four, Vedagarbha twelve, and Chandara eight [*2.6]. The king gave each of these men a village to reside in. And this is how their offspring came to be known as hailing from such and such a village [*2.7–2.11].[31]

Prior to the arrival of Bhattanarayana and the rest of the Brahmins, there had been seven hundred Brahmin households in this land. Henceforth, these families were despised and spurned. They were called "The Seven Hundred" and came to be known as a separate community. Among them they had such villages as Jagai, Bhagai, Sagai, Namasi, Arath, Balathavi, Pithuri, Mulukujuri, etc. The Seven Hundred were not among the five lineages and for that reason the sons of the Brahmins who had come from Kanykubja would not share with them food, rituals, or gifts of exchange. Anyone who did became just as despised and spurned as the Seven Hundred.[32]

Eventually the family line of Adisura ended. The kings of the Sena family line ascended the throne of Gauda [*2.12]. It was during the reign of the celebrated Vallala Sena that the Kulin ranks were established.[33] As time went by there was decay in the learning and conduct of the descendants of the Brahmins who had come from Kanyakubja. The chief purpose of Kulin rank was to arrest this decay. King Vallala Sena determined that if he gave special recognition to nine attributes such as conduct, humility, and learning, then the Brahmins would be sure to preserve them. So he examined the Brahmins to see who had the nine attributes. On those who did, he bestowed Kulin rank. The nine attributes promoting Kulinism are said to be: conduct, humility, learning, fame, pilgrimage, faith, exchange, austerity, and generosity [*2.13]. The meaning of the term "exchange" is "changing one thing for another," and it is of four types: receiving, giving, substituting, and promising before a genealogist [*2.14].[34] The word "receiving" means accepting daughters from homes of similar or more elevated status.[35] The word "giving" means bestowing daughters on homes of similar or more elevated status. The word "substituting" means giving a daughter made of sacred grass in lieu of a real daughter. And "promising before a genealogist" means that both parties, in lieu of a daughter, agree only verbally in front of a genealogist to exchange daughters. The chief mark of a Kulin is to give daughters to good Kulin homes and to receive daughters from good Kulin homes. But the exchange of daughters cannot happen when there are no daughters, so a person with no daughters can lay no claim to the mark of Kulinism. The two practices of exchanging daughters by means of sacred grass and making a verbal assertion before a genealogist were both instituted to remove this fault.[36]

Earlier I mentioned that each of the fifty-six sons of the Brahmins who came from Kanyakubja had settled in a particular village.[37] The various Kulin surnames derive from the names of these villages.[38] Their descendants are known by these Kulin surnames. There are fifty-six Kulin surnames in total; among these the eight Kulin surnames of Bandya, Chatta, Mukhaiti, Ghoshal, Putitunda, Ganguli, Kanjilal, and Kundagrami were preeminently distinguished by possession of the nine attributes [*2.15].[39] Therefore they attained Kulin rank [*2.16–18].

There is a legend that when King Vallala Sena fixed the day for establishing the Kulin ranks, he instructed the Brahmins to come to his royal assembly when their daily rites were completed. As it happened, some Brahmins arrived at one o'clock, others at half past one, and still others at half past two.[40] Those who arrived at two-thirty received Kulin rank; those who arrived at one-thirty were made Shrotriyas; and those who arrived at one o'clock became Lesser Kulins. The purport of this story is that the proper performance of daily rites requires extra time. As such it can be inferred that those who arrived at two-thirty had properly completed their rites. This is how the king was able to recognize them as having the best conduct. And so he bestowed on them the highest rank. Those who arrived at one-thirty were of somewhat lesser conduct and therefore received a correspondingly lower rank. Those who arrived at one o'clock were determined to have fallen from proper conduct and so the king, viewing them with disdain, ranked them among the lowest of Brahmins.

This is how Kulin rank was established. The rule was that Kulins would carry out exchange with Kulins. They were allowed to receive daughters from Shrotriyas, but not to give daughters to Shrotriyas. If they were to do so, they would fall from their clan rank and become known as Vamshaja [*2.19]. And their clan rank would be lost the instant they accepted daughters from Lesser Kulins. This is why Lesser Kulins are known as the enemies of clan rank [*2.20].

After Vallala Sena had established the Kulin ranks, certain Brahmin genealogists received the same status. It was stipulated that their role would be to sing the praises of the Kulins and to recount their genealogies, while paying careful attention to the attributes, faults, and rules pertaining to Kulin rank [*2.21].[41]

Besides the Kulin, Shrotriya, and Lesser Kulins there is one further type of Brahmin known as Vamshaja. All we know is that at the moment when Vallala Sena ranked the Brahmins, he uttered the word Vamshaja. In point of fact, he did not assign any Brahmins to a separate category called Vamshaja. Rulings about Vamshajas would come later.[42] In the course of events, all the Kulin daughters who were married into Shrotriya homes lost their clan status. Anyone losing clan status in such a way came to be called Vamshaja; and when it came to matters of rank, they were classed with the Lesser Kulins. In other words, just as clan status could be lost by taking daughters from Lesser Kulins, it could also be lost by accepting daughters from Vamshaja homes. And so there came to be three types of Vamshaja: First, Kulin Vamshajas who would give daughters to Shrotriya grooms; second, Kulin Vamshajas who would accept daughters from Lesser Kulins; and third, Kulin Vamshajas who accepted daughters from Vamshajas. Basically, the idea is that if one ever loses clan status, one becomes a Vamshaja.[††]

With the establishment of Kulin rank, the Brahmins of this land were divided into five groups: Kulins, Shrotriyas, Vamshaja, Lesser Kulins, and the Seven Hundred, who fell completely outside the five lineages from Kanyakubja.

Eventually, the Lesser Kulins were associated with the Shrotriyas, even if they never were able to attain equality with them. True Shrotriyas started to be called Pure Shrotriyas, while the Lesser Kulins were known as Forced Shrotriyas. And just as they had been disdained and spurned when they were first labelled Lesser Kulins, so too this pattern continued after they were called Forced Shrotriyas.

Ten generations after the establishment of Kulin rank, Devivara Ghataka Visharada organized the Kulins into Assemblages.[43] The Brahmins on whom Vallala had bestowed Kulin rank, gradually lost nearly all their distinctive attributes such as conduct, humility, learning, etc. The only focus

[††] The genealogists do not all agree that Vallala merely pronounced the word "Vamshaja" without ever actually delivering a ruling about Vamshajas. They say that of the fifty-six surnames, thirty-four were established as Shrotriya and fourteen as Lesser Kulin. Of the people comprising the remaining eight surnames, only nineteen were Kulin. No ruling can be found that applies to those not among this group of nineteen. It is possible that Vallala classified all these people as Vamshaja. They were thus possibly the original Vamshajas. Later on all those who lost clan status as a result of errors in marriage became known as Vamshaja. It is also completely possible that these original Vamshajas received the title of genealogist from Vallala. [Translator: this note is quoted verbatim (with no attribution to Vidyasagar) by Lalmohan Vidyanidhi in his influential *Sambandhanirṇaya*, p. 228.]

of their effort and conviction was the attribute of exchange. However, in Devivara's day even this attribute was abandoned. The purity of giving and receiving daughters had remained the only basis for Kulin rank as bestowed by Vallala, and now even that was lost. The very faults that had once led to loss of Kulin rank were now present among all Kulins. Devivara arranged all the Kulins tainted by a particular fault into one community. He called these communities Assemblages. The word "assemblage" means sharing a fault, as if to say all those tainted by the same fault constituted a community [*2.23]. Devivara ruled that clan rank derives from the presence of a fault [*2.24]. If Vallala had issued rulings on Kulin rank based on the presence of attributes, Devivara issued rulings on Kulin rank based on the presence of faults. Devivara arranged the Kulins of his day into thirty-six Assemblages, each depending on a particular fault [*2.25]. Of these, the Assemblages known as Phuliya and Khardaha were the most prevalent. The people of these two Assemblages were regarded as the highest of Kulins.[44] Members of these two Assemblages would become the most egregious offenders against conduct. The faults characteristic of these two Assemblages are noted as follows:

Gangananda Mukhopadhyay and Sripati Bandyopadhyay were both tainted with one fault, and so Devivara placed them in the Phuliya Assemblage.[45] The four faults of Nadha, Dhandha, Baruihati, and Mulukjuri were placed in the Phuliya Assemblage.[46] The Bandyopadhyays living in the place called Nadha were Vamshaja; Gangananda's father Manohar married with their houses. Because of marrying their Vamshaja daughters, he lost his clan and fell to the status of a Vamshaja. In order to save Manohar's clan, the genealogists decreed the Bandhyopadhyays of Nadha to be Shrotriyas. Since that time the Bandhyopadhyays of Nadha, though actually Vamshaja, are reckoned to be Mashcatak Shrotriyas. So in effect, even though Manohar lost his clan through this marriage, by the grace of the genealogists his clan was saved. This is called the Nadha Fault. Srinath Chattopadhyay had two unmarried daughters. A Muslim named Hamsai living in a place called Dhandha took these two daughters by force and caused them to lose caste. Later, one of these daughters married Paramananda Putitunda, the son of a metalsmith; the other married Gangavara Bandyopadhyay. Nilakantha Gangopadhyay entered into exchange relations with this Gangavara. Thereby Gangananda, too, was tainted with the foreign fault, which is called the Dhandha fault [*2.26]. If they eat in the village of Baruihati, Brahmins lose their caste. Kanchnar Mukhopadhyay once fed Arjuna Mishra in this village. Sripati Bandyopadhyay entered into exchange with him, and by engaging in exchange with Sripati Bandyopadhya, Gangananda too was tainted. This is called the Baruihati Fault. Gangananda's nephew Shivacharya married a daughter from Mulukjuri, which led him to lose caste and fall to the rank of the Seven Hundred. Later he married the daughter of Sripati Bandyopadhya. This is known as the Mulukjuri Fault.

Yogeshvara Pandit and Madhu Chattopadhyay were both tainted with one fault, and so Devivara placed them in the Khardaha Assemblage.[47] Yogeshvara's father Hari Mukhopadhyay married a daughter from Gargari, while Yogeshvar himself married a daughter from Piplai. Madhu Chattopadhyay married the daughter of Ray Paramananda from Dingsai. Yogeshvara gave his daughters to this same Madhu Chattopadhyay.

If one marries a daughter from the Vamshaja, Lesser Kulin, or Seven Hundred communities, one's clan is lost immediately and one becomes Vamshaja. It is characteristic of the Phuliya Assemblage that Gangananda Mukhopadhyay's father Manohar married the daughter of a Vamshaja. Gangananda's nephew Shivacharya married a daughter from Mulukjuri. It is the nature of the Khardaha Assemblage that Yogeshvara Pandit's father Hari Mukhopadhyay married a daughter from Gargari; Yogeshvara himself married a daughter from Piplai; and Madhu Chattopadhyay married a daughter from Dingsai. Mulukjuri falls outside the five lineages traced to Kanyakubja and is thus among the community of the Seven Hundred. Gargari, Piplai, and Dingsai are all Lesser Kulins. The pride that the people of the Phuliya and Khardaha Assemblages have in being Kulins is completely misguided; their clan was destroyed a long time ago and they became Vamshajas by virtue of marrying daughters from among the Vamshaja, Lesser Kulin, and the Seven Hundred. Furthermore, due to connection with the Foreign Fault the people of the Phuliya Assemblage lost their caste. This is how the people of all these assemblages lost their caste and fell to the level of Vamshaja, all due to the fault of bad marriages. Put very simply, the system of Kulin rank established by Vallala prior to the creation of the assemblages has been lost. Those today who boast of being Kulin have actually been Vamshaja for a long time. If one follows the rules of Kulin custom, there is not the least difference between those who are reckoned Vamshajas and the proud Kulins of today.[‡‡]

And so it can be shown that for a long time the system of Kulin rank among the Brahmins of Rarh has been vitiated. It is impossible to find anyone today

‡‡ There is a detailed account in the *Doshamalagrantha* regarding which faults lead to which Assemblages. I do not enter into this here for fear of prolixity. Anyone eager to know more should consult the *Doshamalagrantha*. [Translator: I have not been able to locate a text by this name.]

who can be considered a Kulin according to the very rules of the Kulin system. And if this is the case, since the claims of the Kulins are completely inauthentic, then it is unreasonable to object that banning the custom of polygamy would lead to the loss of caste or the destruction of Dharma among the Kulins.

All the homes that Devivara placed into assemblages have established patterns of exchange. Prior to the creation of the assemblages, the Kulins practiced exchange among eight homes. This used to be called mutuality in marriage. In those days there was no difficulty in practicing exchange.[48] There was no need for a man to marry more than once; and Kulin daughters were not forced to go through their lives unmarried. Now, because so few houses are grouped in assemblages, an irrational desire to protect clan status inevitably causes many daughters to be gifted to a single groom. This is how plural marriage got its start among Devivara's Kulins.[49]

According to the Shastras, it is a grievous sin for a daughter to experience her first menses while not yet married. Kashyapa has said:

> The father of an unmarried daughter who experiences her menses while living in his house is tainted with the sin of foeticide. Such a daughter is called Vrishali. Any ignorant Brahmin who marries such a daughter, is to be shunned,[§§] outcasted.[***] and known as the husband of a Vrishali [Kashyapa as quoted in the *Udvahatattva*].[50]

Yama has said:

> If they see an unmarried daughter begin her menses, these three go to hell—the mother, father and eldest brother. Any deluded Brahmin who marries such a daughter, is not to be spoken to[†††], is outcasted, and is known as the husband of a Vrishali [*Yama Samhita* 23–24].[51]

Paithanasi has said:

> A daughter should be given away before the appearance of her breasts. If a daughter has her menses before marriage, both the giver and the receiver

§§ A person who, if invited to a postmortem feast and fed food, spoils the feast.
*** A person one should not sit beside when being served food.
††† A person to whom, if one speaks, it causes one to fall.

> will go to hell. Also the father, grandfather, and great-grandfather will be reborn in feces. Therefore a daughter should be given away in marriage before her first menses [Paithanasi quoted in the *Dayabhaga* 11.2.6].

Vyasa has said

> If a man who is entitled to give away his daughter should allow his daughter to experience her menses, then the number of times that daughter experiences her menses will be the number of times he will be stained with the sin of foeticide; and as long as she remains unmarried, he will be outcasted [*Vyasa Samhita* 2.7].[52]

These days one routinely finds Kulins arranging marriages to daughters who have just begun their menses or to daughters who have already reached puberty.[53] Obedient to Devivara's fanciful customs, the Kulins commit grievous sin. If one heeds the Shastras closely, then they have long been outcaste and have fallen from Dharma.[‡‡‡]

The clan status to which the Kulins are so selfishly attached is not the work of the Creator. If it were the Creator's handiwork, the matter would stand on its own. The Brahmins of this land are unlearned and their conduct is degraded. What counts for learning among them and the very attributes they adore—such as good conduct—are the product of one king's ruling along with the rules established by that king in order to protect Kulin rank. If we followed those royally instituted rules, then we would have to say that Kulins have long since destroyed their clans through improper marriages and other errors. And since it is the case that according to that same king's rules, they should be cut off from Kulin rank, then the pride of today's revered Kulins is completely misguided. There really is no way for them to take pride in the condition and the terms by which Devivara made his rulings. If the Kulins

‡‡‡ Even though it is a grievous sin for unmarried daughters to begin their menses and for daughters who have begun puberty to be given in marriage, the prideful Kulins do not find any fault in this. If they recognized the fault, these prideful Kulins would not consider it a trifling thing; they would seek to avoid hell by not keeping their daughters in an unmarried state. And in that way they would prevent three generations of fathers, grandfathers, and great-grandfathers from being thrown into a pit of filth after death. But perhaps instead they follow this ruling from Manu: "Even if a daughter has begun puberty it is better for her to remain at home until her death than to give her to a groom devoid of the proper attributes" (Manu 9.89). Manu has enjoined against giving daughters to a groom devoid of the proper attributes, and yet today's prideful Kulins are all devoid of proper attributes. They completely lack such attributes as conduct, humility, learning, etc. Which is to say that if one follows the very Shastras they take pride in, one would have to conclude that today's Kulins routinely give their daughters to grooms in ways that are not enjoined.

had any sense, then far from acting proud they would feel ashamed when they introduce their clan. But forget about shame. They are so proud of their clan rank that they dishonor the Shastra. They send themselves to hell and cause their fathers, grandfathers, and great-grandfathers to be cast into rank cesspools after death. Here's to pride! There is no limit to your power and glory. You are an awful enemy of humankind.[54] Just let someone fall victim to your sorcery and their reason is lost, as are all sense of good and evil, right and wrong.

Ten generations after the institution of Kulin rank, Devivara saw that some weakening had occurred and so he established a new framework through the assemblages.[55] Now another ten generations have passed since the forming of the assemblages [*2.36]. As a result the Kulins have been weakened even further. The time has come for establishing a new framework. The first time around, when Vallala Sena saw weakness among the Brahmins, he established Kulin rank as a way to address it. When Devivara saw that weakness had once again befallen the Kulins, he established the assemblages. Today such manifold weakness has befallen the Kulins that there is no good means to address it except through abandoning Kulin pride. If the Kulins had any sense, were true to Dharma, and actually cherished their own well-being, they would relinquish this petty pride and eliminate the stain on the name of Kulinism. And if they think abandoning Kulin pride is impossible or inappropriate, then we will need a new ruling.[56] It may in fact be the case that there is no other path for rescuing the Kulins than through promulgating mutuality in marriage. If we were to take that route, there would be no further need for a Kulin to marry more than once. Nor would any Kulin daughter remain unmarried for a long period of time—let alone for her whole life. She need not fear that her father would go to hell. And if the custom of polygamy should be banned by Government law, this would cause neither harm nor inconvenience. All that is needed is for Kulins and their supporters to apply themselves diligently. Rather than blindly and foolishly seeking to protect this harmful and irreligious Kulin pride, let the supporters of Kulinism use their intelligence, discrimination, and sense of Dharma to begin reforming the errors that cause such harm and loss of Dharma.[57]

Today's arrogant and almighty Kulins take pride in their status and are worshipped by the people of the land. Were their character truly pure and religious, they would not feel injured nor would they raise objections. But their conduct is utterly hideous and vile. Hundreds are the stories told by people about their behavior. There is no need to mention them all here.[58] Suffice it to say that they have lost all mercy, fear of truth, and sense of shame. There is no more room in their hearts for the joys and sorrows of their children, let alone for their welfare. They only think of placing daughters in the most suitable homes. A daughter who finds no home is thought to cause the destruction of clan status; so they are satisfied if they can find a groom for their daughters by any means, without any thought for what might happen to the daughter. If an unmarried daughter goes outside the home, their clan status is destroyed. However, there is no harm if a daughter remains at home and is lured into adultery and stained by repeated foeticide. Protect the clan however you can; get the girl married; if she goes on to become a courtesan, such people feel no anger, shame, or hurt. How can this be? Because despite everything, the goddess of the clan is never shaken; the Kulins remain completely protected. The goddess of the clan has incredible love for them and is endlessly merciful. She will never relinquish her love and mercy. I will give you an amazing example of the love and mercy of the clan goddess.[59]

There once was a certain eminent Kulin in a certain village. He had married three or four times. In one of the villages where he had married, two daughters were born to him. From birth, the girls were raised in their maternal uncle's home. Their father was without a care, content in knowing that their maternal uncle would raise the girls and, in due course, get them married. So their father made no arrangements for them. Unfortunately, the affairs of the maternal uncle took a turn for the worse and he could not arrange to get his nieces married. The first daughter was by then eighteen or nineteen years old; the second was fifteen or sixteen. And then someone deceived them and took them from their home.[60]

After nearly a fortnight the girls' father came to learn of their predicament. He was at a loss, so he went to Kolkata to take the advice of a relation. While telling his relation all the details of his predicament, he choked up and said, "Brother, after all this time the goddess of the clan has abandoned me. My life is ruined. Why am I so unfortunate? Why has the goddess of the clan turned away?" His relation said, "This is the evil result of your never seeking news about your daughters." In the end, after much worrying, the Kulin lord went to the person who had taken the girls away and pleaded with him, "Please, let me have the two girls for three months; after that I will return them to you." The man who had taken the girls was someone who was used to getting his way, but when he saw how wretched the Kulin lord was, he was moved by pity. Considering the father's pleas, he gave the girls back for three months. The Kulin lord was pleased and took his two daughters back to his own house. Once there he told people that someone had stolen the girls to give them away in improper marriages, but that he had rescued them after great effort. To insure the girls could not escape, he employed a guard who watched over them at all times.

Having made these arrangements, the Kulin lord set off to raise money and locate a groom. One month later, at the end of the month of Bhadra, he returned home with the money needed for a wedding. He was accompanied by a six year-old groom. Having managed to learn something about the girls, the groom was unwilling to rescue the clan reputation of the Kulin lord without receiving something above his usual fees. The wedding rites were completed the following night. And so the clan status of the Kulin lord was preserved. Those who were present at the wedding saw for themselves that the goddess of the clan is not fickle. Realizing this, the Brahmin's eyes filled with tears.

Early the next morning the groom returned to his own village. A few days later the newly married girls also disappeared. They have not been heard from since. They had saved their father's clan status. If they led wanton lives after that, it was no threat to the father's clan status. What's more, he had promised the man who had initially taken the girls away that he would return them to him after three months. Shortly after the wedding, as agreed, he did just that. Never mind, the real blessing is that the love and mercy of the goddess of the clan did not waver. It is a great slander to say the goddess of fortune is fickle.

Many came to learn about all the details of this affair, but no one ever showed any disrespect or unkindness to that Kulin lord.

Third Objection: Abolishing Polygamy Would Destroy the Broken Kulins

There are some who object that if the custom of polygamy is abolished, it will spell the end of the Broken Kulins. That is, if one man is not able to marry many times, his clan status would be utterly ruined. In order to fully examine this objection, it will be necessary to introduce the clan of Broken Kulins, their character, and so forth.

Earlier I mentioned that marriage to a Vamshaja daughter destroyed Kulin status, which is why Kulins refuse to marry Vamshaja daughters. For that very reason, Vamshajas are keen to give their daughters to Kulins as a way to enhance the merit of their family line. But this desire is not easily satisfied. Vamshajas with a lot of wealth are an exception, since a Kulin with many sons, if he is hungry for money, will give one of those sons in marriage to a Vamshaja virgin as a way to make money. And a marriage like that only destroys the clan status of the son who marries; it does not violate the Kulin rank of the father or his other sons.

This is how the sons of Kulins lose their clan status by marrying Vamshaja virgins. They are known as Self-Broken Kulins. After this, they show no reluctance about marrying Vamshaja daughters. But since it means breaking the clan status of the Kulin, it costs a great deal to give a daughter to a Kulin—which is why few Vamshajas enjoy this option. However, if you give a Self-Broken Kulin a bit of money he will be happy to oblige. Realizing this, Vamshajas began giving their daughters to Self-Broken Kulins. The Self-Broken have no qualms about rescuing the Vamshajas, especially since a married woman represents little additional burden and might even bring in some additional profit. And so, driven by their desire for profit, the Self-Broken Kulins have made a habit of marrying Vamshaja daughters.

What's more, the Broken Kulins have a rule that their daughters should be given to people of the same exchange series. That is, Self-Broken daughters are supposed to be given to grooms who are also Self-Broken. No matter how many unmarried daughters a Self-Broken Kulin has, they will each be given to Self-Broken grooms for a small fee. And so on, down the generations from son to grandson. It is seen as a matter of pride to give daughters to Self-Broken grooms, and so they are all extremely careful to give their daughters to Self-Broken grooms.

This is how Self-Broken Kulins gradually came to form so many marriages. Nor are their sons any less distinguished in this regard. The number of marriages only begins to decrease after the third generation. Once upon a time, if a Kulin accepted a Vamshaja daughter his status was immediately destroyed and he became like a Vamshaja—despised and rejected. These days he is considered to be a Kulin for up to five generations and is respected as such.

All those unfortunate daughters given to Self-Broken Kulins or Second-hand grooms are left to live their lives in their father's home.[61] Basically, by accepting a certain ritual fee, the almighty recipient of the daughter helps the girl's father preserve his clan status or adds a bit of luster to the family line.[62] It is understood that the recipient of the daughter is not obliged to provide any maintenance for the married woman. These Kulin ladies are thus married in name only; they spend their entire lives in their father's home, just like widows.[63] The Creator has not ordained that they should enjoy the blessings of life with a husband. They entertain no such a hope. If the daughter's family make a special effort, the Kulin son-in-law may spend a few days at his wife's house. But if there is any breach of hospitality or respect, he will never again return to the wife's home.

If one of these Kulin ladies should somehow become pregnant, her relatives have three options for covering it up: First, great care may be taken to bring the son-in-law back. He would be expected to stay for one or two days and then depart. The pregnancy might then be explained. Second, if this cannot be arranged, then it might be necessary to summon the sorts of women who assist with the termination of illicit pregnancies.[64] The third option is very simple—utterly without fault, and actually rather remarkable. Better yet, it requires no expense nor is there any need to call in those who deal with terminating pregnancies. In this case, the girl's mother or some other woman in the household will take a child on their hip and wander around the neighborhood. Going from one house to another, she will say "Look here, Mother" or "Look Sister!" In the course of conversation she will remark that her son-in-law suddenly showed up in the dead of night. "Showing up like that, how can I feed him? So I said to him, 'If you stay for a day or two, then I can arrange to feed you. After that you can depart.' But he wouldn't stay. He just said, 'I cannot stay today; there's a wedding later tonight at the Majumdar's in such and such a village. And after that there is another wedding at the Haldar's. I have to attend those. If I am able, I will come this way on my return.' And so he departed early the next morning. I had said to Svarna, 'Why don't you call Tripura and Kamini so you can all enjoy some time with your husband.' I cannot be there, and as a young lass you cannot be on your own. Then I turned to those other two and said, 'When the groom comes along, you two make yourselves scarce.'" So you see, this is what she would do—wander around the neighborhood, talking openly about the son-in-law's visit. And then later, as news of Svarnamanjuri's pregnancy spread, everyone would chalk it up to the son-in-law's visit.

If these Kulin ladies have sons, the latter are known as Second-hand Kulins. It falls to the maternal relations to raise them and see to their life-cycle rites like the Thread Ceremony. The Kulin father never gets any news about them; nor does he send any assistance. That said, if he receives an invitation to a First-feeding or some other life-cycle rite, he will come in the hopes of making a little something from the ancestral offering. Only after the boy receives his sacred thread will the father begin to show him great affection. Then he will make plans to marry the boy into a well-heeled Vamshaja family, by virtue of which he will make a great deal in terms of dowry and such. About all these things the bride's mother's family has no say, nor any rights. All this is planned while the boy is still young. And if the son happens to become aware of this, the father's plans will be ruined. The son will set out to marry according to his own wishes, and all the dowry will become his. The father would get nothing. In the case of daughters, all the necessary rituals from the cutting of the umbilical cord to the last rites are carried out by the maternal family. The father does nothing to defray the costs of getting such a Kulin daughter married. And since the dignity of the family line would be destroyed if no suitable groom could be found for a Kulin niece, she ends up being married according to the rules of the Broken Kulins. Just like her mother, she will be married in name only and will spend her entire life in her mother's house.

Such is the harsh fate of Kulin daughters and nieces. Whether they live in their husband's family home or with their mother's relations, they do the work of cooks and servants. As long as their own father is alive, these Kulin ladies do not fare too badly. But they are helpless once the brothers take over the family after the father's death. Their brothers' wives heap endless abuse on them. From the time they rise in the morning to the moment they lie down at night, it is nothing but household chores; they never earn the respect of the well-mannered wives of their brothers. The latter are always at their throats. It is hardly an exaggeration to say that they do not even have time to shed a tear. When they can bear no more abuse, they go to their neighbor's house. There they bemoan their fate and lament the nature of the Kulin system. They cry out in distress, "If only I were able to go somewhere else, I would never again set foot in that house." Far too often, Kulin ladies and Kulin daughters take the extreme step of leaving their abusive homes and living as courtesans.

There really is no end to the suffering of Kulin ladies and Kulin daughters. Anyone who gives a moment's thought to their condition will appreciate the afflictions these women face throughout their lives. One's heart aches to contemplate their suffering; and when one investigates the cause of all these unbearable afflictions, one loses faith in humanity. The whole pointless business comes down to this: one party is driven by a trifling desire for prestige while the other party is greedy for profit. And these two parties are assisted by all the other people in our land who simply cannot be bothered to care. Such an unbearable custom will only be banned when people stop trusting or respecting the people who cause the suffering of these Kulin daughters. And yet far from being spurned, the perpetrators of this unbearable custom are respected and worshipped by the people of this land. If such is the case, what means do we have for liberating these Kulin daughters from their awful condition other than petitioning the Government? There is no other region of the world where women live in such an awful condition. If there were any justice, King Vallala and Devivara Ghataka Visharada would certainly be damned.[65] Polygamy is practiced in other parts of India and in other regions of the world, but nowhere else do married women live in such awful conditions as the Kulin women of this land. Other wives live in the same house as their husbands; they receive food and clothing from their husbands; and throughout the year they enjoy the pleasures of living with their husbands. For Kulin daughters, the mere idea of living in their husband's house, enjoying life with him, and being cared for in this way is nothing but a dream.[66]

No one on this earth is as cruel and sinful as the Broken Kulins. They know no mercy, justice, self-respect, or sense of shame. Their character is extraordinary. There is nothing to compare them to. They can only be compared to themselves, and so consider these examples—[67]

—Once someone asked a highly respected Broken Kulin, "Sir, you have married so many times; how is it possible for you to go to all those places?" Without the slightest embarrassment he replied, "I go where I get a 'visit.'"[§§§]

—During the last famine, I met a Broken Kulin who had married many times. He used to boast, "Even though so many people died of starvation during the famine, I suffered nothing. Marriage allowed me to pass my days comfortably."[68]

—Plans are made in some village for a community Puja.[69] The planners need to raise some funds. They pressure some Broken Kulin to marry as a way to raise the money.

—A married woman runs off, taking her husband's family's entire savings. Some Broken Kulin kindly allows her to move into his house. But only as long as the money lasts; after that he throws her out.

—A young wife starts her menses. Her father's greatest wish is to bring the son-in-law and perform the rituals of remarriage.[70] So he announces

§§§ People generally call it a "visit" when a doctor gets paid for making a medical call.

his desire to the girl's father-in-law in a letter. In reply, the father-in-law demands more money. If the girl's father is unwilling or unable to pay, the father-in-law will not let his son go to the bride's house. And so the daughter is prevented from ever going through the rituals of remarriage in her lifetime.

—The wife of a particular Broken Kulin has not seen her husband for ages; somehow she becomes pregnant. To keep a wanton daughter at home would cause her immediate family to be humiliated and rejected by their community. Her well-meaning relations understand that if she is driven from home it will be her ruin. To avoid this they manage by hook or by crook to bring her husband there. This great man, lured by the profit he stands to make, affirms before everyone that the child in the good woman's belly is his own.

In this connection there is an incredible story that gets told about the character of the Broken Kulin. A certain man returns home at midday to take his meal. He sees two unknown women sitting where the food is about to be served. One is about sixty years old and the other is around eighteen or nineteen. It is impossible to ignore the sorry state of their clothing, and their faces betray their evident despair and misery. The man asks his mother, "Who are they? Why are they sitting here?" She points to the elder woman and says, "She is the wife of Mr. Bhattacharya, while she"—gesturing to the younger woman—"is their daughter. They have come to tell you about their misfortune."[71]

Mr. Bhattacharya is a Second-hand Broken Kulin; he has married five or six times. He receives a monthly income from this particular gentleman, and as a result he shows him respect. His sister, nephew, and niece all live with him. No one has ever seen any of his wives stay at his house.

The sight of the faces and clothing on these two women are enough to fill the gentleman's heart with pain. He takes his meal and then hears their story. The elder one tells him, "I am the wife of Mr. Bhattacharya; she is his daughter, to whom I gave birth. I used to stay in my father's house. Then after a while my son said to me, 'Mother, I can no longer provide the two of you with food and clothing.' I asked him, 'What are you saying? I am your mother and she is your sister; if you don't feed us, where will we go? And if you send one of us away, where will the other go? Who else on earth will feed us?' Hearing this, my son said, 'You are my mother, so I will feed and clothe you as best I can, but I can no longer support her.' At this I became angry and said,

'What? Do you want her to become a prostitute?' To which he replied, 'I don't know; you take care of her needs.' This marked a major break with my son. In the end, I took my daughter and left the house."

"Sometime later I came to learn that there was an opening for a cook in the house of one of my aunties. Thinking we could both perform the cooking duties, we went there. Unfortunately they had only just engaged a cook two or three days earlier. This was awful to hear; we worried where we could go or what we might do. My husband has a family in such-and-such a village. His son is well-to-do and kind-hearted.[72] We thought that even though I am his stepmother and she is his step-sister, if we threw ourselves on his mercy he would have pity on us. So we showed up at his place. We told him everything. With tears in our eyes we clasped his hands and said, 'Son, if you don't take pity on us, we have no hope.' "

"Seeing my distress, he showed great love and pity. Even though he was my stepson, he said he would take care of me as long as I should live. I choked up at this statement of trust, and tears flowed down my face. He was very caring, but the women of the house were not. They asked, 'Where did this disaster come from?' They were unkind and abusive. Even after the stepson learned about it, he was powerless to stop the cruelty. When I went to him and asked him about it, he said, 'Ma, I know all about it; but I see no remedy. You two should go off and live somewhere else. Send someone to me now and then and I will be sure to provide you with a little something.' "

"That's how my daughter and I left that place. We were totally disheartened. Eventually it occurred to me that since my husband was still living, we should go and inform him of our predicament. Maybe he would take pity on us. Once we decided on this, it took about four or five days to reach here. Today we learned his answer. He said he cannot keep us at his house nor provide us with food or clothing. People said that if I told you, you might find some solution. And that's why we are sitting here." The gentleman was overwhelmed with anger and pain when he heard this. Tears ran from his eyes. Later he went to Mr. Bhattacharya's house and gave him a proper scolding, saying, "Your conduct astounds me. On what grounds did you throw her out of the house? Tell me right now, are you going to take them back or not?" The comfortably situated Mr. Bhattacharya took fright at the bearing of the gentleman and said, "Go back home. Let me speak to my household. I will come to your place later."

In the afternoon, Mr. Bhattacharya came to see the gentleman. He said, "I have decided to allow the women to stay in my house. However, you will have to contribute something monthly toward the cost." The gentleman agreed to this and gave him funds for three months. He told him, "Here is an advance for the cost of three months. Allow me to cover the cost of their clothing as well." This left Mr. Bhattacharya with no more excuses and so he took his wife and daughter and returned home. He was not a particularly bad man himself, but his sister was a terror. It was only out of fear of her—and out of a desire to placate her—that he behaved so harshly. Once the sister witnessed the anger of the new benefactor and realized he had agreed to pay a bit more each month, she came around. On other occasions Mr. Bhattacharya had expressed his desire to bring home a particular wife, but it had been his sister who rose up in anger. As such he had never before followed through on his desire. It is said that among Broken Kulins the household belongs to the sisters, nephews, and nieces. They have nothing to do with the wives, sons, and daughters.

In any case, having made the aforementioned agreement, the gentleman went away for a while. As agreed, he sent along his monthly payments. Sometime after this, he returned home and inquired about the unfortunate mother and daughter. He learned that Mr. Bhattacharya and his sister had decided that the newly agreed payment from the gentleman benefactor should have been added to the original monthly stipend they received from him and not terminated after three months.[73] And so they threw the mother and daughter out of the house. Those two had no option but to obey his instructions and found themselves with nowhere to go. Since the young girl was attractive and mature, she took to prostitution. She and her mother were able to get by this way.

The behavior displayed by the Broken Kulin in this story would be unusual even among the lowest castes.[74] First off, we see a big man throw his mother and grown sister from his house. Seeking refuge with her husband (who was the father of the girl), the two women once again found themselves chased away by a great man. At that point a gentleman takes pity on the two and agrees to provide for them. Even then they are not given a home. Such misfortune would never befall a grown woman from a refined home if her husband and son were still living. Furthermore, if she had a father and a brother, no daughter of a refined home would be unjustly forced to take up prostitution simply in order to have food and clothing. Yet in this case, even though this poor woman's husband was still living, we are not supposed to call him a sinner. No, he is a Self-Broken Kulin. And what is truly remarkable is that even though Mr. Bhattacharya is tainted by this fault, he and his worthy son are neither despised nor spurned by society.

I have attempted to give a sense of the clan status and character of the Broken Kulin. I would ask everyone to consider whether it is proper or necessary for the custom of polygamy to continue. Only consider that if a man were not allowed to marry many times, such misfortune and ill-repute would not arise for the Kulin. In the beginning, even before the constitution of the assemblages, the clan status of the Kulins was lost. Then later on, after marrying their daughters to Vamshajas, they once again caused the destruction of their newly imagined clan status. When it comes to those who have twice had their own clan status destroyed, what sense does it make to honor their illusory Kulin rank? In fact, if one considers the stark history of their unsanctioned, cruel, and shameful behavior, it does not seem right even to call such people human. It might not really be an offense to Dharma if they were simply cut off, root and branch. When we put it that way, it seems as if the destruction of their petty and imaginary Kulin rank amounts to very little. One way or another, if their clan status perishes, they cease to be Kulins. And if they are no longer Kulins, then they have no Kulin rank. And if they have no Kulin rank, then it makes no sense to talk about the loss of Kulin rank if the custom of polygamy is prohibited.

I should mention here that there are some Broken Kulins who absolutely detest the business of marriage and do not engage in it. They consent to no more than one marriage in their lifetime, and they work toward the goal of getting this detested custom abolished. The behavior of these Broken Kulins is so different that it is difficult to imagine they belong to the same caste or community. While it is sad there are not more of these Broken Kulins, their behavior suggests that it need not be difficult—let alone an insuperable challenge—to get the Broken Kulins to give up the business of marriage.

Fourth Objection: Kulin Polygamy Is Already Fading Away

Some object that the excesses of the Kulin Brahmins of this land are a matter of the distant past. Back then they used to marry many times, but now such misconduct has ceased. What little still goes on will soon completely cease. This being the case, there is no need for a Government decree to prohibit polygamy.[75]

It is completely misleading to say that the misbehavior of Kulins today is nothing like it was in the past. Those who make this claim know absolutely nothing about the conduct and behavior of the Kulins. We see the very same misbehavior around marriage today as there was in the past; do not think there has been any reduction. To avoid pointless debate on this issue, I have gathered the names, ages, places of residence, and corresponding number of marriages for some present-day Kulins [*4.1].

This list indicates the number of marriages among the Kulins, to the best of my knowledge and as far as I have been able to ascertain through my own inquiries. With more focused inquiry still more names could be found for those entering into polygamous marriages. I have not shown the names of individuals who contracted only three to four marriages. The number of Kulins entering into polygamous marriages in districts like Burdwan, Navadwip, Jessore, Barishal, and Dhaka is no lower than what is found in Hooghly District. In fact, in other districts the number of Kulins is even higher. Furthermore, even the number of marriages among Kulins shown here might actually be somewhat higher. Among those contracting multiple marriages, it is simply not possible to say how many marriages they have entered into on their own. That is not something another person can easily ascertain. And yet it does not really matter if in some cases the actual number of marriages might be higher than I have shown. Naturally, if the actual numbers are lower, then those supporters of polygamy who object that the custom is already on the wane, will say I have deliberately inflated the numbers. But I would not do that. I have shown what I have been able to learn through my inquiries. I have not knowingly introduced any error.

The well-known village of Janai is located about twelve miles from Calcutta.[76] I have gathered information for the number of individuals in this single village who have concluded more than one marriage [*4.2].

Now, let my readers consider whether there has been any cessation of the excesses of the Kulins. It does not seem that the excesses of today are any less than those of the past. Rather, it is quite likely that the excesses of today are far greater still. In former times, if a Kulin did not receive a great deal of money, he would not agree to break his Kulin status. There were not really that many people who would break their Kulin status by giving a daughter in marriage just for the offer of a good sum of money. And this is why the actual number of Self-Broken Kulins was much lower in the past. But the Kulins of today are so easily tempted by the prospect of even the smallest gains that they will break their Kulin status. And likewise, the number of people willing to give daughters in marriage and thereby lose their Kulin status has also increased. It used to be that in any given village there was only one person who would break his Kulin status in order to give a daughter in marriage. In due course, that person would have five sons, all of whom would follow their father's example when it came to marrying their daughters. So those five sons would then break their Kulin status by giving their daughters in marriage. Where once there had only been a single person willing to break Kulin status by giving his daughters in marriage, there are now many more people who adopt the custom. Prices are low and the number of possible grooms is high. And as a result the business of breaking Kulin status goes from strength to strength, which means that the number of Self-Broken Kulins today is high and is likely to keep on growing. The Self-Broken Kulins marry more and more; in one place after another the droves of daughters they produce are given to Self-Broken grooms. Since this is how things are, I cannot understand how there is any hope for the excesses of such marriage to decline. It is completely delusional to say, "Don't worry, the excesses of the Kulins are almost over and those few who remain will very soon pass away."

The majority of modern folks living in Calcutta have no connection to village life.[77] They are completely unaware of what goes on there. Curiously, when someone attempts to make such matters known, then all of a sudden they act as if they understand completely. Taking their cue from how things are in Calcutta, they assume it must be the same in the villages. Observers like these say that thanks to the special progress of learning in this land, evil customs like polygamy have almost ceased.

It is true that after a long time, during which English learning has been cultivated and interactions with the British have increased, we do see some cessation of evil customs in Calcutta and surrounding areas. But elsewhere there has not been a similar cultivation of English learning, nor has there been the same increase in interaction with the British. Consequently, in those places the evil customs and traditions are as strong as ever. And so it really is inappropriate to say that the condition of the villages is in any way like that of Calcutta. If you look at the matter in terms of cause and effect, this should not be surprising.[78] The factors determining why Calcutta has developed as it has are not replicated in those other places; we should not expect to see similar results there. Calcutta has cultivated English learning for a long time; it has seen increasing interaction with the British. Neither of these things can be said for the villages. It simply is not possible to find the same results there.

All of which is to say that there is no scope for comparing conditions in the villages with life in Calcutta.

The fact of the matter is, it is generally not a good idea to express an opinion on matters about which one has no special knowledge. And one cannot gain special knowledge about something without careful investigation. Therefore, unless one's goal is to mislead people, one should not say that this hideous and cruel custom is on the decline or is not as prevalent was in the past. Whether informed or not, a person whose only goal is to express opposition to the proposed matter—whether out of jealousy, hatred, or slavery to some evil tradition—is perfectly happy to spread information that supports his own position or undermines that of his opponents. His claims might even be utterly baseless. Even so, he feels absolutely no compunction about telling people how things really stand. If someone proposes a particular course of action, motivated by the best of intentions, the aforementioned person will shamelessly claim that this new proposal is driven by harmful intentions. Committed only to victory, these people have no compunction about confounding their opponents with falsehoods.

Fifth Objection: Kayasthas Will Lose the Right to Second Marriage

Some object that if polygamy is banned, the Kayastha caste will lose their right to Second Marriage.[79] This is a weak and trifling objection. Take away Second Marriage and there is no loss of caste nor is there a decay of Dharma among the Kayasthas. Nor will there be any problem in the matter of marriage.

The Kayastha caste falls into two categories. First, the Kulins, then the Mauliks. There are three families of Kulin Kayasthas: Ghosh, Basu, and Mitra. The Mauliks are of two types, Accomplished and Potential. There are eight families of Accomplished Mauliks: De, Datta, Kara, Sinha, Sen, Das, Guha, and Palit. And of the seventy-two families of Kayasthas, the following are Potential Mauliks: Soma, Rudra, Pala, etc.[80] According to rank, the Potential Mauliks are somewhat lower than the Accomplished. One often hears the Accomplished Mauliks called True Mauliks and the Potential Mauliks called the Seventy-Two.

The established rule regarding marriage within the Kayastha caste is this: a Kulin daughter is given to the eldest son of a Kulin. If he were to marry a

Maulik daughter there would be loss of Kulin status. As long as his first marriage is to a Kulin daughter, his Kulin status does not suffer from subsequently marrying a Maulik daughter. The other sons of the same Kulin father may marry Maulik daughters; this is quite common. It is necessary for every Maulik to give his daughter to Kulin grooms and to marry his sons to Kulin daughters. If Mauliks engage in reciprocal giving and receiving, there is no loss of caste or destruction of Dharma; but this pattern of reciprocal giving and receiving of daughters has fallen out of favor in Kayastha society. Sixty or seventy years ago it was not rare at all for Mauliks to marry among themselves and they were not particularly blamed for it.

The Mauliks give their daughters to the second son of Kulins, and so forth, even though there are some Maulik families who have resolved to give their daughters to the eldest son of Kulins. The eldest son of a Kulin is not permitted to contract his first marriage with a Maulik daughter. Maulik Kayasthas go to great effort and expense to give their daughters to those Kulins who would otherwise protect their Kulin status by marrying the daughters of Kulins. Those Kulins whose eldest sons make second marriages with Maulik households are known as those with the right to Second Marriage. All Maulik households that marry in this fashion are called Second Marriage households.

Mauliks who practice Second Marriage take great care of their sons-in-laws, who live in their homes. No doubt this is because the eldest sons of Kulins have their father's rank. The goal of Second Marriage Mauliks is to see the sons of their daughters gain this rank. And yet among men with two families there can be no certainty as to which wife will be the first to bear him a son. If the Kulin daughter who was married first happens to give birth to a son, then the goal of Second Marriage is never attained. Therefore the best way to attain this goal is to prevent the son-in-law from living with the Kulin virgin he wed first. This makes it essential to keep the son-in-law satisfied. In such cases, the Kulin daughter who was married first may never see her husband's face. As such, a daughter like this is really married in name only; she lives like a widow in her father's house. It is very expensive to keep a son-in-law, so if a Second Marriage Maulik does not have the means, he will not succeed in this kind of effort; the thing he most wants will never be his. In that case, the eldest son of a Kulin takes both the Kulin daughter and the Maulik daughter and lives together as a family.

Previously I mentioned that if Second Marriage were not practiced there would be no loss of caste or destruction of Dharma for the Mauliks; nor would there be any problem in the matter of marriage. Maulik status is completely preserved by giving Maulik daughters to the middle sons of Kulins. Which is why almost all Mauliks give their daughters to such grooms. Those few Maulik families who make Second Marriages do so merely so they can boast, "We have given away a daughter to the eldest son of a Kulin." They do not pause to think that thereby they ruin a sinless Kulin daughter who just happened to have married first. In a land where there is no habit of looking after the welfare of one's own daughters, it is obviously too much to think that people might consider the welfare of someone else's daughter.

All these Second Marriage families are destitute. Honestly, they cannot afford the expense of Second Marriages, which for them represent the worst sort of disaster. They secretly wish to see the custom of Second Marriage abolished by law. They believe that if this vile custom were to be prevented by Government decree it would be their salvation. And yet they lack the courage to lead the way. If they were to abandon the practice of Second Marriage and were to begin giving their daughters to the younger sons of Kulins, they would actually not suffer any loss of caste nor decay of Dharma. Sadly, it is their neighbors who heap scorn and abuse on them if they do not—or cannot—contract Second Marriages. And fear of such scorn and abuse is the one thing that prevents them from giving up Second Marriages. Honestly, it leads me to think that the people of our land are both foolish and cowardly.

Clearly if the custom of polygamy is banned by Government decree, it will be a blow to Second Marriage. But there is no evidence, nor is there any reason to infer, that the Kayastha caste would suffer any inconvenience or harm; at most it would be a blow to the trifling sense of pride cherished by some Maulik families. Second Marriage is not a practice essential to the Kayastha caste. Far from it. This practice is surely both harmful and contrary to Dharma.[81] Once this practice is abolished and people see that the Kayastha caste has not suffered any harm nor experienced any loss of Dharma—let alone other inconveniences—it will no longer be necessary or proper for people to put forward objections to the banning of polygamy. But to be clear: even if the custom of needlessly marrying more than once is abolished by Government legislation or by some other means, it will not really mark the end of Second Marriages. All those Kulin families whose eldest sons might become widowers would still be able to accept brides from Second Marriage families. This is why anyone who objects that it is wrong to ban the custom of polygamy because it would harm Second Marriage just sounds like a fool.

Sixth Objection: It Is Up To Bengali Society to Eradicate This Evil

There are some who freely acknowledge that the continued practice of the custom of polygamy in this land is a cause of great harm, and they admit that it should be incumbent on us all to make every effort to ban it. However, they also object that since it represents a social evil, its eradication should remain a social duty. They do not think it is appropriate for Government to interfere.[82]

I have to smile when I hear this objection. I suppose it is reassuring to say that the eradication of social evil is a social duty. If the people of this land were to commit themselves to the eradication of this social evil, the realization of that goal would surely be a joyous and blessed moment. However, judging by what we know about the inclination, intelligence, and powers of discrimination possessed by the people of this land, it is hard to believe they are capable of demonstrating the type of care and effort it will take to realize such a goal. To be honest, the blessed day has not yet arrived when the eradication of this social evil can be accomplished through our own care and effort. And looking at the present state of society, it is difficult to say how long it might take. It is possible that such a blessed moment might never come.

The people who raise this sort of objection belong to the "new community."[83] There are members of this new community who are a bit older and more worldly and who are therefore less likely to indulge in baseless talk the way some of the more immature people now do—even though there was once a time when the older folks made a lot of noise on such topics. Indeed, the eradication of social evil and promotion of social welfare had once been their avowed goals in life; such words used to be constantly on their lips. But it was all schoolboy talk. Once they left school and took up worldly concerns, their schoolboy dreams evaporated. Forget about eradicating social evils, it did not take long for them to be completely tainted by precisely the same evils. They lived happily with them. They became worldly. Now you don't hear them talking about such things—mere illusions!—like the eradication of social evil or the promotion of social welfare. Far from it; if they hear such talk or see anyone engaged in such work, they mock and deride them.

The younger members of this community are still in the thrall of their schooldays; indeed, those who dropped out of school early make the most noise. Looking at this younger group, one could be forgiven for thinking they are ready to commit their lives to the eradication of social evil and the promotion of social welfare. But people fail to realize it is all just talk, with no conviction to back it up. These people get on their high horses and proclaim that the eradication of social evil is a social duty. They say it is inappropriate for Government to intervene in such matters. But ask them about the sort of work it would take to eradicate social evil; ask them what kind of people in society are capable of undertaking such work, especially without the help of others. Ask these people how the eradication of social evil is to be accomplished, when they are smart and discerning enough to see the condition of our land. Who is bold enough to claim we will ever succeed in eradicating this type of social evil solely through our own dedication and hard work? We are too weak and too impoverished. Our poor society is completely overrun with detestable traditions. Those who cry for the moon in this way do not have the strength to eradicate social evil.[84] The members of the new community say such wise things, but what they say exceeds their own wisdom, learning, and strength. It is much easier said than done.

I will give you two examples that illustrate the sort of inclination and strength we have for eradicating social evil. The first has to do with the sale of daughters among the Brahmin caste; the second with the sale of sons among the Kayastha caste. Most of the Shrotriya Brahmins and many Vamshajas sell their daughters. And all the Shrotriyas and most Vamshajas marry through the purchase of daughters.[85] According to the Shastras, this buying and selling of daughters is utterly improper. It is also completely vile. Atri says:

> A daughter who is sold for marriage is not a wife. Any sons born to her are not entitled to perform their father's last rites [*Atri Samhita*].
>
> A woman who is sold for marriage is not a wife. She cannot be a co-performer of her husband's duties to the gods or the fathers [*Atri Samhita* quoted in the *Dattaka Mimamsa*].[86]

When Harisharma was living in Vaikuntha, the god Brahma said to him:

> O twice-born man, any deluded person who sells a daughter out of the desire for profit will go to the Hell known as the Cesspool. O twice-born man, the son born to a woman sold into marriage is a Chandala, unfit to perform any rites [*Kriya-yoga-sara*, chapter 19].[87]

See for yourselves! The purchase of daughters in order to marry is condemned by the Shastras. The authors of the Shastras did not consider such a woman to be a wife, nor did they consider her offspring to be a son. In their opinion, such a woman was a slave, and her son was a Chandala, outcasted from all Dharma. One must be married to perform rituals, but according to the Shastras, a woman like this cannot assist her husband with his rituals. People pray for sons to perform their last rites, but according to the Shastras, a son from a marriage like this is not qualified to perform those rituals. Furthermore, anyone who sells daughters out of a desire for profit will be cast into Hell.

Everyone acknowledges that selling daughters for profit and marrying by the purchase of daughters are vile practices. Even those who engage in such practices admit that this buying and selling is an improper business. Everyone feels keenly what an unrighteous and harmful practice it is. If we actually had the inclination and strength to eradicate such social evils, this nasty business would not have gone on for so long in this land.

Compared to the business of selling daughters as found among Brahmins, the sale of sons among the Kayasthas is an even more horrific business. If a middling or impoverished Kayastha has a daughter, it marks his ruin. As the daughter grows older she drains the last drop of her father's blood. People say, "It is a disaster to have a daughter, but to have a son is a celebration."[88] When arrangements are made for a marriage, a son is worth so much that his father can demand jewelry and all sorts of gifts, to the extent that the middling or impoverished Kayastha has great difficulty securing his daughter against the debt. In this matter the groom's family can be so shameless and despicable that people lose all respect for them. The remarkable thing is that while people go to great lengths and incur enormous misery in order to get a daughter married, when it comes to arranging a son's marriage, they view things entirely differently. This is why it is commonly assumed that for Kayasthas a daughter's marriage is a cause of great misfortune, while that of a son is a major celebration. Every Kayastha will admit that the business of selling sons is vile, but when it comes time to see their son married, they don't feel this way at all; they just don't see it this way. Amazingly, those who are as well-educated as their sons are equally heartless when it comes to this business. Boys who have passed their entrance exams for the university are highly valued; those who have passed their higher examinations are valued even more highly still. Most people cannot even imagine marrying their daughter to someone with such an education. It is a cause for certain disaster if you add on top of this demands for a brick-built house and arrangements for ongoing support. Only the extremely wealthy can consider marriage in such circumstances. What is even more surprising is the fact that this business is far more prevalent in Kolkata than in the villages. It is a real marvel to think that while the value of a Brahmin's daughter is gradually decreasing, the value of a Kayastha's son is rising ever higher. With this kind of market, and with things heating up in this fashion, we will undoubtedly see more daughters from middling or impoverished Kayastha families remaining unmarried, just as we see with the Kulin daughters of Brahmin families.[89]

As far as I can tell, every Kayastha is outraged about this state of affairs. Everyone agrees the practice is shameful and detestable, and yet if the Kayastha caste is unified on this point, why does it still go on? If the people of our land had the inclination and strength to eradicate social evils, the sale of sons among the Kayasthas caste would have ceased long ago.

Hindu society in our land is immersed in the transmission of evil. I ask those who embrace new ways, how much time and effort have you spent on the eradication of evil?[90] Have your efforts led to the eradication of particular evils? What evils are making efforts to eradicate right now?

As long as the custom of polygamy is practiced, Hindu society will be greatly harmed. Thousands of married women experience unimaginable suffering. They are swept away by waves of adultery and foeticide. There is no chance that the people of our land will make an effort to prevent this; if there were, there would be no need to submit a petition to the Government. But now we recognize how important it is that polygamy be abolished, and so we must submit a petition to the Government. If not, then let us decide that it is wrong to petition Government in this way and remain content to see the practice persist. Day in, day out, people observe what an awful chain of events follows from our allowing this vile and cruel custom. And seeing this, their hearts are tormented; they conclude that for the well-being of society the custom must be abolished—by whatever means. The truth is there is no reason to think society will be harmed by a Government decree that seeks the termination of this cruel custom. Nor is it possible to imagine that those who choose to petition the Government for this purpose are doing something unjust or ill-considered. It is childish to claim we cannot place our strength in the hands of the Government. Where is our strength? If we really were strong enough, we would never have had to take this matter to the Government; we would be capable of reforming society on our own.[91] Without the will, effort, and strength to do this, there can be no talk of eradicating social evil. And to be honest, I doubt there are many people who think petitioning the

Government in this way leads to humiliation or social decay. And if that is true, then it is a blessing for our land and our society.

Seventh Objection: It Is Wrong for the People of Bengal to Petition the Government

Others object as follows: The custom of polygamy is practiced in all regions of India, among both Hindu and Muslim communities. Among these, it is only members of the Bengali Hindu community who petition for the abolition of polygamy. Bengal is only one part of India. It is wrong for the Government to upset the people of India at the request of just one community in one part of India.

This objection is entirely without merit. It may be that the evils and dire consequences wrought by the custom of polygamy as found in the Bengali Hindu community are not found to the same degree in other regions of India; nor does one hear of such evils and dire consequences in the Muslim community of Bengal. Nevertheless, the petitioners seek to prohibit polygamy because of its dire consequences for the Bengali Hindu community; this is their goal and this is their appeal. The Muslim community in this region practices polygamy; let them continue to do so. The petitioners have no objection to this. They do not seek, nor do they wish, for the Government to use this occasion to interfere in their practice of polygamy. What is more, they do not intend for the Government to enact a law regarding marriage that would universally apply to the public of India. They are saddened by the sorry condition of their native land occasioned by polygamy, and seeing no other means to redress the matter, they are appealing to the Government. Their sole goal is to liberate their region and their community from this sorry condition.[92] Should the Government be moved to accept this petition and enact a rule applying to the Hindu community of this region, it need not upset the Muslim community in this region, nor the Hindu and Muslim communities in other regions of India. The Hindu community of this region are the Government's people. An extremely harmful matter has befallen their society. The people lack the care and strength to put an end to this matter. Yet it must be ended. And so, finding no other recourse, the people take refuge in the ruler and request his assistance. In such cases, it is the ruler's obligation to grant the people's request. It would contravene royal duty were the ruler to turn away just because the residents in some other region might be disappointed to learn that he had listened to his people and enacted a law that benefitted one particular region.

It is common knowledge that when, at an earlier point in India's past, the great-souled Governor-General Lord Bentinck decided to put an end to the heinous custom of widow immolation, he took the advice of the most eminent Government officials. They all told him clearly that if he undertook this action, the people would be exceedingly aggrieved from one end of India to the other; he was warned they would instantly rebel against the Government. The great-minded, beneficent Governor-General heard all this but was neither frightened nor dissuaded. He said, "If after preventing this custom our rule lasts but a single day then even so the worthiness of the name of the English people and their right to rule will have been completely fulfilled."[93] He accomplished this great deed after being struck to the core and driven to action by the sight of the people's suffering. We still live under the authority of the English, but look how much things have changed. The English were once so committed to removing the suffering of the people that they set aside even their fear of losing power. And now? You might as well forget about their being committed; even after repeated petitions from the people they will not see it done. Oh dear!

"Those days are gone!"[94]

Be that as it may, the Government nonetheless needs to enact a law in keeping with the views of the petitioners; it should not for a moment turn away from the task it is called to perform, whether out of fear that the Muslims of this region might be aggrieved or that the Hindus or Muslims of some other region might hold them to account. The English are not as stupid, incompetent, or weak as that. In fact, they tell us that they never intended to extend their authority over this land out of a simple desire for the delights of ruling power; the one and only goal of their ruling authority was supposed to be to increase the welfare of this region in every way possible.

In this connection I cannot resist citing the complaint of one young Kulin woman. When I met this Kulin woman and her youngest sister, the older one asked me, "Aren't you making some effort at the eradication of polygamy?" I said, "Not just an effort; if fate wills it, we shall succeed this time." She told me, "If fate does not so will it, and you cannot succeed, then the fate of the Kulin girl is dire. I know all too well just how dire this fate is." Saying this she remained silent for a while, looking into the face of the young girl seated on her lap. Then she looked at me with tears in her eyes and said, "If polygamy is eradicated, we two stand to gain nothing more. Whatever happiness we now enjoy, we will continue to enjoy. But we do not wish to see the unfortunate girls born to us suffer in the same way. Preventing that would ease our misery." After further lamentations like this, the Kulin woman said, "Everyone says there is a woman who rules over our land, but we don't believe it. How could women suffer like this in a realm ruled over by a woman?" As she said this, her face grew pale with distress and hopelessness. I was overcome with grief, and tears flowed from my eyes.

O Fate! Why have you ordained nothing but misery for our Kulin daughters? If the lamentations I have just mentioned should reach the ears of our merciful Queen in England, I am sure she will feel immense shame and sorrow.[95]

Let me quickly provide some background details for these Kulin women: They are the daughters of Second-hand Broken Kulin fathers and are themselves the wives of Self-Broken Kulin men. When we met, the eldest was around twenty-one or twenty-two years old, while the youngest was about sixteen or seventeen. The husband of the eldest woman was thirty years old; he had already married twelve times. The husband of the youngest was twenty-five or twenty-six and had married more than thirty-two times.

Conclusion

I have now done all I can to refute the objections I have heard regarding efforts to ban the custom of polygamy. I cannot say to what degree I have been successful. Those who are gracious enough to read this book may decide for themselves. There are just a few more objections that tend to arise and I should address them now.[96]

First, some men voluntarily enter into marriages; they marry as they choose. Such men are the heads of their own families; they obey no one else's will when it comes to domestic matters. They marry two, three, or four times, just as they desire. They could object that when it comes to domestic matters everyone should have complete agency to decide, not to mention the complete power to do as they please. Opponents have no right to say anything or to throw up obstacles. Let those with no desire to marry more than once spend their lives satisfied with just one marriage. We will not encourage them to enter into more marriages. We wish to marry more than once. And that we shall do. Why must they cast aspersions or raise objections?

Second, a father and a mother give away a son in marriage. After marriage, the family of the daughter offers all sorts of items as gifts for the son-in-law.[97] If these gifts are not to the liking of the women on the son-in-law's side, they tend to become dissatisfied. This dissatisfaction can become intense enough to cause the groom's family to feel it is necessary to get him married again.

Third, sometimes for the most trivial reasons, friction develops between the parties to a marriage. In these cases too, the father and mother, out of anger at the other parties, will give their son away again in marriage.

Fourth, occasionally in some cases and for some reason a mother-in-law will form an animosity toward the young bride. Under the sway of this animosity, she will give her husband permission to give their son once again in marriage.

Fifth, some mothers and fathers are so driven by the desire to acquire ample gifts of jewelry and other items that they give their sons in marriage to unattractive daughters. The son never comes to love his new wife and so in the end, in order to placate him, he is allowed to marry again.

Sixth, there are times when the father and mother are not greedy as much as they are keen to promote the happiness of their own families; so they give their son away in marriage, ignoring his own welfare. In such cases, it may be the son who feels the need to marry again.

If the custom of polygamy is abolished by Government decree, then sons would no longer be married off in this fashion by selfish fathers and mothers. This is why even these fathers and mothers feel the need to raise objections to the idea of banning polygamy. And yet, at least for the time being, no one group has given voice to these sorts of objections. And so I feel no need to go about refuting them.

When the petition calling for a ban on the custom of polygamy was submitted, there were hateful things said about some of the more eminent proponents of the ban.[98] People claimed the proponents were supporting something harmful to our land simply as a means to advance their own interests. I need only reply that more than twenty thousand people signed the petition. These people were not so senseless or mean that they suddenly lost the ability to tell right from wrong. They did not sign on merely to help satisfy the desire of a handful of people to promote themselves. Here are the names of some of the signatories [*C.1].

I would like my readers to decide whether or not it is appropriate to suggest that all these individuals are just senseless and mean. These are the type of people who would only sign a petition if they were convinced that banning the custom of polygamy was necessary and proper; this is why they supported the idea of submitting a petition to the Government. They did not do so merely to please someone else or because they were pressured by others.[99] Nor would they have agreed with the claim that banning the custom of polygamy would prove harmful to our land. Anyone with eyes and ears and a heart will admit that the custom of polygamy is the cause of immeasurable harm. It is really hard to imagine that these people were somehow less astute than those august opponents who like to protest that if such a harmful matter is banned it will harm our land. Never mind; this much can be said without hesitation or doubt: Those who petitioned the Government to ban the custom of polygamy did so for no other reason than to liberate women from their pitiable condition and to eradicate evils from society.[100]

Appendices

1

A number of Sanskrit sources have been cited as proof-texts in the second chapter of this book, but I have not indicated in every instance the books from which they were taken. I gathered all these sources from the renowned genealogist of Vikrampur, Ishvarchandra Tarkabhushan. Sadly, Tarkabhushan inadvertently failed to note the names of the books from which he had taken these passages. Since Tarkabhushan has now passed away, I have not been able to benefit from his continued assistance. Nowadays, most of these collections are the common memory of the genealogists, even if they themselves do not own the books. This makes it difficult to determine where these sources may be found. Finding myself at a loss, I am not able to provide the names for all the books.

2

I should say something about the information I have provided under the fourth topic regarding the residences and number of marriages among Broken Kulins who practice the business of marriage. In the case of these Broken Kulins, one cannot identify the paternal home. Some of them live in the homes of their father's maternal uncle; some live in their own maternal uncle's home; and some live in the home of their son's maternal uncle. For others it is unclear at any given time precisely where they reside. As a result, there is bound to be some discrepancy regarding their actual places of residence. As far as their ages are concerned, I should note that this data was collected five years ago.[101] Some of these men would now be another five years older, while others will have passed away. As to the number of marriages, readers may notice that this figure is higher for the older men than it is for the younger men. One might wonder whether this reflects a relative decline in the business of marriage today. However, it is worth noting that when it comes to men who have contracted a high number of marriages, these marriages did not all take place in a single day, nor even a single year; instead, the number of marriages just went on increasing over time. Just as they continue to do right down to the present. Among the Broken Kulins, marriages take place up until the day a man dies. This would therefore suggest that over the past five years the number of marriages indicated above has actually increased among the younger men. One has to imagine that by the time the younger Kulins reach the age of the older men listed above, the number of their marriages will have increased to a comparable level. Therefore, readers should not look at the discrepancy between the two groups and conclude that the business of marriage is any less robust among today's Broken Kulins.

3

A BILL TO REGULATE THE PLURALITY OF MARRIAGES BETWEEN HINDUS IN BRITISH INDIA

Preamble

Whereas the institution of marriage among Hindus has become subject to great abuses, which are alike repugnant to the principles of Hindu Law and the feelings of the people generally;[****] and whereas the practice of unlimited polygamy has led to the perpetration of revolting crimes; and whereas it is expedient to make Legislative provision for the prevention of those abuses and crimes, alike at variance with sound policy, justice, and morality: It is enacted as follows:—

[****] This is a copy of the draft manuscript of the bill opposing polygamy prepared by Raja Devnarayan Singh. [Trans.: in English in the original text from 1871.]

I. No marriage, contracted by any male person of the Hindu religion, who has a wife alive, shall be valid, unless such person, on his remarriage, shall comply with the provisions of this act relative to remarriages.

II. Every male person of the Hindu religion, who desires to contract a fresh marriage, while he has a wife alive, shall prepare a written application, setting forth the grounds on which he claims to be allowed to remarry, and shall present the same to the Local Committee or Punchayet appointed to receive such applications. Every such Local Committee or Punchayet shall consist of persons conversant with the laws or usages of Hindus.

III. On receipt of an application under the last preceding section, the Local Committee or Punchayet shall proceed to inquire whether there are sufficient grounds for allowing the claim therein set forth. Every such claim shall be summarily disallowed, unless one of the following grounds be alleged in the application.

1. That the living wife of the applicant has committed adultery.
2. That the living wife of the applicant is a confirmed Lunatic.
3. That the living wife of the applicant is afflicted with incurable Leprosy or some other such incurable and loathsome disease.
4. That the living wife of the applicant has been incapable of bearing male children, for a period of not less than eight years after the consummation of marriage.
5. That the living wife of the applicant is guilty of practices by which a Hindu becomes an outcaste.
6. That the living wife of the applicant is a person with whom, according to the law and usages of the Hindus, he could not lawfully contract a marriage; and that his marriage with her had been contracted in ignorance of the true state of the case, or in consequence of fraud practiced upon him.

IV. If the grounds alleged in an application relate exclusively to matters of private concernment, the Local Committee or Punchayet may require the applicant to testify to the facts on solemn affirmation and may record such testimony as sufficient prima facia evidence of the facts so testified. Provided, that nothing in this act shall exempt any applicant, in respect to any fact so testified, from liability to prosecution in a charge of giving false evidence.

V. If any of the grounds, stated above, be alleged in the application for permission to remarry, the Local Committee or Punchayet shall proceed to investigate the claim and shall pass an award allowing or disallowing the same.

VI. Every such award of a Local Committee or Punchayet shall be treated as an award of arbitrators and shall be forwarded without delay to the District Court, for registration.

VII. The District Judge, on receipt of any such award, shall issue a notice to every person concerned, allowing a stated period in which to shew cause why the award should not be registered. Provided, that such notice shall not state the grounds upon which the award is based; the party wishing to know them, may apply to the Local Committee or Punchayet for a copy of their award.

VIII. If, within the period allowed, any of the parties concerned appear to shew cause, the District Judge shall appoint a day for hearing the objection, and after such hearing shall pass judgment rejecting or admitting such objection. Provided, that if the objection relate to some point of Hindu Law or usage or to some matter of private concernment, it shall be competent to the District Judge without passing judgment, to refer the objection to the Local Committee or Punchayet, by whom the award was made, for further investigation and report, and proceed, on receipt of their reply, to pass judgment as aforesaid.

IX. If the objection be admitted, the award shall be of no effect and shall not be registered.

X. If the objection be rejected, or if no objection be made within the period stated, the award shall be duly registered.

XI. When any such award shall be registered in the District Court, any party concerned may, at any time, obtain a copy of the same and may put it in as sufficient prima facie evidence that the remarriage, to which it refers, is not invalid.

XII. Any person infringing the provisions of this act shall, on conviction before a competent Court, be punished with imprisonment, with or without hard labor, for a period not exceeding five years, or a fine not exceeding five thousand Rupees, or both.

XIII. Any person or persons, who shall knowingly aid or abet any person in infringing the provisions of this act, shall, on conviction before a competent Court, be punished with imprisonment, with or without hard labor, for a period not exceeding two years, or a fine not exceeding two thousand Rupees, or both.

XIV. On the registration, under this act, of an award of a Local Committee or Punchayet, a fee shall be chargeable at such rate as the Local Government shall from time to time prescribe.

Supplement One

Recently thirteen individuals, including Kshetrapal Smritiratna and Narayan Vedaratna, circulated a signed opinion entitled, "Polygamy is sanctioned by the Shastras."[102] The opinion came to me after I had circulated my own book entitled, *Bahuvivaha rahita haoya uchita ki na etadvishayaka vichara* [i.e., *Against High-Caste Polygamy*]. The purpose of their opinion is to convince the public that polygamy is sanctioned by the Shastras and thus should not be abolished. The signatories of that petition cite some passages from the Smritis and Puranas as proof-texts. The first and second of these are:

1. A married man who out of desire for pleasure wishes to marry another woman may do so if he is able to satisfy his first wife financially [A passage of Smriti from the *Madanparijata*].[103]
2. It is necessary for a man seeking to fulfill his duties to accept a wife, but if he is requested by someone willing to give a daughter in marriage or if he has a strong need for passion, then he may take several wives [Section on the duties of an independent householder from the *Brahmanda Purana*].[††††]

On first seeing these two proof-texts, many will conclude that polygamy is clearly sanctioned by the Shastras. I should clarify. In my book, *Against High-Caste Polygamy*, I have demonstrated[‡‡‡‡] that the creators of the Shastras have provided four injunctions regarding marriage. According to those four injunctions, marriage is determined to be of three types: Required, Contingent, and Desired. Marriage according to the first injunction is Required; if one does not marry, one is not qualified for the stage of householder. Marriage according to the second injunction is also Required; if one does not marry, one is outcasted for falling out of one's stage of life. Marriage according to the third injunction is Contingent, because in such cases a man marries due to the barrenness, long-term illness, or otherwise, of his wife. Marriage according to the fourth injunction is Desired; it is not necessary as is the case with both Required and Contingent marriages. It is done purely from

†††† I follow the textual reading and explanation preferred by Smritiratna. However, in my opinion there is a problem with how they read the first half of the second proof-text, and as such their understanding is also discordant. I believe the proper reading should be: "A man should marry one wife who is fit for fulfilling duties."

‡‡‡‡ See the discussion under the First Objection.

a man's desire. If a man desires it, such a marriage is allowed; that's all there is to it. The purpose of the householder stage is the gaining of sons and the performance of duties and rites. These goals cannot be reached without taking a wife. This is why in the first injunction the taking of a wife is described as the door to the householder stage of life, and as the essential means for fulfilling that stage. Should a man lose his wife while carrying out the life of a householder, but fail to take another wife, then he will be outcasted; devoid of a wife he cannot fulfill that stage of life. This is why the creators of the Shastras promulgated the second injunction, which communicates the necessity for a man in such a situation to take another wife. Should a wife be barren or have a long-term illness, etc., then those faults frustrate the goals of having a son and completing one's duties. Hence the creators of the Shastras promulgated the third injunction as a way to address such situations; this allows for another marriage even when a man is already married. The purpose of marriage within one's class is to make it possible to follow the injunctions of the Shastras regarding completion of the householder's duties. But if a man from a superior class desires to marry, the creators of the Shastra promulgated the fourth injunction, which communicates the right to marry outside one's class. And by the same injunction they absolutely prohibited a man in this position from marrying within his own class.

It is clear from the first and second proof-texts cited by Smritiratna that these particular injunctions have to do with Desired marriages. The first refers to "A married man who out of desire", while the second notes that "if he has a strong desire." Marriages that come about from a desire for pleasure or a need for passion cannot be called anything but Desired. In the context of marriage based on desire, Manu has issued an injunction regarding marriage outside one's class. From this injunction it is clear that in such cases marriage within one's class is strictly prohibited. As such, it may be concluded from the first and second proof-text provided by Smritiratna that a man who has made a marriage within his class and desires to marry again out of a need for passion may make a marriage outside his class. However, it cannot be demonstrated that a man who sets out to marry voluntarily as a way to fulfill his desire is allowed to marry again within his own class while his first wife is still living. The passages of Smriti selected from the *Madanparijata* and the *Brahmanda Purana* appear to be general injunctions about desired marriage; they do not indicate whether the man may marry within or outside of his class. Manu has given an injunction about desired marriage; he clearly indicates that a man who so desires may marry outside his class.[104] There can be no legitimate grounds for doubt or objection here. If they are to conform with the passage from Manu, the true meaning of the two passages from the Smriti and Purana above must be taken to apply to marriage outside one's class. And so it is pointless to conclude that these two proof-texts demonstrate polygamy is approved by the Shastras.

The third, fourth, fifth, eighth, ninth and tenth proof-texts cited by Smritiratna all apply to marriage outside of one's class. Since the practice of marrying outside one's class has been abolished for the Kali Yuga, there is no need to say anything more on this score.[105] The remaining proof-texts they cite refer to one man having many wives; but these do not allow us to conclude that the matter of voluntary polygamy is approved by the Shastras. These proof-texts are all so similar that it is sufficient to consider just one in order to make my point. Therefore, for present purposes I choose the following:

> 7. Among several wives of the same caste, if one has a son, Manu declares that all the wives have a son [*Manu-smriti* 9.183].[106]

This passage from Manu, like so many similar passages from the sages, does not mean that people may voluntarily form plural marriages for reasons other than those specified by the Shastras. On the contrary, it is clear that passages like this, which raise the issue of marrying plural wives, apply only to the practice of supersession.[§§§§] What it comes down to is this: (1) when the creators of Shastra have ruled that Desired marriage is only allowed outside of one's class; (2) when according to this injunction marriage within one's class is absolutely prohibited as long as a previously married wife is alive; (3) and when it is completely possible to make plural marriages as long as all the aforementioned conditions apply; (4) then there is no way to conclude that the creators of the Shastras approved the idea of making as many voluntary marriages as one wished. In short, the matter of voluntary pilgrimage is not a practice approved by the Shastras. It is thus utterly pointless to ask whether the matter of voluntary polygamy is reasonable or not. Anyone with a basic intelligence and the capacity for reflection can easily see that polygamy is a hideous and cruel practice that cannot be justified.[107]

To be honest, I had not hitherto realized how those almighty men tainted by the sin of polygamy, or those who worked to protect the practice of

[§§§§] See the discussion under the First Objection.

polygamy, could be so saddened by efforts to prohibit the custom; nor did I realize there are some who actually worry that if polygamy is prohibited our land will somehow be ruined. I really have been astounded by the perseverance of men like Smritiratna. They are saddened and even outraged by efforts to prohibit polygamy; and seeing the officers of the Society for the Protection of Dharma making an effort in this direction, they hurl abuse at them, saying they are selfish, saying they don't know the Shastras, saying they are devious and rash. I believe the opinion circulated by Smritiratna was ill-considered.

Many people have told me that Smritiratna's opinion in favor of polygamy was approved by, benefitted from, and encouraged by the efforts of Taranath Tarkavachaspati, Professor of Grammar at the Calcutta Government Sanskrit College. I find this hard to believe.[108] Tarkavachaspati is not so unlearned as to enter into such an improper business. Just five years earlier, at the time of the petition to the Government pleading for the prohibition of polygamy, he was a strong supporter. He signed the petition himself eagerly. It cannot be possible that he has now joined the party of those who seek to protect polygamy. He cannot really be arguing that this shameful, detested, deleterious, and unjust practice is approved by the Shastras.

Shri Ishvarchandra Sharma
Kashipur
24th of Shravan | Samvat 1928

Supplement Two

It is my firm conviction that the custom of polygamy as practiced in this land is not approved by the Shastras, but has its roots in voluntary behavior. This is why I have provided the relevant Shastric prohibitions concerning marriage in my book, *Against High-Caste Polygamy*. Even so, Taranath Tarkavachaspati, Professor of Grammar, and Dwarkanath Vidyabhushan, Professor of Poetics—both of the Calcutta Government Sanskrit College—hold the opinion that the practice of polygamy is in accord with the Shastras. They have each made their views known on this matter. Both Tarkavachaspati and Vidyabhushan are renowned scholars. When people see opposing rulings from two such scholars, they may feel inclined to think that the matter of voluntary polygamy is approved by the Shastras. Hence it is important to review this matter.

Let us begin with the views of Tarkavachaspati as expressed in the following passage:[109]

> Recently the respected Ishvarchandra Vidyasagar published a Supplement on polygamy, in the Conclusion of which he wrote that, 'Many people have told me that Smritiratna's opinion in favor of polygamy was approved by, benefitted from, and encouraged by the efforts of Taranath Tarkavachaspati, Professor of Grammar at the Calcutta Government Sanskrit College.[110] I find this hard to believe.' I have such a long-standing affection, friendship, and bond with Vidyasagar that he really ought to have asked me before reporting something he had only heard reported by others. It ill befits Vidyasagar to circulate something he happened to overhear. Is he not aware of the authority his words convey? I was astounded by his rashness and it deeply pained me. In truth, Vidyasagar was misled by someone who spoke falsely. I did not approve, assist, or provide encouragement in this connection. As a matter of fact, about a month ago I parted ways with the Society for the Protection of the Eternal Dharma. I based my decision on a passage proving that polygamy is in accord with the Shastras. I therefore said that it was wrong for the Society to assist in efforts to prohibit the practice. I cannot say who told Vidyasagar that this constituted lending assistance, but may it please the editors: it has long been my conviction that polygamy is approved by the Shastras. I have repeatedly stated, and I say it now, that polygamy is practiced in all lands, is approved by the Shastras, and is of longstanding practice. It pains me that my views on this matter are not in accord with those of Vidyasagar. It is certainly proof of his intellect that he has advanced innovative interpretations and reasons in his effort to demonstrate that polygamy contravenes the Shastras. But reflection shows that his interpretations and his reasons do not conform to the Shastras. That said, I should add that even though polygamy is approved by the Shastras, the framework by which the Broken Kulin Brahmins arrange their marriages, not to mention the changes that have taken place over time, have made it a hideous, shameful, and cruel affair. This has become manifestly clear to me. My deepest desire has been—and remains—to see this practice banned. And let me add that five or six years ago I was active in the preparation of a petition to the Government (which I eagerly signed), calling for a bill to ban the practice, feeling at the time that 'even though it is a social matter, the present moment left room for no other course of action.'[111] However, now I realize that this detested framework has been significantly weakened, whether through the force of learned reflection

> or some other reason. I now think there is no need for a law, since very soon it will completely disappear. Laws are not always the solution. This is why from one year to the next the Legislative Council continues to revise legislation.
>
> —Taranath Tarkavachaspati*****

In the selection above Tarkavachaspati tells us he has long held that polygamy is approved by the Shastras. And yet his conclusion is not supported by any proof. In a letter he wrote to the Society for the Protection of the Eternal Dharma, on 16th Shravan last, he provided both Shastric sources and reasoned arguments. In a relevant portion of that letter we find the following:

> A married man who out of desire for pleasure wishes to marry another woman may do so if he is able to satisfy his first wife financially [*Madanparijata*].[112]
>
> This passage of Smriti taken from the *Madanparijata*, determines that a man who has married once and wishes to marry another woman for pleasure is able to do so as long as he satisfies his first wife financially. We are aware of passages like this; and we know that great souls like Dharma married the daughters of Daksha Prajapati; and we know that Sages like Yajnavalkya, as well as kings like Dasharatha and Yudhishthira conducted themselves similarly. All this is well attested in the Vedas and Puranas. So it can be ascertained that the celebrated and longstanding tradition of polygamy among the learned is in accord with the Shastras. Now a ruling has been made to prohibit this custom, which is practiced among the Kulins and other great men of this land, as well as among Hindu societies in many other lands.

Tarkavachaspati will surely acknowledge that the type of injunction on marriage found in the passage of Smriti from the *Madanparijata* is a Desired marriage. On the topic of Desired marriage, Manu has given a ruling providing for marriage outside one's class; but the same injunction makes it clear that marriage within one's class is completely prohibited. So this much can be concluded on the basis of the passage from the *Madanparijata*: a man who has married within his class according to the injunctions may voluntarily

***** *Somprakash* (13 Bhadra) 1278 Sal.

undertake to marry again, as long as he marries outside his class. Otherwise, a man who voluntarily sets out to marry from a desire for pleasure, may in no way marry again within his class so long as his first wife—from a marriage within his class—is still living. At first glance, the passage of Smriti from the *Madanparijata* appears to be an injunction about Desired marriage. It makes no mention of whether the man desiring to marry should marry within or outside his class. But Manu provides an injunction on Desired marriage which clearly indicates that a man who so desires should do so outside his class. This being the case, if we are to reconcile the passage of Smriti from the *Madanparijata* with the passage from Manu, then the proper interpretation has to be that it applies to marriage outside one's class. There is no room for doubt or objection here. And as such, there is no way to demonstrate that voluntary marriage within one's class is in accord with the Shastras as Tarkavachaspati hopes to show by citing the passage of Smriti from the *Madanparijata*.

In order to demonstrate that there are Shastric authorities for the validity of voluntary polygamy, Tarkavachaspati mentions the well-known and respectable conduct of Gods, sages, and kings from earlier eras. We should review what sort of proof such conduct provides.

> Manu says:
> The highest Dharma is that conduct enjoined by the Veda and the Smriti [*Manu-smriti* 1.109].

The creators of the Shastras intended to say that conduct in accord with the Vedas and Puranas is the highest Dharma. Let people follow that sort of conduct. Otherwise, conduct opposed to the Vedas or Smritis is not commended nor should it be followed. To follow such conduct is to fall into sin. Many who are unable to heed the injunctions and prohibitions become tainted by unsanctioned conduct. What we notice today in this regard seems to have been just as true in the past. By which I mean that there many in the past who were tainted by unsanctioned conduct after finding themselves unable to heed the injunctions and prohibitions of the Shastras. The difference is that people back then were powerful; they didn't fall into sin by unsanctioned conduct. They were more learned in the Shastras and more devoted to Dharma, and so their conduct was completely faultless. It would be inappropriate to think that since everything people did in the past was viewed as respectable conduct one might therefore avoid sin merely by following their example. If their conduct is prohibited by the Shastras, then it cannot be followed. If ordinary people follow such conduct they will fall into sin.

Apastamba says:

> We can see that people in older times violated Dharma and practiced unsanctioned conduct. They were powerful and so they were not touched by sin. Anyone who tries to follow their example will be ruined [*Apastamba Dharmasutra* 2.6.8-10].[113]

This passage allows us to conclude that ordinary people should follow conduct in accord with the injunctions of the Vedas and Smritis, while shunning any conduct that is opposed to them. I have demonstrated in my *Against High-Caste Polygamy* that voluntary marriage other than what is indicated by the Shastras is a form of conduct opposed to the Smritis. Thus, even though Gods like Dharma, sages like Yajnavalkya, and kings like Yudhishthira voluntarily married more than once, it is by no means appropriate for ordinary people to follow their example. It is therefore wrong for learned scholars to present the Gods, sages, and kings of old as examples for ordinary people to follow when it comes to voluntary polygamy. I should mention here the deliberation of the Vedic commentator Madhavacharya on the authoritativeness of respected conduct.

> What authority can be ascribed to the conduct of the learned in relation to things like marriage of daughters from one's maternal family? It might be argued that just as with other examples of learned conduct, this is authoritative. However, since it is in opposition to the Smriti it is not authoritative. All learned conduct has its root in the Smriti. In this case, one might wish to infer the Smriti from the learned conduct, except that a Smriti learned by inference is negated by one that is learned from direct perception [*Jaiminiya-nyaya-mala-vistara*, 1.3.5].

The conduct of the learned is understood as what we see practiced in refined society.[114] The creators of the Shastra reckoned the conduct of the learned to be authoritative in matters of Dharma, just like Veda and Smriti. All learned conduct is rooted in the Smriti. So, if we see learned conduct, we might think it conforms to what is found in the Smriti. Except that learned conduct is of two types: (1) that which is rooted in direct knowledge of the Smriti and (2) that which is rooted in inference about the Smriti. We say learned conduct is rooted in direct knowledge of the Smriti whenever we observe that what is practiced as learned conduct in a particular place is rooted in the Smriti. And whenever we see learned conduct that is not rooted in the Smriti, we infer that this learned conduct used to be rooted in the Smriti but over time has become degraded; in such a case we say that this learned conduct is rooted in inference. Directly observed Smriti overrides inferred Smriti. So, whenever we observe learned conduct in a particular place and we know it is a practice that is prohibited by the Smriti Shastra, then knowing it to be opposed to directly observed Smriti, we can say it is not authoritative. In some southern places, there is a practice in refined society of marrying daughters from one's maternal family. As such one might say this constitutes the conduct of the learned in those places. However, in the Smriti Shastra, marriage of daughters from one's maternal family is always prohibited. For this reason, this type of learned conduct is opposed to direct observation of Smriti.[115] Learned conduct opposed to what is directly observed about Smriti cannot be accepted as authoritative on the basis of inference. Learned conduct involving the marriage of daughters from one's maternal family is never authoritative. In the same way, it may well be that the practice of voluntary polygamy counts as learned conduct in this land; but it is opposed to what is directly observed in Smriti. And therefore it is wrong for it to be celebrated under the category of learned conduct or treated as authoritative in terms of Dharma. After all, if every sort of conduct found among the Gods and kings of old were to be counted as learned conduct and deemed authoritative, then we would also have to practice things like sex with unwed daughters, theft of a guru's wife, marriage with daughters of one's maternal family and the taking of one wife by five men.[116]

Thus it will not work for Tarkavachaspati to claim that the practice of voluntary polygamy is approved by the Shastras on the basis of passages from Smriti and other celebrated examples of learned conduct. If he has no authorities stronger than this, his long-held conclusion must be in error. That is, Tarkavachaspati cannot simply assert that "it is my long-held conclusion that polygamy is approved by the Shastras." He is required to furnish solid proof of the validity of this conclusion. It seems unlikely people will simply take his word for it and pay no heed to other authorities. Tarkavachaspati says,

> "I have said it over and over and I say it again that polygamy is practiced in all lands, is in accord with the Shastras, and is a practice of long standing."

There is no other proof for this claim, beyond asserting again and again that voluntary polygamy is approved by the Shastras. Tarkavachaspati himself knows firsthand that polygamy is not approved by all the Shastras. If it were, then surely he could provide countless proof texts from the Shastras. But after diligently combing through the standard collections of texts, he has not been able to satisfy himself with even one passage. And since he cannot find support for his own opinion in the books on Dharmashastra by Manu, Vishnu, Vashishtha, Gautama, Yajnavalkya, Apastamba, Parashara, and Vedavyasasa, he seeks refuge in the *Madanparijata*.

Tarkavachaspati says,

> It is certainly a proof of (Vidyasagar's) intellect that he has advanced innovative interpretations and reasons in his effort to demonstrate that polygamy contravenes the Shastras. But reflection shows that his interpretations and reasons do not conform to the Shastras.

Let me just say that in my book, *Against High-Caste Polygamy*, I have quoted six passages from Manu pertaining to marriage. I fail to see where Tarkavachaspati finds my interpretation to be "innovative." I do not think it is possible to say there are different interpretations for the individual words used to compose these passages. Tarkavachaspati says that the interpretation and meanings I have provided are neither in accord with the Shastras nor appropriate. What concerns me is that he never indicates what sort of interpretation or reasoning would be appropriate or in accord with the Shastras. It is considered learned conduct to provide one's own sense of interpretation and reasoning when raising objections to someone else's interpretation and reasoning. Tarkavachaspati is required to do the same, since only then will people be able to decide which interpretation and reasoning is appropriate and conforms to the Shastras. Otherwise, it is only his word that my interpretation and reasoning are unacceptable. That is not right.

Tarkavachaspati writes in *Somprakash*,

> Even though polygamy is approved by the Shastras, the framework by which the Broken Kulin Brahmins arrange their marriages, not to mention the changes that have taken place over time, have made it a hideous, shameful, and cruel affair. This has become strikingly clear to me. My deepest desire has been—and remains—to see this practice banned.

And to the Society for the Protection of the Eternal Dharma, he writes,

> This custom is practiced among the Kulins and great men of this land as well as the Hindu societies in many other lands.

In one context the practice of Kulin polygamy is hideous, shameful, and cruel; in another context the Kulins are called great men, among whom the practice of polygamy is considered learned conduct. Reading Tarkavachaspati's letter to the Society for the Protection of the Eternal Dharma, one would think that every polygamous Kulin is worshipped as a great soul. One would have no idea that he feels revulsion and aversion toward the Broken Kulins:

> Five or six years ago, I was active in the preparation of a petition to the Government (which I eagerly signed), calling for a bill to ban the practice, feeling at the time that 'even though it is a social matter, the present moment left room for no other course of action.'[117] However, now I realize that this detested framework has been significantly weakened, whether through the force of learned reflection or some other reason. I now think there is no need for a law, since very soon it will completely disappear.
>
> "About a month ago I parted ways with the Society for the Protection of the Eternal Dharma, and among the reasons I listed was a passage I selected which proves that polygamy is in accord with the Shastras. I said that it was wrong for the Society to assist in efforts to prohibit the practice."

Here we might note that Tarkavachaspati took up this matter for the same reasons and with the same intention as the Society for the Protection of the Eternal Dharma. The only difference is that thanks to his genius, Tarkavachaspati knew that the excesses committed by the Kulins with respect to marriage would soon completely vanish; therefore there was no need for a law. Apparently the dim-witted administrators of the Society for the Protection of the Eternal Dharma do not appreciate this fact even today. It bears noting that back when Tarkavachaspati chose to sign—of his own free will and enthusiastically—the petition calling for a ban on the practice of polygamy, it was a cruel, hideous, and shameful matter. Now, seeing that the times have changed, it is a practice that is "in accord with all the Shastras" and a "celebrated and long-standing tradition among the learned." Basically, Tarkavachaspati sought to ban a cruel, hideous, and shameful matter, whereas the Society for the Protection of the Eternal Dharma sought to put an end to a celebrated and long-standing tradition among the learned. Tarkavachaspati's pristine conscience was revolted by such an injustice. The Society for the Protection of the Eternal Dharma only needed to realize that with the expansion of learning, not to mention the efforts and signatures of men like Tarkavachaspati, another five years would witness a gradual decrease in the excesses related to polygamy. Then in another two and a half years there would be a further diminution, until eventually, after another five years, the practice would have completely ceased. And if that is the case, then it should have been perfectly legitimate for the Society for the Protection of the Eternal Dharma to wait another two and a half or even five years. There was no need for Tarkavachaspati to unleash his wrath on them.

Now let us review the opinions of Dwarkanath Vidyabhushan on the matter of polygamy.[118] Vidyabhushan writes:

> The chief proof that polygamy is not prohibited by the Shastras of this land is the practice of this land itself. Were it prohibited, it would not be so widespread. The men of this land have long done just as they please and have long sought their own comfort and convenience, while caring not a whit for the welfare of women. Having secured for themselves the prerogative of creating the Shastras, it is simply not possible to imagine these selfish men would then work to block the chief pathway to enjoyment. The Vedas, Puranas, Smritis, and Kavya serve to refute the idea that polygamy is prohibited, as the following passages show:[119]
>
> 1. Veda:
> Just as two tethers can be tied to a single post, so one man may marry two women. Just as one tether cannot be tied to two posts, so one woman may not marry two men [*Taittiriya Samhita* 6.6.4.3].
>
> 2. *Dayabhaga* of Jimutavahana:
> The phrase "but, if lust impels them, they may have further wives" is there to indicate that the flaw is a minor one, not that there is no flaw at all. That is why Shankha and Likhita say: "The primary rule is that men should wed women of their own castes; these are best for all. The secondary rule is as follows: a Brahmin may wed four in descending order; a Kshatriya three, a Vaishya two, and a Shudra one" [*Dayabhaga* 9.4-5, quoting *Shankha-Likhita* 64].[120]
>
> 3. Achyutananda's commentary on the *Dayabhaga*:
> The meaning here is that because the phrase "limited by caste" is used, there is no objection to Brahmins and others taking five or six wives of the same caste [*Dayabhaga-siddhanta-kumudachandrika*].

4. *Bhagavata Purana*:
Vasudeva's wife Rohini is living in the home of Nanda; his other wives are living in seclusion out of fear of Kamsa [*Bhagavata Purana* 10.2.7].

5. Shakuntala:
Vetravati! Since he was so wealthy, the merchant Dhanamitra must have had many wives. Please inquire whether one of his wives had a child [Kalidasa, *Abhijnanashakuntalam*, Act 6].

6. Bharatachandra Ray:[121]
My mother-in-law is a tyrant, my sister-in-law is a tigress, and my co-wife is a viper full of poison.[†††††]

Vidyabhushan says, "The chief proof that polygamy is not prohibited by the Shastras of this land is the practice of this land itself. Were it prohibited, it would not be so widespread." If we follow this sort of ruling, tomorrow someone is likely to say, "The practice of this land is the chief proof that the sale of daughters is not contrary to the Shastras, since if it were forbidden by the Shastras it would not be so widespread." And the next day someone else will say, "The practice of this land is the chief proof that abortion is not contrary to the Shastras, since if it were forbidden by the Shastras it would not be so widespread." And then a third person will say, "The custom of this land is the chief proof that bearing false witness is not contrary to the Shastras, since if it were forbidden by the Shastras it would not be so widespread." The very next day a fourth person will say, "The custom of this land is the chief proof that forgery is not contrary to the Shastras, since if it were forbidden by the Shastras it would not be so widespread." Then a fifth person will say, "The custom of this land is the chief proof that bribery and unethical business conduct are not contrary to the Shastras, since if they were forbidden by the Shastras they would not be so widespread." And so on. Every kind of evil behavior can be said to be in accordance with the Shastras. Rest assured that with this sort of ruling, Vidyabhushan will win the undying affection of a great many people.

Vidyabhushan is no more arrogant nor rash than Tarkavachaspati. He is no more likely to reach a conclusion blindly than Tarkavachaspati. He applies his own rigorous reasoning. Consider the following amazing logic,

††††† *Somprakash* 13 Bhadra 1278.

> The men of this land have long done just as they please and have long sought their own comfort and convenience, while caring not a whit for the welfare of women. Having secured for themselves the prerogative of creating the Shastras, it is simply not possible to imagine these selfish men would then work to block the chief pathway to enjoyment. .

Vidyabhushan is relentless in advancing his own position; he casts aside all concern with what is proper and what is not. It is essential for him to demonstrate that the matter of voluntary polygamy is approved by the creators of the Shastra. And so he came up with the crazy notion that the Indian creators of Shastra were selfish, unrestrained, and devoted to pleasure; they gave no thought to the well-being of women. Their pursuit of pleasure could not be fulfilled if people were not free in matters of marriage. It was inconceivable to them that a man's chief path to the enjoyment of pleasure should be blocked by the prohibition of freedom in marriage. Thus it is inconceivable that the creators of Shastra did not approve of freedom in marriage. I don't think anyone has ever before heard such strange exegesis from the mouth of a scholar. Even though Vidyabhushan is most learned and wise, the kinds of hideous intentions he ascribes to the humble and sinless creators of Shastra are absolutely unheard of.[122]

As to the sorts of rulings one finds in the Shastras regarding practices with respect to women, we find this:

> Fathers, brothers, husbands and brothers-in-law, anxious for their own well-being will honor their women, ornamenting them with clothing and jewelry (55). That family in which women are honored will be blessed by the gods, whereas the family in which women are not honored will see no fruit from any rites like sacrifice and giving (56). Any family in which the women suffer, will quickly decline, whereas the family in which women are content will enjoy continual happiness (57). Where women are mistreated, they bring curses, and all those families will suffer as if by sorcery (58) [*Manu-smriti* 3.55-58].

Parashara says,

> Always honor women with food, ornaments, and clothing. Men should always behave in such a way that women suffer no displeasure (41). If women are content, then men will gain endless life, wealth, glory, and sons. Where they are not content, then by their curse all of those things will be

> lost (42). The gods, the fathers, and all of humanity will bless the family in which women are forever honored and ornamented, etc. (43). Women are Lakshmi herself when pleased, but when angered are the very form of an angry god. The clan prospers when they are content, and is destroyed when they are disrespected (44). If they are of good character, a husband, father-in-law, brother-in-law, father, mother, brother and all other relations will never disrespect women (45) [*Brihat Parashara Samhita* 4.41-45].[123]

If men disregard this ruling and treat women wrongly, it is not the fault of the creators of the Shastra.

Here are all the injunctions and prohibitions regarding marriage in the Shastras:

> A twice born man, having taken his guru's permission, and having bathed and performed the ritual of return,[‡‡‡‡‡] should marry an attractive woman of his own caste [*Manu-smriti* 3.4].

> Having properly completed the last rites for his first wife, a man should take another wife and re-establish his sacred fires [*Manu-smriti* 5.168].

> A man should practice supersession, which is to say he should marry again, in cases where his wife is addicted to drink, wanton, fractious, continually ill, harsh or wastes his income [*Manu-smriti* 9.80].

> A wife should be superseded in the eight year if she is barren, in the tenth year if her son dies, in the eleventh year if she bears only daughters, but immediately if she speaks harshly [*Manu-smriti* 9.81].

> As long as she remains alive, a man should marry no other woman than the one he joined with in order to perform the rites and gain sons [*Apastamba Dharmasutra*, 2.5.12].

> Marriage within one's class is enjoined for the twice-born, but those who undertake to marry voluntarily should marry into other classes according to order. That is, a Brahmin may marry a Brahmin, Kshatriya, Vaishya, or Shudra; a Kshatriya may marry a Kshatriya, Vaishya or Shudra; a Vaishya

‡‡‡‡‡ A particular ritual ceremony following on completion of Vedic study and studentship and prior to entering the householder stage.

may marry a Vaishya or Shudra; and a Shudra may only marry a Shudra [*Manu-smriti* 3.12].

A man is able to marry again, even if his wife is living, in order to enjoy pleasure; he may take another wife provided he satisfies his previously married wife with money [A passage from Devala quoted in the *Smritichandrika*].[124]

Garga says that a man should never marry a third time to enjoy pleasure. If, out of delusion or lack of knowledge, he does take a third wife, he will certainly fall from caste [*Matsya Purana* quoted in the *Nirnaya Sindhu*].[125]

You see from the first passage, that an injunction is given about marriage at the time of entering the householder stage of life. From the second passage we have an injunction about marrying again upon the loss of a wife. The third and fourth passage enjoin another marriage if a wife, though living, is barren, etc. The fifth injunction absolutely prohibits another marriage within one's caste while a previously married wife is living, if one has completed one's duties and gained a son. The sixth passage promulgates an injunction regarding marriage outside one's caste for someone whose wife is alive and who wished to marry again to enjoy pleasure. In the seventh passage a ruling is given that if a man desires to marry again in order to enjoy pleasure, he may marry outside his caste provided he has the consent of his previously married wife.[126] The eighth passage makes it clear that marrying for a third time in order to enjoy pleasure is completely prohibited. All these injunctions and prohibitions on the matter of marriage are crystal clear. It is one thing to say that people have ignorantly transgressed the injunctions and prohibitions in order to marry selfishly. But it is the height of insolence—and betrays a real ignorance of Dharmashastra—to say with a straight face that the creators of Shastra composed these texts to satisfy their selfishness and unrestrained appetites.

In addition to the reasons already mentioned, Vidyabhushan attempts to bolster his conclusion with proof texts selected from the Veda, Smriti, Purana, Sanskrit and Bengali poetry.[127]

1—As to the Vedic passages he provides, his interpretation goes like this. Just as at the time of a sacrifice two ropes may be attached to a single sacrificial post, so too one man may marry two wives.[128] And just as a single rope may not be tied to two sacrificial posts, it is not possible for one woman to be married to two men. With these Vedic passages Vidyabhushan attempts to demonstrate that, if necessary, a man whose wife is still living may marry a second time. I cannot tell you how far this is from proving that the matter of voluntary polygamy is in accord with the Shastras—let alone from showing that the creators of Shastra were selfish and had unrestrained appetites.

2—The passage from Shankha and Likhita quoted in the *Dayabhaga* is exactly the same as the passage from Manu on the topic of marriage outside one's class. In other words, it announces a prohibition on marriage within one's caste in the case of voluntarily marrying while one's original wife is still living. Therefore, this cannot be taken as proof that voluntary polygamy is approved by the Shastras; nor does it prove the selfishness or unrestrained appetites of the creators of the Shastras.

3—In his commentary on the *Dayabhaga*, Achyutananda uses the phrase "limited by caste" with the intention of saying that Brahmins and other classes may not be censured for making five or six marriages within their caste. Shankha and Likhita state that in the proper order Brahmins may take four wives, Kshatriyas three, Vaishyas two, and Shudras one. The author of the *Dayabhaga* says that in this passage the words "four, three, two, and one" are used to refer to the four castes, three castes, two castes, and one caste. In other words, Brahmins may marry into four castes, Kshatriyas into three, Vaishyas into two, and Shudras into one. Writing on the *Dayabhaga*, Achyutananda expresses his personal opinion that five or six marriages are not to be censured. But Manu, in his fourth injunction regarding marriage, completely prohibits voluntary marriages within one's caste. Putting this together, one realizes that Achyutananda's personal opinion mentioned above is unacceptable. It certainly reveals the sorry state of one's intellect and one's own sense of Dharma to disregard the words of a sage in order to follow the ruling of a modern digest writer or commentator.[129]

4—As for the passage selected from the *Bhagavata Purana*, it means that when Vasudeva's wife Rohini was in Nanda's house, his other wives went abroad out of fear of Kamsa. Vasudeva had married voluntarily, and in so doing he had transgressed the injunctions of the Shastras. But we cannot blame the creators of Shastra for that. We have already seen that in their opinion such selfish behavior by people in prior ages is not sanctioned; it should not be copied by ordinary people. This is precisely why the creators of Shastra advise ordinary people to remain vigilant and not to follow the example of such unsanctioned behavior. So once again, we see that this neither establishes that the matter of voluntary polygamy is in accord with the

Shastras nor shows that their creators were selfish and unrestrained in their appetites.

5—From the passage selected from the drama *Abhijnana-Shakuntalam*, it can merely be established that during the Satya Yuga there was an illustrious merchant named Dhanamitra who made many marriages.

6—And the passage from *Vidyasundara* merely shows that there were co-wives at that time.[130]

If an argument arose around the question of whether in this land at some time and for some reasons men had married again while their first wives were still living, then the passages from Shakuntala and *Vidyasundara* would serve as sufficient proof. We have seen over and over again evidence that people have disregarded the Shastric prohibitions in order to voluntarily marry again. Such unsanctioned behavior does not prove that the matter of voluntary polygamy is in accord with the Shastras, nor does it show that the creators of the Shastras were selfish or unrestrained in their appetites. If you were to think that the people of this land have not—at various times and for various reasons—disregarded the rulings of the Shastras; and if you were to think that whatever they did was in accord with the injunctions and prohibitions of the Shastras; then it stands to reason that you would look at the practice of voluntary polygamy in this land and conclude that such behavior was not prohibited by the Shastras. However, once you see that in the opinion of the creators of the Shastra the practice of voluntary polygamy is completely prohibited, then it would be completely wrong to use this kind of behavior as proof that it was not prohibited. And yet, the people of our land have disregarded the prohibitions of the Shastras in many situations, not least when it comes to marriage. So I suppose that if you look at it this way, then you may feel they deserve no special blame for their behavior; in fact you might even think they were justified in doing so.

Conclusion to the Second Supplement

In closing I simply want to say,

> Marriage within one's class is enjoined for the twice-born, but those who undertake to marry voluntarily should marry into other classes according to order. That is, a Brahmin may marry a Brahmin, Kshatriya, Vaishya, or Shudra; a Kshatriya may marry a Kshatriya, Vaishya or Shudra; a Vaishya

may marry a Vaishya or Shudra; and a Shudra may only marry a Shudra [*Manu-smriti* 3.12-13].

The injunction we find here is Exclusionary. From this Exclusionary injunction it is established that as long as a man's first wife is living he is always prohibited from voluntarily marrying again within his caste.[131] As long as one fails to see that this injunction is Exclusionary it is possible to claim that polygamy is "approved by all the Shastras" and to say that it is "not prohibited by the Shastras." Thus it is incumbent on those who wish to claim that the practice of voluntary polygamy is approved by the Shastras, or on those who claim that it is not prohibited by the Shastras, to refute the idea that this injunction is Exclusionary.[132] Unless or until they do that, they may raise all the objections they want; they may quote as many proof texts as they like—Vedas, Smritis, Puranas, Shakuntala, Vidyasundar, whatever. They will still not be able to demonstrate that the practice of voluntary polygamy is not prohibited by the Shastras, let alone that it is approved by the Shastras. The only thing that will come from further pointless debate and wrangling among themselves and other curious readers will be a waste of time.

Shri Ishvarchandra Sharma
Kashipur
1st of Ashvin | Samvat 1928

Supporting Evidence

*1.10–*2.36: Additional text and footnotes

Note: because the original Sanskrit and Bengali passages adduced by Vidyasagar are likely to be of interest largely to specialists, I leave them untranslated and employ diacritical marks for greater clarity. My thanks to the anonymous reader who helped correct some of my transcriptions and improved the sense of one or two passages.

Vidyasagar provides only minimal information regarding the sources for these passages, and in some cases, no source at all. Where possible I have provided further citations within brackets or in additional endnotes.

*1.10 footnote on exclusionary injunctions:

viniyogavidhir apy apūrvvavidhiniyamavidhiparisaṃkhyāvidhibhedāt trividhaḥ | vidhiṃ vinā kathamapi yadarthagocarapravṛttir nopapadyate asāv apūrvvavidhiḥ | niyatapravṛttiphalako vidhir niyamavidhiḥ | svaviṣayād anyatra pravṛttivirodhī vidhiḥ parisaṃkhyāvidhiḥ | tad uktaṃ

> *vidhiratyantamaprāptau niyamaḥ pākṣike sati |*
> *tatra cānyatra ca prāptau parisaṃkhyeti gīyate ||*

Source: *Vidhisvarūpa Vicāra*

[The text cited varies from the text as found in *Vidhiswarup Vichar*, 41. I follow Vidyasagar, but have added additional *daṇḍas* (or full stops) and set the *śloka* as a block quotation at the suggestion of one anonymous reader, who felt these emendations would help clarify the passage.]

*1.14 footnote on how the passage from *Udvahatattva* applies to men with three wives

etadvacanaṃ varttamānastrītrikaparam iti vadanti |

—Source: *Udvāhatattva* [*Gṛhastharatnākara*, cited in *Raghunandanakrita Udvahatattvam* (39), where the word *vacanam* is omitted; cp. the 1835 Serampore edition of *Institutes of the Hindoo Religion by Rughoo Nundun*, which contains the passage as quoted by Vidyasagar]

*2.1 footnote on the date of Adisura

ādisūro navanavatryadhikanavaśatīśatābde pañca brāhmaṇān ānāyayāmāsa |

—Source: *Kṣitīśavaṃśāvalīcarita* [cited in Vidyanidhi, *Sambandhanirnaya*, 157]

*2.2 footnote on the five Brahmins and their lineages

bhaṭṭanārāyaṇo dakṣo vedagarbho' tha chāndaṛaḥ |
atha śrīharṣanāmā ca kānyakubjāt samāgatāḥ ||
śāṇḍilyagotrajaśreṣṭho bhaṭṭanārāyaṇaḥ kaviḥ |
dakṣo 'tha kāśyapaśreṣṭho vātsyaśreṣṭho' tha chāndaṛaḥ ||
bharadvājakulaśreṣṭhaḥ śrīharṣo harṣavarddhanaḥ |
vedagarbho' tha sāvarṇo yathā veda iti smṛtaḥ ||

—Source not given [likely from Vācaspati Miśra, *Kularāma*; partially cited in Basu, *Banger Jatiya Itihas*, vol. 1, part 1, 105]

*2.5 footnote on the original five villages

pañcakoṭiḥ kāmakoṭir harikoṭis tathaiva ca |
kaṅkagrāmo vaṭagrāmas teṣāṃ sthānāni ca ||

—Source not given [cp. the similar verse cited in Basu, *Banger Jatiya Itihas*, vol. 1, part 1, 111; Basu refers to the Kulācāryas Harimiśtra, Eḍumiśra, and Vācaspati Miśra]

*2.6 footnote on the fifty-six sons

bhaṭṭataḥ ṣoḍaśodbhutā dakṣataścāpi ṣoḍaśa |
catvāraḥ śrīharṣajātā dvādaśa vedagarbhataḥ |
aṣṭāvatha parijñeyā udbhutāśchāndaṛāmuneḥ ||
—Source not given [cited in Raychaudhuri and Raychaudhuri, *The Brahmans of Bengal*, from a manuscript they refer to as "Mishra Grantha" (120n7), perhaps referring to a work by Vācaspati Miśra]

*2.7–11 text and footnotes regarding the assignment of villages and surnames

In the family line of Bhattanarayana in Shandilya's lineage there are these sixteen surnames: Bandya, Kusum, Dirghangi, Ghoshali, Batbyal, Pariha, Kulakuli, Kushari, Kulabhi, Seyak, Gargari, Akash, Keshari, Maschatak, Vasuyari, Koral.[1] In the family line of Daksha in Kashyapa's lineage there are these sixteen surnames: Chatta, Ambuli, Tailavati, Podari, Hara, Gura, Bhurishthal, Palasi, Pakrashi, Pushali, Mulagrami, Koyari, Palasayi, Pitatundi, Simalayi, and Bhatta.[2] In the family line of Shriharsha in Bharadvaja's linage there are these four surnames: Mukhuti, Dimsai, Sahari, and Rai.[3] In the family of Vedagarbha in Savarna's lineage there are these twelve surnames: Ganguli, Pumsik, Nandigrami, Ghanteshvari, Kundagrami, Siyari, Sateshvari, Dayi, Nayeri, Parihal, Baliya, and Siddhala.[4] In the family line of Chandara in Vatsya's lineage there are these eight surnames: Kanjilal, Mahinta, Putitunda, Piplai, Ghoshal, Bapuli, Kanjari, and Simlal.[5]

*2.12 footnote on the decline of Adisura and advent of Vallala Sena

ādisūrer vaṃśadhvaṃsa senavaṃśa tājā ||
viṣkakasener kṣetraja putra vallālasena rājā |
—Source not given [cited in Vidyanidhi, *Sambandhanirnaya*, 208]

*2.13 footnote on nine attributes along with Vidyasagar's comment

ācāro vinayo vidyā pratiṣṭhā tīrthadarśanam |
niṣṭhāvṛttis tapo dānaṃ navadhā kulalakṣaṇam ||

There is a legend that whereas the verse originally featured *śānti* ("peace") in place of *niṣṭhā*, Vallala's genealogists replaced that term with the word, *āvṛtti*.

—Source not given [from Vallala Sen's *Kulamanjari*; the verse appears widely in texts like Vācaspati Miśra's *Kulasarvasva* and Sarvānanda Miśra's *Kulatattvārṇava*; it is translated in Inden, *Marriage and Rank in Bengali Culture* (61)]

*2.14 footnote on exchange

ādānaṃ ca pradānaṃ ca kuśatyāgas tathaiva ca |
pratijñā ghaṭakāgreṣu parivarttaś caturvidhaḥ ||

—Source not given [Raychaudhuri and Raychaudhuri, *The Brahmans of Bengal*, cite a variant from Vācaspati Miśra's *Kularāma* (129n32)]

*2.15 footnote on the attributes of the surnames

bandyaś caṭṭo 'tha mukhuṭī ghoṣālaś ca tataḥ paraḥ |
putituṇḍaś ca gāṅguliḥ kāñjiḥ kundena cāṣṭamaḥ ||

—Source not given [cited in Vidyanidhi, *Sambandhanirṇaya*, 224]

*2.16-18 text and footnotes detailing the various surnames

Among these eight surnames there are five in the Chattopadhyay lineage: Bahurupa, Sucha, Arabinda, Halayudha, Bangala; in the Putitunda lineage there is one: Govardhanacharya; in the Ghoshal lineage there is one: Shira; in the Gangopadhyay lineage there is one: Shisha; in the Kundugrami lineage there is one: Roshakara; in the Bandyopadhyay lineage there are six: Jahlana, Maheshvara, Devala, Vamana, Ishana, Makaranda; in the Mukhopadhyay lineage there are two: Utsaha and Garuda; in the Kanjilal lineage there are two: Kanu and Kutuhala. All nineteen are Kulin.[6] The following thirty-four surnames possessed eight attributes: Palathi, Pakrashi, Simalayi, Bapuli, Bhurishthal, Kulakuli, Batbyal, Kushari, Seyak, Kusuma, Ghoshali, Mashchatak, Vasuyari, Koral, Ambuli, Tailavati, Mulgrami, Pushali, Akash, Palasayi, Koyari, Sahari, Bhattacharya, Sateshvari Nayeri, Dayi, Parihal, Siyari, Siddhala, Pumsik, Nandigrami, Kanjari, Simlal, and Bali. For this reason they were ranked as Shrotriyas.[7] Of the nine attributes mentioned above, they were lacking the attribute of exchange. In other words, whereas the eight surnames of Bandya and the rest were careful in matters of giving and receiving, the thirty-four surnames of Palathi and the rest were not. This is why they did not attain the rank of Kulin. And there were fourteen surnames that fell away from good conduct: Dirghangi, Pariha, Kulabhi, Podari, Rai, Keshari, Ghanteshvari, Dimsai, Pitamundi, Mahinta, Gura, Piplai, Haṛa, and Gargari. As a result they were counted as Lesser Kulins.[8]

*2.19 footnote on Vamshaja

śrotriyāya sutāṃ dattvā kulīno vaṃśajo bhavet |
—Source not given [cited in Vidyanidhi, *Sambandhanirṇaya*, 226]

*2.20 footnote on Lesser Kulins as enemies of clan rank

. . . *arayaḥ kulanāśakāḥ* |
yatkanyālābhamātrena samūlas tu vināśyati ||
—Source not given [cited in Vidyanidhi, *Sambandhanirṇaya*, 227]

*2.21 footnote on genealogists receiving Kulin rank

vallālaviṣaye nūnaṃ kulīnā devatāḥ svayaṃ |
śrotriyā meravo jñeyā ghaṭakāḥ stutipāṭhakāḥ ||
aṃśaṃ vaṃśaṃ tathā doṣaṃ ye jānanti mahājanāḥ |
ta eva ghaṭakā jñeyā na nāmagrahaṇāt param ||
—Source not given [amending Vidyasagar's *aśaṃ* to *aṃśaṃ* in the final couplet]

*2.23 footnote on the term *mela*

doṣān melayatīti melaḥ |

—Source not given [a similar passage—*doṣāṇām milanaṃ yatra tatra mela prajāyate*—is quoted without a source in Raychaudhuri and Raychaudhuri, *The Brahmans of Bengal*, 135n39]

*2.24 footnote on the connection between fault and rank

doṣo yatra kulaṃ tatra |

—Source not given

*2.25 footnote providing the names of the thirty-six Assemblages

1 Phuliyā, 2 Khaṛdaha, 3 Sarvvānandī, 4 Vallabhī, 5 Surāi, 6 Ācāryaśekharī, 7 Paṇḍitaratnī, 8 Bāṅgāla, 9 Gopālaghaṭakī, 10 Chāyānarendrī, 11 Vijayapaṇḍitī, 12 Cādāi, 13 Mādhāi, 14 Vidyādharī, 15 Pārihāla, 16 Śrīraṅgabhaṭṭī, 17 Mālādharakhānī, 18 Kākusthī, 19 Harimajumdārī, 20 Śrīvarddhanī, 21 Pramodinī, 22 Daśarathaghaṭakī, 23 Śubharājakhānī, 24 Naṛiyā, 25 Rāyamela, 26 Caṭṭarāghavī, 27 Dehāṭī, 28 Chayī, 29 Bhairavaghaṭakī, 30 Ācambitā, 31 Dharādharī, 32 Bālī, 33 Rāghavaghoṣālī, 34 Śuṅgosarvvānandī, 35 Sadānandakhānī, 36 Candravatī.

—Source not given

*2.26 footnote on the Dhandha fault

anūḍhā śrīnāthasutā dhandhaghāṭasthale gatā |
hāsāikhānadāreṇa yavanena valātkṛtā ||
dhandhasthānagatā kanyā Śrīnāthacaṭṭajātmajā |
yavanena ca saṃsṛṣṭā soḍhā kaṃsasutena vai ||
nāthāicaṭṭera kanyā hāsāikhānadāre |
sei kanyā vibhā kaila vandya gaṅgāvare ||

—Source not given

*2.36 footnote listing Kulin generations

1 Śrīharṣa, 2 Śrīgarbha, 3 Śrīnivāsa, 4 Ārava, 5 Trivikrama, 6 Kāka, 7 Sādhu, 8 Jalāśaya, 9 Vāṇeśvara, 10 Guha, 11 Mādhava, 12 Kolāhala. Śrīharṣa was the first to come to Bengal.

1 Utsāha, 2 Āhita, 3 Uddhava, 4 Śiva, 5 Nṛsiṃha, 6 Garbheśvara, 7 Murāri, 8 Aniruddha, 9 Lakṣmīdhara, 10 Manohara. Utsāha was the first Kulin in the Mukhuṭi lineage.

1 Gaṅgānanda, 2 Rāmācārya, 3 Rāghavendra, 4 Nīlakaṇṭha, 5 Viṣṇu, 6 Rāmadeva, 7 Sītārāma, 8 Sadāśiva, 9 Gorācād, 10 Īśvara. Gaṅgānanda is in the Phuliyā Assemblage; Iśvara is in the Khaṛdaha Assemblage.

—Source not given

Supporting evidence *4.1–*4.2: Data on polygamous marriages

4.1 HOOGHLY DISTRICT

Name	Marriages	Age	Place of residence[a]
Bholanath Bandyopadhyay	80	55	Baso
Bhagavan Chattopadhyay	72	64	Desh Mukho
Purnachandra Mukhopadhyay	62	55	Chitrashali
Madhusudan Mukhopadhyay	56	40	"
Tituram Ganguli	55	70	"
Ramamay Mukhopadhyay	52	50	Tajpur
Vaidyanath Mukhopadhyay	50	60	Bhuipara
Shyamcharan Chattopadhyay	50	60	Pakhuda
Navakumar Bandyopadhyay	50	52	Kshirpai
Ishanchandra Bandyopadhyay	44	52	Ankrishrirampur
Yadunath Bandyopadhyay	41	47	Chitrashali
Shivchandra Mukhopadhyay	40	45	Tirna
Ramkumar Bandyopadhyay	40	50	Konnagar
Shyamcharan Bandyopadhyay	40	50	Chunchura

Name	Marriages	Age	Place of residence[a]
Thakurdas Mukhopadhyay	40	55	Dandipur
Navakumar Bandyopadhyay	36	44	Gaurhati
Raghunath Bandyopadhyay	30	40	Khamargachi
Shashishekhar Mukhopadhyay	30	60	"
Taracharan Mukhopadhyay	30	35	Barijhati
Ishanchandra Bandyopadhyay	28	40	Gurapa
Shricharan Mukhopadhyay	27	40	Sangai
Krishnadhan Bandyopadhyay	25	40	Khamargachi
Bhavanarayan Chattopadhyay	23	40	Jaimpara
Maheshchandra Bandyopadhyay	22	35	Khamargachi
Girischchandra Bandyopadhyay	22	34	Kuchundiya
Prasannakumar Chattopadhyay	21	35	Kapsit
Parvaticharan Mukhopadhyay	20	40	Bhaite
Yadunath Mukhopadhyay	20	37	Mahesh
Krishnaprasad Mukhopadhyay	20	45	Vasantpur
Harachandra Bandyopadhyay	20	40	Ranjitbati
Ramanath Chattopadhyay	20	50	Garalgacha
Anandachandra Chattopadhyay	20	45	Bhaite
Dinanath Chattopadhyay	19	28	Vasantpur
Ramaratna Mukhopadhyay	17	48	Jayrampur
Kedarnath Mukhopadhyay	17	32	Mahesh
Durgacharan Bandyopadhyay	16	20	Chitrashali
Gopalchandra Mukhopadhyay	16	35	Maheshvarpur
Abhayacharan Bandyopadhyay	15	30	Malipara
Annadacharan Mukhopadhyay	15	35	Goyara
Shyamcharan Mukhopadhyay	15	35	Santiya
Jagacchandra Mukhopadhyay	15	40	Khamargachi
Aghoranath Mukhopadhyay	15	36	Bhuipara
Harishchandra Mukhopadhyay	15	32	Mogalpur
Nanigopal Bandyopadhyay	15	24	Pata
Yadunath Bandyopadhyay	15	22	"
Dinanath Bandyopadhyay	15	25	Belesikare
Bhuvanmohan Mukhopadhyay	15	20	Bhaite
Kaliprasad Ganguli	15	45	Pashpur
Suryakanta Mukhopadhyay	15	35	Bhaite

Name	Marriages	Age	Place of residence[a]
Ramkumar Mukhopadhyay	14	32	Kshirpai
Kailashchandra Mukhopadhyay	14	45	Madhukhand
Kalikumar Mukhopadhyay	14	21	Siyakhala
Madhavchandra Mukhopadhyay	13	50	Bainchi
Harishchandra Bandyopadhyay	13	40	Garalgacha
Karittikeya Mukhopadhyay	12	30	Deora
Yadunath Bandyopadhyay	12	30	Tantisal
Mohinimohan Bandyopadhyay	12	30	Malipara
Satkari Bandyopadhyay	12	40	"
Brajarama Chattopadhyay	12	25	Chandrakona
Kailashchandra Bandyopadhyay	12	32	Krishnanagar
Ramtarak Bandyopadhyay	12	28	Jayrampur
Kalidas Mukhopadhyay	12	40	Bhuipara
Vishvambhar Mukhopadhyay	12	30	Balagarh
Tituram Mukhopadhyay	12	40	Natibpur
Prasannakumar Ganguli	12	36	Gaja
Manasaram Chattopadhyay	11	65	Bhanjpur
Ashutosh Bandyopadhyay	11	18	Tantisal
Pyarimohan Mukhopadhyay	11	30	Garalgacha
Lakshminarayan Chattopadhyay	10	25	Vidyabatipur
Shivchandra Mukhopadhyay	10	45	"
Kaliprasad Mukhopadhyay	10	30	Bhaite
Ramkamal Mukhopadhyay	10	40	Nityanandapur
Kaliprasad Bandyopadhyay	10	28	Bainchi
Dvarkanath Mukhopadhyay	10	25	"
Matilal Mukhopadhyay	10	45	"
Ishvarchandra Bandyopadhyay	10	45	Dhasa
Durgaram Bandyopadhyay	10	50	Shyambati
Yajneshvar Bandyopadhyay	10	45	Anur
Prasannakumar Chattopadhyay	10	35	Bengai
Chandicharan Bandyopadhyay	10	30	Baital
Pratapchandra Mukhopadhyay	10	40	Vasantpur
Kailashchandra Chattopadhyay	10	40	Siyakhala
Ramchand Mukhopadhyay	9	36	Yadupur
Kailashchandra Bandyopadhyay	9	30	Napara

Name	Marriages	Age	Place of residence[a]
Suryakanta Bandyopadhyay	8	40	Bainchi
Gopalchandra Mukhopadhyay	8	45	"
Chunilal Bandyopadhyay	8	32	"
Kalikumar Bandyopadhyay	8	40	Mollai
Ganeshchandra Mukhopadhyay	8	20	Deora
Digambar Bandyopadhyay	8	35	Gurapa
Kalidas Mukhopadhyay	8	40	Malipara
Yadavchandra Ganguli	8	35	Baharkuli
Madhavchandra Bandyopadhyay	8	25	Sikare
Kedarnath Mukhopadhyay	8	32	Barijhati
Ishvarchandra Mukhopadhyay	8	45	Patul
Shyamcharan Mukhopadhyay	8	45	Jayrampur
Harishchandra Bandyopadhyay	8	60	Shyambati
Ramchand Chattopadhyay	8	40	Bhanjpur
Ishvarchandra Chattopadhyay	7	32	"
Digambar Mukhopadhyay	7	36	Ratnapur
Kudaraam Mukhopadhyay	7	32	Natibpur
Durgaprasad Bandyopadhyay	7	62	Mathura
Vaikunthanath Bandyopadhyay	7	34	Vasantpur
Shridhar Bandyopadhyay	7	35	Bhursuva
Ramsundar Mukhopadhyay	7	50	Antpur
Venimadhav Ganguli	7	50	Chitrashali
Shyamcharan Bandyopadhyay	6	30	Mogalpur
Navakumar Mukhopadhyay	6	22	Chandrakona
Yadunath Mukhopadhyay	6	30	Bakharchak
Chandranath Bandyopadhyay	6	30	Vasantpur
Umacharan Chattopadhyay	6	40	Ranjitbati
Umeshchandra Mukhopadhyay	6	26	Nandanpur
Ganganarayan Mukhopadhyay	5	30	Gaurhati
Ishvarchandra Bandyopadhyay	5	32	Pashpur
Kalachand Mukhopadhyay	5	50	Sultanpur
Manasaram Chattopadhyay	5	45	Tarakeshvar
Ganganarayan Bandyopadhyay	5	22	Amrapat
Vishvambhar Mukhopadhyay	5	40	Baligora
Ishvarchandra Chattopadhyay	5	35	Tarakeshvar

Name	Marriages	Age	Place of residence[a]
Madhavchandra Mukhopadhyay	5	40	Talai
Bholanath Chattopadhyay	5	26	Tekra
Harashambhu Bandyopadhyay	5	40	Maju
Nilambar Bandyopadhyay	5	32	Sandhipur
Kalidas Mukhopadhyay	5	30	Kalidanga
Bholanath Bandyopadhyay	5	36	Gaurangapur
Dvarkanath Bandyopadhyay	5	30	Krishnanagar
Sitaram Mukhopadhyay	5	35	Chandrakona
Ramdhan Mukhopadhyay	5	40	"
Navakumar Mukhopadhyay	5	43	Barada
Dharmadas Mukhopadhyay	5	35	Narit
Suryakuma Mukhopadhyay	5	26	Barada
Sharacchandra Bandyopadhyay	5	19	Napara
Mahendranath Mukhopadhyay	5	18	Dandipur

[a]District lines have changed since Vidyasagar's day, and thus some of the places surveyed may no longer fall within the current boundary of Hooghly District in the state of West Bengal. Some of these villages likely now fall inside the district of Paschim Midnapore.

4.2 THE VILLAGE OF JANAI

Name	Marriages	Age
Mahananda Mukhopadhyay	10	35
Yadunath Bandyopadhyay	10	29
Anandachandra Ganguli	7	65
Dwarkanath Ganguli	5	32
Bholanath Mukhopadhyay	5	50
Chandrakanta Mukhopadhyay	5	64
Shyamcharan Bandyopadhyay	4	18
Dinanath Chattopadhyay	4	26
Trailokyanath Mukhopadhyay	4	45
Trailokyanath Mukhopadhyay	4	27

Name	Marriages	Age
Nilakantha Bandyopadhyay	4	50
Sitanath Bandyopadhyay	3	29
Tripuracharan Mukhopadhyay	3	35
Kalidas Ganguli	3	26
Dinanath Ganguli	3	19
Kalipada Bandyopadhyay	3	40
Kshetramohan Chattopadhyay	3	40
Kalipada Mukhopadhyay	3	50
Madhavchandra Mukhopadhyay	3	35
Navakumar Mukhopadhyay	3	43
Nilamani Ganguli	3	48
Kalikumar Mukhopadhyay	3	55
Chandranath Ganguli	3	50
Shrinath Chattopadhyay	3	43
Harananda Mukhopadhyay	3	60
Pyarimohan Chattopadhyay	2	40
Suryakumar Mukhopadhyay	2	40
Bholanath Bandyopadhyay	2	55
Sitanath Bandyopadhyay	2	55
Chandrakumar Mukhopadhyay	2	60
Chandrakumar Chattopadhyay	2	52
Ramanath Bandyopadhyay	2	52
Harinath Mukhopadhyay	2	62
Rajmohan Bandyopadhyay	2	57
Bholanath Mukhopadhyay	2	50
Dinanath Mukhopadhyay	2	50
Vishvambhar Mukhopadhyay	2	50
Ramkumar Bandyopadhyay	2	50
Pyarimohan Mukhopadhyay	2	35
Chandrakumar Bandyopadhyay	2	32
Kalikumar Ganguli	2	25
Ashutosh Ganguli	2	20
Yadunath Bandyopadhyay	2	31
Navinchandra Bandyopadhyay	2	33
Kedarnath Mukhopadhyay	2	28
Gauricharan Mukhopadhyay	2	28

Name	Marriages	Age
Bhagavanchandra Mukhopadhyay	2	32
Dvarkanath Ganguli	2	30
Kalimohan Bandyopadhyay	2	32
Harihar Ganguli	2	35
Kamakhyanath Mukhopadhyay	2	28
Pyarimohan Ganguli	2	33
Kalidas Mukhopadhyay	2	35
Chandrakumar Chattopadhyay	2	28
Navinchandra Mukhopadhyay	2	24
Nandalal Bandyopadhyay	2	28
Dinanath Mukhopadhyay	2	30
Yadunath Ganguli	2	27
Vishveshvar Mukhopadhyay	2	27
Gopalchandra Bandyopadhyay	2	27
Chandrakumar Ganguli	2	21
Mahendranath Mukhopadhyay	2	21
Priyanath Bandyopadhyay	2	22
Yogendranath Bandyopadhyay	2	20

Supporting evidence *C.1: List of signatories to the 1855 petition

Śrīyuta Mahārājādhirāja Mahātāpacandra Bāhādur, Ruler of Burdwan
Śrīyuta Mahārāja Satīśacandra Rāy Bāhādur, Ruler of Navadvīpa
Śrīyuta Rājā Pratāpacandra Siṃha Bāhādur (Pāikpāṛā)
Śrīyuta Rājā Satyaśaraṇa Ghoṣāla Bāhādur (Bhukailāsa)
Śrīyuta Bābu Jayakṛṣṇa Mukhopādhyāya (Uttarpāḍā)
Śrīyuta Bābu Rājakumāra Rāy Caudhurī (Bāripur)
Śrīyuta Rājā Pūrṇacandra Rāy (Sāoṛāpulī)
Śrīyuta Bābu Sāradāprasāda Rāy (Cakdighī)
Śrīyuta Bābu Yajñeśvara Siṃha (Bhāstāṛā)
Śrīyuta Bābu Rāy Priyanātha Caudhurī (Ṭākī)
Śrīyuta Bābu Śambhunātha Paṇḍita

Śrīyuta Bābu Devendranātha Ṭhākura
Śrīyuta Bābu Rāmagopāla Ghoṣa
Śrīyuta Bābu Hīrālāla Śīla
Śrīyuta Bābu Śyāmacaraṇa Mallika
Śrīyuta Bābu Rājendra Mallika
Śrīyuta Bābu Rāmacandra Ghoṣāla
Śrīyuta Bābu Īśvaracandra Ghoṣāla
Śrīyuta Bābu Dvārakānāth Mallika
Śrīyuta Bābu Kṛṣṇakiśora Ghoṣa
Śrīyuta Bābu Dvārakānātha Mitra
Śrīyuta Bābu Dayālacād Mitra
Śrīyuta Bābu Rājendra Datta
Śrīyuta Bābu Nṛsiṃha Datta
Śrīyuta Bābu Govindacandra Sena
Śrīyuta Bābu Harimohana Sena
Śrīyuta Bābu Mādhavacandra Sena
Śrīyuta Bābu Rājendralāla Mitra
Śrīyuta Bābu Pyārīcād Mitra
Śrīyuta Bābu Durgācaraṇa Lāhā
Śrīyuta Bābu Śivacandra Deva
Śrīyuta Bābu Śyāmācaraṇa Sarakāra
Śrīyuta Bābu Kṛṣṇadāsa Pāla

Notes

Note on the Text and Translation

1. In some reprint editions, the word *vichara* is replaced by *prastava* ("proposal"); see Haldar, *Vidyasagar-rachanasamgraha*, vol. 2, 167. I believe this error creeps in because Vidyasagar had used the term *prastava* prominently in the titles of books one and two of his work promoting widow marriage, whose title is very similar to *Bahuvivaha*, namely *Vidhavavivaha prachalita haoya ucita ki na etadvishayaka prastava* (1855).
2. See https://archive.org/details/in.ernet.dli.2015.291855/page/n127/mode/2up.
3. Blumhardt's 1886 *Catalogue of Bengali Printed Books in the Library of the British Museum* confirms that the Second Edition ran to only 94 octavo pages, as compared to the First Edition's 116.
4. On the relationship between Vidyasagar and Taranath, see Hatcher, *Vidyasagar: The Life and After-Life of an Eminent Indian*, ch. 6.
5. For this reason, in the case of texts like *Manu-smriti* I provide only basic information on chapter and verse. For less familiar texts, I have done my best to trace the provenance of Vidyasagar's citations, although even so some of these remain unclear.
6. On the relationship between the language of abolishing and banning, see my comments at 138n6.
7. The prevalence of Kulin traditions was strongest among the subcastes of Rarhi and Barendra Brahmin and Kayasthas. Bengali Vaidya communities also followed Kulin marriage customs, but these are not taken up by Vidyasagar.
8. The tracts on widow marriage were published in January and October of 1855; for a complete translation and notes, see Vidyasagar, *Hindu Widow Marriage*. As noted above (note 1), whereas Vidyasagar called the work on widow marriage a "proposal" (*prastava*), he framed the present work as an "examination" (*vichara*).

Introduction

1. See Kelly Elizabeth Phipps, "Marriage and Redemption: Mormon Polygamy in the Congressional Imagination, 1862–1887," 481.
2. On Vidyasagar as *abala-bandhu*, see Brian A. Hatcher, *Vidyasagar: The Life and After-life of an Eminent Indian*, 89.
3. On this, see Vidyasagar, *Hindu Widow Marriage: An Epochal Work on Social Reform from Colonial India*.
4. Thomas Metcalf notes that in the decade after the mutiny, the British enacted only one major social reform measure; he refers explicitly to the failure of efforts to suppress

polygamy as clear evidence of official reluctance to move more aggressively in this direction; see *The Aftermath of Revolt: India, 1857–1870*, 112.

5. See Metcalf, *The Aftermath of Revolt*, 92–93.
6. Quoted in Swapan Basu, "The Development of Journalism and Public Opinion in Bengal 1818–1910," 765. Benoy Ghosh found evidence of widespread support for government intervention up until the outbreak of the Rebellion; see his *Vidyasagar o Bangali Samaj*, 281–82.
7. Beginning around 1860 a few remarkable women began publishing essays on the living conditions for Hindu wives and widows. One thinks of Kailashbashini Debi's "The Pitiful State of Hindu Women" (*Hindu mahilaganer hinavastha*, 1864) and Bamasundari Debi's, "What Are the Evil Customs that Need to Disappear for This Land to Prosper?" (*Ki ki kusanskar tirahitha haile ei desher srivridhi haite pare*, 1861); for brief translations, see Malini Bhattacharya and Abhijit Sen, eds., *Talking of Power: Early Writings of Bengali Women from the Mid-Nineteenth Century to the Beginning of the Twentieth Century*.
8. See *Against High-Caste Polygamy*, Objection Seven, the second paragraph of which contains a remarkable appeal for government intervention, in which Vidyasagar speaks of social emancipation being promoted by a ruler (*raja*) who heeds the appeals of his subjects (*praja*).
9. The quixotic dimensions of Vidyasagar's career were famously highlighted by Amalesh Tripathi in his *Vidyasagar: The Traditional Moderniser*, see esp. 64.
10. A forceful account of Vidyasagar's frustrations can be found in Asok Sen, *Vidyasagar and his Elusive Milestones*.
11. For a review of important legal developments in the period from 1820 to 1860, see Julia Stephens, *Governing Islam: Law, Empire, and Secularism in South Asia*, ch. 1.
12. Partha Chatterjee famously argued that the quest to promote the sanctity of the Indian nation led thinkers in the last quarter of the century to abandon appeals for government assistance on the so-called women's question in favor of celebrating Indian women as a the cherished site of spiritual dignity; see his *The Nation and its Fragments: Colonial and Postcolonial Histories*, 132.
13. On the Brahmo Marriage Act, see Nandini Chatterjee, "English Law, Brahmo Marriage, and the Problem of Religious Difference: Civil Marriage Laws in Britain and India."
14. In "Reflections on Kulin Polygamy," Malavika Karlekar notes how Vidyasagar supported his pleas with "solid academic and empirical research" (1995, 137).
15. I am indebted to Shuvatri Dasgupta for pointing out (in a personal communication) that Henry Beverley commented that publication of the 1872 Census marked an "epochal" moment in the history of statistics in Bengal; see *Report on the Census of Bengal 1872*, 1.
16. Vidyasagar viewed passage of Act XV permitting widow marriage as the "single greatest good deed" of his lifetime; see Vidyasagar, *Hindu Widow Marriage*, 1.
17. See Tripathi, *Vidyasagar*, 64, and Sekhar Bandyopadhyay, *Caste, Culture and Hegemony: Social Domination in Colonial Bengal*, 122–23.
18. See Mitra, *Isvar Chandra Vidyasagar*, 462.

19. Mitra, *Isvar Chandra Vidyasagar*, 541.
20. For a detailed and influential study of Kulin rank in terms of shared "coded substance," see Ronald Inden, *Marriage and Rank in Bengali Culture: A History of Caste and Clan in Middle-Period Bengal.*
21. See Sarkar, *Vidyasagar*, 23, and Indra Mitra, *Karunasagar Vidyasagar*, 341. As will be discussed subsequently, the figure of Mr. Bhattacharya in *Against High-Caste Polygamy* (Third Objection) may be loosely based on Vidyasagar's former teacher.
22. See Karlekar, "Reflections on Kulin Polygamy," 137. In a private communication, Karlekar reminded me of a report by Dwarkanath Ganguly in the journal *Abalabandhabh* ("Friend of the Weak/Woman") indicating that in cases where Kulin families saw no hope of marrying their daughters, they might choose to murder them.
23. Writing in the context of the widow marriage campaign, Lucy Carroll notes that the problem of widows generally was "largely a prerogative of the higher Hindu castes"; see her "Law, Custom and Statutory Reform: The Hindu Widows' Remarriage Act of 1856," in S. Sarkar and T. Sarkar, eds., *Women and Social Reform in Modern India: A Reader*, 79.
24. Sekhar Bandyopadhyay speaks of Vidyasagar's "sympathetic self" being undone by the "orthodox disciplinarian in him"; see his *Caste, Culture and Hegemony*, 131.
25. On Vidyasagar's reforms and "masculinist anxiety," see Bandyopadhyay, *Caste, Culture and Hegemony*, 127. The role played by claims about deviant sexuality in solidifying modern norms of patriarchy and conjugal life is explored in Mitra, *Indian Sex Life: Sexuality and the Colonial Origins of Modern Social Thought.*
26. See Carroll, "Law, Custom and Statutory Reform," 80.
27. On modes of Brahmanical patriarchy fostered in the context of reform, see Tanika Sarkar, "Conjugality and Hindu Nationalism: Resisting Colonial Reason and the Death of a Child-Wife," in her *Hindu Wife, Hindu Nation*; see also Rachel Sturman, "Marriage and Family in Colonial Hindu Law," in T. Lubin and D. Davis, eds., *Hinduism and Law: An Introduction.*
28. On this, see Karlekar's study of Nistarini Debi, in her "Reflections on Kulin Polygamy."
29. See especially his *Banger Jatiya Itihas*, vol. 1, part 1.
30. Inden's book belonged to the heyday of ethnosociology, which drew criticism for its essentialist understanding of Hindu culture; in time Inden would himself question some of this earlier work; see Inden, *Imagining India*. However, even an early critic like Thomas Trautman accurately predicted the book's value would "outlive its theoretical trappings"; see his review in *Journal of Asian Studies* (1980), 524.
31. This picture could be further complicated by inclusion of other groups like the Baidyas, who also followed Kulin ideology and practice; see Sen, *Vidyasagar*, 172.
32. The dating here is subject to debate, as is the historical evidence for the ruler named Adisura. Taking the tradition at face value, H. H. Risley remarked that Adisura did what any king on the margin of the Brahmanical heartland would do in order to gain legitimacy for his reign; see his *The Tribes and Castes of Bengal*, vol. 1, 145. It is sometimes suggested that the earliest Brahmin communities in Bengal had been corrupted by the prevalence of Jainism and Buddhism; on this see Tarak Ch. Raychaudhuri

and B. Raychaudhuri, *The Brahmans of Bengal*, 13–14, 20, who refer to Lalmohan Vidyanidhi, *Sambandhanirnaya*, 15.

33. Inden, *Marriage and Rank in Bengali Culture*, 59.
34. See *Against High-Caste Polygamy*, Second Objection.
35. Inden, *Marriage and Rank in Bengali Culture*, 59.
36. Raychaudhuri and Raychaudhuri quote a well-known verse indicating that "conduct is the highest law" (*acharah paramo dharmah*); *The Brahmans of Bengal*, 124.
37. This vignette appears in *Against High-Caste Polygamy*, Second Objection.
38. For simplicity's sake, I am limiting discussion to the regional subcaste of Rarhi Brahmins and not focusing on either the Rarhi Kayasthas or other regional Brahmin subcastes like the Varendra Brahmins.
39. The modern perception of the pain wrought by this system is registered by Bibhutibhushan Bandyopadhyay in his novel, *Pather Panchali*, the first chapter of which bears a title that might be translated as "The Evils of Vallala's System" (*Ballali Balai*).
40. Vamshajas were deemed to have already lost their Kulin status through improper marriages; see Raychaudhuri and Raychaudhuri, *The Brahmans of Bengal*, 34.
41. Narottam Kundu, "Caste and Class in Pre-Muslim Bengal," 179; see Inden, *Marriage and Rank in Bengali Culture*, 69.
42. Raychaudhuri and Raychaudhuri, *The Brahmans of Bengal*, 32. As early as 1817 Rammohun Roy had blamed "Ballalsen" for "this departure from law and justice" and suggested that the "innovation" of Kulin rank was the "chief source of that decay of learning and virtue, which . . . may at present be observed." See his *Second Defence of the Monotheistical System of the Vedas* in *The English Works of Raja Rammohun Roy*, 121.
43. See his remarks in *Against High-Caste Polygamy*, under the Second Objection.
44. Risley, *The Tribes and Castes of Bengal*, vol. 1, 146. For colonial-era observers, "hypergamy" was the defining feature of Kulinism. On this, see Inden, *Marriage and Rank in Bengali Culture*, 5, where we learn that Denzil Ibbetson originally coined the concept when discussing marriage customs in Punjab. The concept was then applied by H. H. Risley to Kulinism in his *Tribes and Castes of Bengal*, vol. 1, 146.
45. Inden, *Marriage and Rank in Bengali Culture*, 76.
46. Risley, *The Tribes and Castes of Bengal*, vol. 1, 147.
47. Inden, *Marriage and Rank in Bengali Culture*, 46.
48. Vidyasagar drew on the Kulin lore of the genealogists himself. Their digests are known variously as *kulajis*, *kula-panjikas*, or *kula-granthas*. One of the earliest published modern attempts to collate data from these texts was Lalmohan Vidyanidhi's *Sambandhanirnaya*, which was published in 1875. A close reading of Vidyasagar's tract translated here makes it evident that Lalmohan drew upon Vidyasagar's account and some of Vidyasagar's genealogical sources when compiling his text.
49. Vidyanidhi, *Sambandhanirnaya*, 180–81. N. K. Dutt calls Devivara a "great social organizer and reformer" in *The Origin and Growth of Caste in India*, vol. 2, 9.
50. Faults were numerous and varied. They included marrying a Kulin woman into a Shrotriya family, undertaking a marriage forbidden by the *dharmashastras*, marrying

a Vamshaja or a widow, marrying or dining with Muslims (*yavanas*), or eating in the house of a degraded caste.

51. Raychaudhuri and Raychaudhuri, *The Brahmans of Bengal*, 46.
52. Borrowing an example used by Risley in *The Tribes and Castes of Bengal*, vol. 1, 147–48.
53. Risley, *The Tribes and Castes of Bengal*, vol. 1, lxxv (note).
54. In addition to Karlekar's, "Reflections on Kulin Polygamy," I have benefitted from an unpublished manuscript she kindly shared with me, entitled "Nistarini Debi: A Kulin Widow's Life."
55. In his poem, *Kulinmahilavilap* ["The Lament of the Kulin Women"], composed in support of Vidyasagar's initiative, Hemchandra Bandyopadhyay imagined Kulin brides pleading their case to Queen Victoria, lamenting, "Our friends turn away, God turns away; our fathers and our brothers, too—even the heartless ones we call our husbands." See his *Granthavali*, vol. 1, part 1, 173–76.
56. Karlekar, "Reflections on Kulin Polygamy," 6.
57. See Aishika Chakraborty, "Gender, Caste, and Marriage: Kulinism in Nineteenth-Century Bengal," in S. Sen et. al., eds., *Intimate Others: Marriage and Sexualities in India*, 49.
58. See Inden, *Marriage and Rank in Bengali Culture*, 118–22, and Karlekar, "Reflections on Kulin Polygamy," 4.
59. Chakraborty, "Gender, Caste, and Marriage," 50.
60. Karlekar, "Reflections on Kulin Polygamy," 13.
61. Inden, *Marriage and Rank in Bengali Culture*, 120. Amiya Sen refers to the case of Rashbehari Mukhopadhyay (1826–95), who would become a vocal opponent of Kulin polygamy, but who admitted to having been married eight times before reaching the age of twenty, simply as one way for his family to fend off poverty; see Sen, *Vidyasagar: Reflections on a Notable Life*, 175.
62. Vidyasagar's *Shakuntala* is a prose retelling of Kalidasa's Sanskrit classic, which itself draws on the story of Shakuntala as found in the Mahabharata.
63. See Hatcher, "The Shakuntala Paradigm: Vidyasagar, Widow Marriage and the Morality of Recognition."
64. Vidyasagar, *Hindu Widow Marriage*, 205.
65. Shuvatri Dasgupta offers a trenchant analysis of the colonial "crisis of care" in places like Bengal where due to capitalism and the fiscalization of life, old grammars of belonging were displaced, while longing for alternate social worlds took on the apocaplyptic imaginary of the Kali Yuga (on which more below); see her "A History of Conjugality: On Care, and Capital, in the British Empire c. 1872–1947."
66. I refer, for example, to the way a biographer like Chandicharan Bandyopadhyay speaks of Vidyasagar as someone "tender hearted" (*komal hrdaya*), with a particular affection for women (*nari-suhrta*); see Bandyopadhyay, *Vidyasagar*, 268.
67. The quote is taken from Rosemary Hennessy's review of Nancy Fraser's *Justice Interruptus*, 131.
68. These examples are taken up at greater length in Hatcher, *Vidyasagar*, esp. ch. 3.

69. In a personal communication, Malavika Karlekar pressed me to acknowledge the role of the Brahmo Samaj in fostering the development of progressive ideas and in shaping a more expansive space for women's participation in social life; the point is well taken, and Vidyasagar's ethics does run close to the Brahmos' in some important ways; however, I prefer to train my focus on what remain the distinctive lineaments of his moral vision and public projects, which do not map neatly onto Brahmo commitments.
70. Quoted in N. N. Vaidya, *A Collection Containing Proceedings which led to the passing of Act XV of 1856*, 4.
71. Vidyasagar's silence is all the more stunning, given the fact that the question of women's property rights had been clearly adumbrated by Rammohun Roy a half-century earlier; see the latter's *Brief Remarks regarding Modern Encroachments on the Ancient Rights of Females, according to the Hindu Law of Inheritance*, in *The English Works of Raja Rammohun Roy*, 374–84.
72. Fraser, "Recognition without Ethics?," 26.
73. See Lata Mani, "Contentious Traditions: The Debate on *Sati* in Colonial India," in K. Sangari and S. Vaid, eds., *Recasting Women: Essays in Indian Colonial History*. There is a good deal to say in favor of this interpretation. Vidyasagar's reliance on the truth of shastra over the validity of local conduct or *deshachara*, and his willingness to imagine that the colonial state could begin framing new laws in accordance with an idealized scriptural Hinduism, are both problematic assumptions. Not only does he miss or suppress the legal pluralism inherent in Hindu approaches to family life and property, but the legislation he supported (in the case of 1856) was ill-suited to foster positive change. If anything, Act XV actually caused unintended harm, especially to women outside of the elite caste contexts on which Vidyasagar had focused. On this latter point, see Carroll, "Law, Custom and Statutory Reform."
74. See Sen, *Vidyasagar and his Elusive Milestones* and Barun De, "The Colonial Context of the Bengal Renaissance."
75. Tripathi, *Vidyasagar: The Traditional Moderniser*, 65.
76. Unlike Vidyasagar, Rammohun married more than once. He was initially married while still a child; when his first wife died, his father married him to two more women; see Sophia Dobson Collet, *The Life and Letters of Raja Rammohun Roy*, 6.
77. See Rammohun Roy, *A Second Conference between an Advocate for, and an Opponent of the Practice of Burning Widows Alive*, in *The English Works of Raja Rammohun Roy*, 361–62; for the Bengali text, see *Rammohun-Rachanavali*, 202.
78. The essay, "Bahuvivaha," from 1842 (1764 Shaka), is reprinted in B. Ghosh, ed., *Samayikpatre Banglar Samajchitra*, vol. 3, 5–8. I want to thank Sumit Chakrabarti for sharing this text with me.
79. "Bahuvivaha," in Ghosh, ed., *Samayikpatre Banglar Samajchitra*, vol. 3, 7.
80. See Ghosh, ed., *Samayikpatre Banglar Samajchitra*, vol. 3, 15–16.
81. Similar works from this period include the 1857 drama, *Sapatni Nataka*, of Tarakchandra Chudamani, and Dinabandhu Mitra's *Lilavati Nataka* from 1869.
82. Mitra, *Karunasagar Vidyasagar*, 383.
83. See the "Advertisement" to *Kulin Kulasarvasva*, in S. Bakshi, ed., *Ramnarayan Tarkaratna Rachanavali*, 3.

84. On the practice of petitioning in early modern and colonial South Asia, see Rohit De and Robert Travers, "Petitions and Political Cultures in South Asia"; for examples of early nineteenth-century petitions around colonial educational policy, see Lynn Zastoupil and Martin Moir, eds., *The Great Indian Education Debate*. Summaries of petitions in relation to Kulin polygamy can be found in Beman Behari Majumdar, *History of Indian Social and Political Ideas*, 17–22; Benoy Ghosh, *Iswar Chandra Vidyasagar*, 110–24; and Mitra, *Karunasagar Vidyasagar*, 339–40.
85. Mitra, *Isvar Chandra Vidyasagar*, 555; see also France Bhattacharya, *Pandit Iswarchandra Vidyasagar*, 178.
86. Ghosh, *Iswar Chandra Vidyasagar*, 110.
87. Ghosh, *Iswar Chandra Vidyasagar*, 114, mentions "no less than 127 petitions"; cp. Mitra, *Karunasagar Vidyasagar*, 338.
88. Ramaprasad was the son of Rammohun Roy. He was a member of the Legislative Council and the first Indian member of the Calcutta High Court. Around the time of the widow marriage movement he took the trouble of reprinting his father's 1822 essay, *Brief Remarks regarding Modern Encroachments on the Ancient Rights of Females* (cited above).
89. Quoted in Mitra, *Karunasagar Vidyasagar*, 340.
90. See the Author's Notice to *Against High-Caste Polygamy*.
91. This argument was still being made over a decade later; see Vaidya, *A Collection Containing Proceedings*, xiii: "Whenever there is a large amount of unredressed evil suffered by people who cannot adopt their own remedy, the State has a function to regulate and minimize the evil, if by so regulating it, the evil can be minimized better than by individual effort and without leading to other worse abuses."
92. Radhakanta was a scion of the influential Shobha Bazaar Raj and son of Gopimohan Deb, who had founded the Dharma Sabha in opposition to Rammohun Roy's support for the abolition of widow immolation.
93. For the text of the petition, which was dated 1 February 1866, see Mitra, *Isvar Chandra Vidyasagar*, 557–60.
94. Another thirty petitions were sent; see Ghosh, *Iswar Chandra Vidyasagar*, 116.
95. See the quoted remarks in Mitra, *Isvar Chandra Vidyasagar*, 560.
96. To borrow from Nancy Gardner Cassels, we see here the tension between nineteenth-century programs for public justice (via reforms like Act XV of 1856) and those predicated on the expansion of education; see her *Social Legislation of the East India Company: Public Justice versus Public Instruction*.
97. We should bear in mind that as late as the 1880s and 1890s there were still reports of Kulin men with fifty wives, and of elderly men whose new brides were only four or five years old; see Basu, "The Development of Journalism and Public Opinion in Bengal 1818–1910."
98. Quoted in Ghosh, *Iswar Chandra Vidyasagar*, 120.
99. Joykrishna, a progressive Zamindar from Uttarpara and prominent public figure, had long been a friend and ally of Vidyasagar. As often happened, Vidyasagar found his friendships strained by differences of opinion on major issues like this; see Hatcher, *Vidyasagar*, ch. 6.

100. Quoted in Ghosh, *Vidyasagar o Bangali Samaj*, 535. A subsequent report to the secretary of India in March 1867 reveals that Vidyasagar's opinion was ignored completely. There it is reported that the "Native Members" on the committee gave assurance that Bengalis were becoming increasingly enlightened on this matter; see *Abstract of Letters Received, 18590–1867*, 221.
101. This matter is explained in the context of the First Objection. Vidyasagar returns to this point at the end of *Bahuvivaha*, Book Two (which is not translated here); see Haldar, *Vidyasagar-racanasaṃgraha*, vol. 2, 413.
102. Rammohun Roy had envisioned just such a plan, writing, "Had a Magistrate or other public officer been authorized by the rulers of the empire to receive applications for his sanction to a second marriage during the life of a first wife, and to grant his consent only on such accusations as the foregoing being substantiated, the above Law might have been rendered effectual, and the distress of the female sex in Bengal, and the number of suicides, would have been necessarily very much reduced"; see his *Brief Remarks regarding Modern Encroachments on the Ancient Rights of Females* in *The English Works of Raja Rammohun Roy*, 380.
103. Vidyasagar had used a similar argument in his campaign to promote widow marriage. On the four *yugas* and the *kalivarjya* duties, see Vidyasagar, *Hindu Widow Marriage*, xxi–xxiii.
104. In Supplement Two of *Against High-Caste Polygamy*, Vidyasagar refers to the theory of the *yugas* to argue that while kings in past eons may have done things that were forbidden by the shastras—such as marry more than one woman—they could only do this because they represented something like a special case from a special time. After all, theirs was a more righteous era; for people living in the degraded Kali Yuga, it would be wrong to follow the example of such kings.
105. Taranath was among those arguing against the need for legislation, claiming that Kulinism was already fast waning in Bengal. Vidyasagar's impatience with Taranath mirrors his impatience with the educated public, whom he accuses of being out of touch with reality.
106. See *Against High-Caste Polygamy*, Second Objection.
107. For more on this, see the Introduction to Vidyasagar, *Hindu Widow Marriage*, and also Brian A. Hatcher, "Sastric Modernity: Mediating Sanskrit Knowledge in Colonial Bengal," in K. Bandyopadhyay, ed., *Modernities in Asian Perspective: Polity, Society, Culture, Economy*.
108. I address this in my essay, "Pandits at Work: The Modern Sastric Imaginary in Early Colonial Bengal."
109. See Vidyasagar, "The Evils of Child Marriage."
110. Sen, *Vidyasagar and his Elusive Milestones*, 54.
111. That said, it should be noted that Book Two of *Bahuvivaha* does indulge in an extensive review of scriptural arguments as found in the work of five scholars: Taranatha Tarkavachaspati, Ramakumara Nyayaratna, Kshetrapala Smritiratna, Satyavrati Samashrami, and Gangadhara Kaviratna. Published in 1873, it can be found in Gopal Haldar, *Vidyasagar-racanasamgraha*, vol. 2, 244–416.

112. On this, see my short article, "Samajvijnani Vidyasagar," in *Anandabazar Patrika* (4 June 2022). The argument is developed further in Hatcher, *A Less Familiar Vidyasagar: Pioneer of Social Research*.
113. In all fairness, Vidyasagar does occasionally betray his pundit predilections. While he writes for a general readership, he rarely uses an ordinary word if there is a more technical term that applies. Thus instead of the straightforward word *papa* for "sin," he adopts *pratyavaya*. He seems happiest in the language and traditions of shastric interpretation, and thus routinely employs terms like *tatparya*, *vyavastha*, *artha*, and *mimamsa*. This lends some irony to his criticism of Taranatha Tarkavachaspati in Book Two of *Bahuvivaha* for writing in Sanskrit instead of Bengali. One could almost say Vidyasagar's Bengali is so Sanskritic that he barely escapes the same failing; on this, see Hatcher, *Vidyasagar*, 137–38.
114. See the last paragraph of the Fourth Objection in *Against High-Caste Polygamy*.
115. *Against High-Caste Polygamy*, Seventh Objection.
116. See the opening paragraph of the main text in *Against High-Caste Polygamy*.
117. That Vidyasagar was unable to transcend some of these limitations makes him far from unique in his day. Only a few years later, Gooroodass Banerjee would quote Jeremy Bentham to make the point that since equality between the sexes was unthinkable, it made sense that authority should reside with men; see his *Hindu Law of Marriage and Stridhan*, 115.
118. See the final paragraph of the First Objection in *Against High-Caste Polygamy*. For more on this theme, see Brian A. Hatcher, *Idioms of Improvement: Vidyasagar and Cultural Encounter in Bengal*, 254–55.
119. See Sudipta Kaviraj, *The Unhappy Consciousness: Bankimchandra Chattopadhyay and the Formation of Nationalist Discourse in India*, ch. 4.
120. On the limited horizon of Bankim's histories, see Kaviraj, *The Imaginary Institution of India: Politics and Ideas*, 172–73.
121. Vidyasagar's *Bangalar Itihasa* was a close translation of John Clark Marshman's *History of Bengal*, but Vidyasagar also created his own critical editions of Sanskrit texts like *Sarvadarshana Samgraha* (1858), *Uttararamacharitam* (1870), and *Abhijnana-Shakuntalam* (1871) for use by university students. He was also capable of employing historical-critical tools to argue that a text like the *Dattaka-chandrika*, routinely ascribed to the premodern author Kubera, was in fact a modern work; see Vidyasagar, *Hindu Widow Marriage*, 203.
122. On genealogies and nationalist historiography, see Rochona Majumdar, "Looking for Brides and Grooms: *Ghataks*, Matrimonials and the Marriage Market in Colonial Calcutta, circa 1875–1940," 918.
123. In his 1842 essay "Bahuvivaha" (cited above), Akshaykumar Datta had reminded his readers that Vallala Sena was just another human being and therefore as prone to error as any other man; it is reprinted in B. Ghosh, ed., *Samayikpatre Banglar Samajchitra*, vol. 3, 5–8.
124. His biographer Chandicharan Bandyopadhyay praised Vidyasagar's skillful use of history in this way; see *Vidyasagara*, 267.
125. See *Against High-Caste Polygamy*, Second Objection.

126. In fact, at one point Vidyanidhi copies a single footnote from Vidyasagar's work *verbatim*; see *Sambandhanirnaya*, 227–28.
127. In time, another generation of historically minded scholars like R. P. Chanda would go on to question the historical utility of this genealogical literature and would turn to archaeology to develop new positivist histories of India. On this, see Kumkum Chatterjee, "The King of Controversy: History and Nation-Making in Late Colonial India," 1461. I am indebted to Rajat Sanyal for orienting me to the work of R. P. Chanda.
128. I saw this point more clearly in light of comments during a question and answer session after presenting some this material in a lecture to the English Department at Presidency University in June 2021.
129. See Geraldine Forbes, "Jogendro Chandra Ghosh and Hindu Positivism: A Case Study in Cultural Adaptation."
130. This is to set aside for the moment critical debates over their respective merits as authors—not to mention Bankim's dismissal of Vidyasagar's literary work as little more than imitative translation.
131. This was a fate that often befell neglected Kulin women; see Ghosh, "'Birds in a Cage,'" 40. At the same time, the tropics of unrestrained sexuality, social deviance, and the "traffic in women" played powerful disciplinary roles in the discourse about Indian social life in colonial literature; see Mitra, *Indian Sex Life*, 8.
132. See Shambhuchandra Vidyaratna, *Vidyasagara Jivanacharita*, 149–54, and Mitra, *Karunasagar Vidyasagar*, 341–43.
133. See Ghosh, "'Birds in a Cage,'" 42, and Chakraborty, "Gender, Caste, and Marriage," 51
134. See *Against High-Caste Polygamy*, Fourth Objection. These lists attracted the critical attention of Bankimchandra Chatterjee, who wondered if they had not been padded out, perhaps with the names of dead individuals; see *Bankim-rachanavali*, vol. 2, 315.
135. See Brian A. Hatcher, "*Samajvijnani Vidyasagar*," in *Anandabazar Patrika* (4 June 2022).
136. See *Against High-Caste Polygamy*, Fourth Objection.
137. The village of Janai is described briefly by Sudhir Kumar Mitra in his *Hugli Jelar Itihas*, vol. 2.
138. Bear in mind that Vidyasagar does not actually calculate the rate of marriages, but his data indicates a total of 182 marriages among sixty-four individuals, ranging from two to five wives per individual, with an overall average of three wives per Kulin. Once again, it should be noted that Bankim questioned the scale of the problem suggested by Vidyasagar's data, speculating instead that the rate might be more like one in ten thousand individuals who practiced *adhivedana* or "supersession"; see *Bankim-rachanavali*, vol. 2, 315.
139. When polygamy first began to be debated in the public sphere, an editor for the *Friend of India* had remarked, "Surely in a measure so important the collection of data ought not to be forgotten." Quoted in Ghose, *Selections from English Periodicals*, vol. 3, 94.

140. Benoy Ghosh notes that Vidyasagar collected "some important statistical data" about Kulinism in Hooghly, but does not pause to explore the novelty of the method; see *Iswar Chandra Vidyasagar*, 121–22. At a biographical level, Chandicharan Bandyopadhyay could not say how Vidyasagar gathered his data; see his *Vidyasagar*, 271. However, according to Vidyasagar's younger brother, there was at least one occasion when he requested local villagers to send him lists of marriages in their area; see Vidyaratna, *Vidyasagar-jivanacarita*, 155.
141. See Asad, "Ethnographic Representation, Statistics, and Modern Power." Asad refers briefly to the work of Frédéric Le Play, a contemporary of Vidyasagar, who was a minerologist turned social scientist and reformer. See Mogey, "The Contribution of Frédéric Le Play to Family Research."
142. One British author, writing in the *Friend of India* (3 July 1856), argued against legislation, since in his words polygamy was "not very frequent even among profligates," was "not considered reputable by the better Hindoos," and was in any case "slowly dying out"; see Ghose, *Selections from English Periodicals*, vol. 3, 94.
143. Bankim's position reflects what Patricia Uberoi refers to as the modality of "community self-reform" as opposed to the kind of state-centered legislative project proposed by Vidyasagar; see Uberoi, ed., *Social Reform, Sexuality and the State*, xxiii.
144. See the essay, "The Nationalist Resolution of the Women's Question." Compare this to Chatterjee's treatment of a figure like Kailashabashini Debi, wife of Vidyasagar's associate, Kishorichand Mitra, in *The Nation and its Fragments*, ch. 7
145. On Vidyasagar's educational project, see Hatcher, *Idioms of Improvement*, part 2.
146. See *Against High-Caste Polygamy*, Sixth Objection.
147. In 1879, Gooroodass Banerjee acknowledged the validity of Vidyasagar's argument, but felt confident that the custom was already "fast becoming obsolete" (*Hindu Law of Marriage and Stridhan*, 44). By the early twentieth century, British administrators were reporting that Kulinism had "practically died out"; see L. S. S. O'Malley, *Hooghly: Bengal District Gazetteers*, 101.
148. See *The Hindu Marriage Act, 1955* (Act 25 of 1955), Section 5, which stipulates, among several conditions, that "neither party has a spouse living at the time of the marriage."

Chapter 1

1. This was in 1855, and the reference is to the *Bandhuvargasamavaya Sabha*, whose Secretaries were Kishorichand Mitra and Akshaykumar Datta. Kishorichand's wife, Kailashbashini Debi provided a fascinating account of her married life that reveals both her good fortune and the direction in which female domesticity would become framed in late colonial Bengal; on this, see Partha Chatterjee, *The Nation and its Fragments*, ch. 7.
2. Vidyasagar refers to another petition from 1857. On these prior petitions, see the Introduction to the present translation.

3. Asok Sen confirms that popular support for a law banning high-caste polygamy was about as strong as it had been for legislation allowing widow marriage; see his *Vidyasagar and his Elusive Milestones*, 63.
4. This was in 1862–63. Devnarayan Singh was Raja of Varanasi. His petition garnered 1500 signatories; see Ghosh, *Vidyasagar o Bangali Samaj*, 281–82.
5. This was in 1865, during the Governor Generalship of Cecil Beadon, who served from 1862–67.
6. Here we see how key Bengali terms operate in the text. Vidyasagar refers to those who seek a possible government "ban" (*nivarana*) on polygamy, which would be tantamount to seeing the custom "abolished" (*rahita*). Even though the latter term figures prominently in the title of *Bahuvivaha rahita haoya uchita ki na etadvishayaka vichara*, the former term occurs far more frequently throughout the text. A third term, not invoked here but important in the main text, has to do with the exegesis of Shastric texts, which turns on the question of whether (or when) polygamy might be "prohibited" (*nishiddha*) by Hindu law.
7. On this period in Vidyasagar's life, see Vidyaratna, *Vidyasagar jivanacharita*, 214.
8. This is the closest language to "reform" that Vidyasagar employs, speaking more literally of the "purification" (*samshodhana*) of "social faults" (*samajika dosha*). Such language is used again in answering the Sixth Objection.
9. The Draft Bill, entitled "A Bill to Regulate the Plurality of Marriages between Hindus in British India," can be found in Appendix 3 of *Against High-Caste Polygamy*.
10. In what follows, Vidyasagar proceeds by answering a set seven of objections. The original text of *Bahuvivaha* does not include descriptive headings for the numbered objections. I introduce them to provide readers with a sense for the main concern addressed under each objection.
11. It is worth noting that Vidyasagar's position in this section had been anticipated by Rammohun Roy in his 1822 essay, *Brief Remarks regarding Modern Encroachments on the Ancient Rights of Females,* wherein Rammohun cites some of the same passages as Vidyasagar, while concluding, "This horrible polygamy among Brahmans is directly contrary to the law given by ancient authors"; see *The English Works of Raja Rammohun Roy*, 380. It is therefore curious that Vidyasagar makes no mention of Rammohun, despite having praised the work of Rammohun's son in the Notice.
12. For the original, see *Unavimshati Samhita*, edited and translated by Panchanan Tarkaratna, 421. While Vidyasagar provides brief footnotes for such quotations, they are often minimal, e.g. "Daksha Samhita, chapter one." I have chosen to eliminate most of these footnotes and replace them with an in-text reference as here.
13. Readers familiar with Hinduism may find Vidyasagar's statement curious, since the Shudra class is not ranked among the "twice-born" classes. However, Vidyasagar indicates that by *upalakshana*, or "implication," we are to understand the inclusion of something not otherwise mentioned, in other words that "twice-born" (*dvija*) refers not to the highest three classes, but to "the four classes."
14. See *Raghunandanakrita Udvahatattvam*, edited by Manabendu Bandyopadhyay Shastri, 151.
15. The technical term here for "taking a wife" is *daraparigraha*.

16. Supersession, or *adhivedana*, refers to the act of marrying of an additional wife, which may happen if the original wife has any of the faults listed here. See John Ernst Trevelyan, *Hindu Family Law*, 30, who cites the *Mitakshara*. Vidyasagar will return to this issue below.
17. Gooroodass Banerjee would later refer to Vidyasagar's claim that Manu 3.12-13 constitutes a prohibition on polygamy, but conclude that in this case the prohibition is "merely directory and not imperative" (see his *Hindu Law of Marriage and Stridhan*, 43).
18. The concept of the exclusionary injunction (*parisamkhya vidhi*) is an important one, to which Vidyasagar will return. Stephanie Jamison defines it as "an injunction involving an exhaustive enumeration, the force of which is not in the enumeration itself, but in the implication of exclusion, in effect forbidding what is absent from the list"; see her "Rhinoceros Toes, Manu V17-18, and the Development of the Dharma System," 250.
19. For simplicity's sake I speak of "the group of five animals," while recognizing that Manu 5.17-18 actually lists seven animals, not five: porcupine, hedgehog, monitor lizard, rhinoceros, tortoise and rabbit. For more detail, see Jamison, "Rhinoceros Toes, Manu V17-18, and the Development of the Dharma System."
20. This bracketed reference directs readers to the section entitled Supporting Evidence, where they may examine the specific materials Vidyasagar cites in support of his exposition.
21. Here I employ the idiom of "plural marriage" to render the two-word phrase *bahu vivaha*, which Vidyasagar employs here, instead of the usual compound form, *bahuvivaha*.
22. See *Unavimshati Samhita*, edited and translated by Panchanan Tarkaratna, 208.
23. See *Unavimshati Samhita*, edited and translated by Panchanan Tarkaratna, 63.
24. Patrick Olivelle states that this passage from Manu "clearly refers to a polygamous marriage" (*The Law Code of Manu*, 280), but Vidyasagar understands Manu as envisioning a situation in which a husband has had to take additional wives due to the barrenness of his other wives; in this reading, Manu's point is that even though barren, these other wives should all be allowed to say they have a son.
25. See *Raghunandakrita Udvahatattvam*, 39; cp. *The Institutes of the Hindoo Religion by Rughoo Nundun*, vol. 2, 64.
26. The passage from the *Grihastharatnakara* quoted in the *Udvahatattva* is not one I have found discussed in secondary literature on marriage and polygamy, other than certain commentarial passages stressing that *trivivaha* or "three marriages" should be taken in the sense of "three wives"; see *Raghunandanakrita Udvahatattva*, 39–40.
27. The sacrifice in question is the *putreshti yaga*; see Vidyanidhi, *Sambandhanirnaya*, 161.
28. In the footnote [*2.1] Vidyasagar cites a passage from the *Kshitishvamshavalicharita* that mentions only the "year" (*abda*) and not the calendar or era in question. He takes it to refer to the Samvat era, as have others; on the dilemmas around dating, see Vidyanidhi, *Sambandhanirnaya* 157–161 and Basu, *Banger Jatiya Itihas*, vol. 1, part 1, 100. On the legend as found in Kulin genealogies, see Chanda, *Gaudarajamala*, 57. The reliability of these narratives was rejected by the likes of R. C. Majumdar and

D. C. Sircar; see the latter's *Studies in the Society and Administration of Ancient and Mediaeval India*, vol. 1, 16.

29. As will subsequently be demonstrated by the king's reaction, the behavior and dress of the five Brahmins contravened expectations for the proper conduct of such men; see Basu, *Banger Jatiya Itihas*, vol. 1, part 1, 108.
30. As mentioned above, the historicity of such traditions has been the subject of intense debate. For a useful overview, see Swati Datta, *Migrant Brahmanas in Northern India*, ch. 2.
31. The point is more obvious in the Bengali, where the term *gramin*, or "the one with a village" (*grama*), yields the term *gai*, or "surname."
32. On the Seven Hundred and their relationship to the descendants of the five Brahmins from Kanyakubja, see Basu, *Banger Jatiya Itihas*, Vol. 1, part 1, ch. 4.
33. Vallala Sen ruled ca. 1158–79 CE; see R. C. Majumdar, ed., *History of Bengal*, vol. 1, 216–218.
34. One scholar has noted that exchange is the very "essence" of Kulinism; see Kundu, "Caste and Class in Pre-Muslim Bengal," 179. The term "genealogist" (*ghatak*) mentioned here, has shifting valences, not least during the nineteenth century. Often called "matchmakers," they represented much more than this, being revered as "leaders of the clan" (*kulacharya*). In the latter role, the most respected genealogists preserved and celebrated particular clan lineages. During Vidyasagar's day, they carried immense influence within the caste politics of colonial Calcutta; see Majumdar, "Looking for Brides and Grooms" and Chatterjee, "King of Controversy."
35. I typically translate *kanya* as "daughter," although a more narrow meaning would be "prepubescent virgin." The rite of marriage is known as *kanya-dana* or the "gift of a virgin" by her father to a suitable groom (*patra*).
36. On the practices of "substituting" and "promising" see Inden, *Marriage and Rank*, 110.
37. Material in this and several succeeding paragraphs (including Vidyasagar's footnotes) is repeated verbatim by Lalmohan Vidyanidhi, with no explicit reference to Vidyasagar; see *Sambandhanirnaya*, 224–230.
38. Here again we see the explicit connection between the ones with villages (*gramin*) and their surnames (*gai*).
39. Vidyasagar refers here to the so-called *mukhya* Kulin families. As the material found at Supporting *2.16–18 reveals, the picture is complicated by further distinctions among other ranks, notably the Shotriyas and the Lesser or *gauna* Kulins (sometimes called "secondary" Kulins). The legendary account of how these distinctions arose is taken up in the following paragraph.
40. I translate these distinctions into modern clock time. The unit of time here is actually the *prahara*, but the basic purport remains the same.
41. While this is a passage Vidyanidhi repeats verbatim from Vidyasagar, he does not quote the Sanskrit passage adduced by Vidyasagar in the footnote reproduced in Supporting Evidence [*2.21]; see *Sambandhanirnaya*, 227–228.
42. See Basu, *Banger Jatiya Itihas*, vol. 1, part 1, 157.
43. This took place circa 1480 CE.

44. On this complex system of ranking, see Basu, *Banger Jatiya Itihas*, vol. 1, part 1, 219. Vidyanidhi says Phuliya was the preeminent assemblage; see *Sambandhanirnaya*, 193. See also Dutt, *The Origin and Growth of Caste in India*, vol. 2, 11.
45. On Gangananda, see Vidyanidhi, *Sambandhanirnaya*, 243.
46. Dutt summarizes these four faults as follows: (1) Gangananda's father had married a Vamshaja; (2) Gangananda made a marriage alliance with the family of Arjuna Mishra of Baruihati, whose family had served as priests to Shudras; (3) Gangananda married into the Mulukjuri family of Seven Hundred Brahmins; (4) Gangananda made marriage alliances with a family who had married their sons to some daughters who had been abducted by a Muslim; *The Origin and Growth of Caste in India*, vol. 2, 10–11.
47. According to legend, Yogeshvara and Devivara were cousins (the former was Devivara's mother's sister's son). Yogeshvara was a Kulin of the Mukhuti surname, while Devivara was a Vamshaja. Yogeshvara insulted Devivara by refusing to take food at his home. Later, when Devivara received from the goddess a boon (hence his name, *devi-vara*) to appoint Kulin rank, he demoted Yogeshvara. When the latter repented, Devivara granted him Kulin rank; see Dutt, *The Origin and Growth of Caste in India*, vol. 2, 10–12, who argues that this pattern of resentment and jealousy is one legacy of Devivara's so-called reforms.
48. As Amiya Sen notes, prior to Devivara's scheme, "an exchange of Brahmin daughters could take place across ranks"; *Vidyasagar*, 173.
49. Writing in 1883, James Wise spoke of the "contrivance" whereby "marriages in certain corresponding families of equal rank were enjoined, and any violation of the law was visited by dishonour and degradation." Wise argued that this fostered the rise of polygamy, since a Mukhuti family would be "obliged to marry their sons to Chatarji daughters, and the Chatarji sons to Mukhuti daughters. When it happened that the Mukhuti had only one son, and the Chatarji ten daughters, the former was compelled to marry the whole ten, or all remained spinsters. The Kulin boy with hundreds of rich offers of marriage must decline all, until he had fulfilled this obligation"; see his *Notes on the Races, Castes and Trades of Eastern Bengal*, 233.
50. Raghunandana attributes this passage to both Atri and Kashyapa; see *Raghunandakrita Udvahatattvam*, 70.
51. See *Unavimshati Samhita*, edited and translated by Panchanan Tarkaratna, 270.
52. See *Unavimshati Samhita*, edited and translated by Panchanan Tarkaratna, 380.
53. On this see J. N. Bhattacharya, *Hindu Castes and Sects: An Exposition of the Origin of the Hindu Caste System and the Bearing of the Sects towards each other and towards other Religious Systems*, 38.
54. Vidyasagar uses the informal second-person pronoun *tui* to mock the pretensions of a personified pride (*abhimana*).
55. Traditional genealogies cite a figure of ten generations between Vallala and Devivara; see Wise, *Notes on the Races, Castes and Trades of Eastern Bengal*, 231.
56. On the significance of this call for a "new ruling" (*nutan vyavastha*), see my comments in the Introduction. As he reveals in the next sentence, his solution would be to return

to the pre-Devivara pattern of mutuality in marriage, whereby Kulins could exchange their daughters across ranks.

57. Here is another point where Vidyasagar uses the term *samshodhana* ("purification") to speak of what I have translated as the "reform" of social errors.
58. Colonial-era rhetoric echoes Vidyasagar: "The amount of immorality developed by the Kulins is incalculable. . . The two main obstacles to reform are, the opposition of the Ghataks, an influential body, whose existence depends on the continuance of the system, and the selfishness of the Kulins themselves, who prefer certain wealth and ease to the precariousness of a learned, or the exertion of a mercantile, life"; Wise, *Notes on the Races, Castes and Trades of Eastern Bengal*, 234.
59. Vidyasagar's sarcastic references to the sacralizing role played by the clan goddess, or *kula-lakshmi*, are a further indication of the sometimes radical nature of his critique of religious custom.
60. Vidyasagar leaves the circumstances vague, but he seems to suggest that the girls were trafficked into prostitution. It has been shown that some unscrupulous genealogists would present families with false marriage offers as a way to lure their daughters into prostitution; see Majumdar, "Looking for Brides and Grooms", 917. For more on the reality and the rhetoric around sex trafficking in colonial India, see Mitra, *Indian Sex Life*, 68–77.
61. As Vidyasagar will clarify below, a Second-hand Kulin is defined as the son of a Kulin woman by a man who is not her husband, and who is thus raised in her maternal uncle's home.
62. Here I take the *vivaha-karta* as the Kulin father who agrees to marry his son to the daughter of the *kanyakarta* or father of the bride. This is the first time Vidyasagar has used these terms, which emphasize the instrumental agency (*kartritva*) of the male actors. As defined by Gooroodass Banerjee, "Marriage is viewed as a gift of the bride by her father or other guardian to the bridegroom: the bride, therefore, is regarded more as the subject of the gift than as a party to the transaction"; see *Hindu Law of Marriage and Stridhan*, 45.
63. As noted in the Introduction, Rammohun Roy noted in 1820 that some Kulin men took up to fifteen wives and never saw most of them again once the marriage ceremonies were completed; see his *A Second Conference between an Advocate for, and an Opponent of the Practice of Burning Widows Alive*, in *The English Works of Raja Rammohun Roy*, 361–362; for the Bengali text, see *Rammohun-Rachanavali*, 202.
64. Here Vidyasagar refers to the work of those who were said to come to the aid of adulterers through the practice of abortion or *foeticide*.
65. Here again is remarkably strong statement from someone who is himself a Kulin Brahmin pandit.
66. Vidyasagar may be thinking of Manu 9.95, which enjoins that a husband should always support his wife; see Olivelle, *The Law Code of Manu*, 161.
67. I take the liberty of breaking out the following examples as short paragraphs, to make it clear that Vidyasagar is here compiling something like a charge sheet of indictments against the behavior of Broken Kulin families.

68. Kulins could draw on the resources of their various wives' families in this way because, as Shrabani Ghosh reminds us, they frequently kept lists of their marriages and the kinds of gifts they could expect to receive from particular families; see her "'Birds in a Cage,'" 42. That the practice of the Kulin husband periodically visiting his many wives in order to pick up gifts was well established in the eighteenth century is attested by Bharatacandra Ray's couplet, delivered from the mouth of a Kulin bride: "Should he lie with me only once every few years, he would ask, 'What parting gifts will you be giving me?'"; France Bhattacharya, trans., *In Praise of Annada*, vol. 2, 305.
69. As Vidyasagar will note under the Fourth Objection, the majority of his readers lived in the city of Kolkata and were not well informed about daily life in the village. By contrast, Vidyasagar travelled frequently around southwestern Bengal in a variety of capacities: while working as an Assistant Inspector of schools, conducting voluntary relief work during famines and epidemics, and pursuing friendships and professional connections with other Sanskrit scholars in places like Nadia, Hugli, and Burdwan.
70. Here Vidyasagar refers to a ritual known in Bengali as *punarbiye*, which is performed in the case of a young woman who has been married (*parapurva*) but has not yet had sexual intercourse with her husband. The ritual should only happen after she has experienced her first menses; see *Narada-Smriti*, Stripumsa, v. 46; and Manu 9.81-72. In Bharatacandra Ray, we meet a Kulin wife who jokes that at her wedding the scholars couldn't decide whether it constituted her first marriage or her *punarbiye*; see Bhattacharya, *In Praise of Annada*, vol. 2, 302–03.
71. As discussed in the Introduction, while Vidyasagar presents this story as common knowledge, this vignette may in fact be based on events he experienced in his own home village of Birsingha. He had a schoolmaster, Kalikanta Chattopadhyay, who was a Self-Broken Kulin with many wives; see Mitra, *Isvar Chandra Vidyasagar*, 23, which draws on Sarkar, *Vidyasagar*, 23. Kalikanta's polygamy left Vidyasagar feeling ashamed and angry; see Vidyaratna, *Vidyasagar jivancharita*, 149–54.
72. This would appear to be one of Mr. Bhattacharya's sons by another of his wives.
73. One has to imagine that the Second-hand Broken Kulin was already receiving a monthly stipend from the unnamed gentleman in this story, perhaps as the legacy of his family's standing in the village or as compensation for some ritual services. We are to further understand that the greed of Mr. Bhattacharya and his sister led them to demand the additional increment in perpetuity.
74. This brief editorial comment disparaging low-caste habits—especially when followed by remarks celebrating the qualities found in "refined" (*bhadra*) homes—provides an unfortunate reminder of the way elite norms around caste hierarchy constrained Vidyasagar's views on respectability and social order; see Hatcher, *Idioms of Improvement*, 106.
75. In January of 1867 Vidyasagar had written to the Law Commission to express his belief that time and education would not be enough to eradicate polygamy and to express his support for passage of a Declaratory Law on the matter; see Ghosh, *Vidyasagar o Bangali Samaj*, 286.
76. Janai is a small Census Town in Hooghly District, located about twelve miles northwest of Kolkata.

77. See note 58 above.
78. Vidyasagar embraces a mode of historical-contextual thinking here; I translate his *karya karana-vyavastha* as "in terms of cause and effect."
79. The topic of the Fifth Objection is devoted to the impact of the proposed legislation on a specific category of marriages known as *adyarasa*; the meaning of this term will become clear in the following paragraphs, where it emerges as a strategy used by lower-ranking Maulik Kayasthas to promote their clan status over higher-ranking Kulin Kayasthas; see Vidyanidhi, *Sambandhanirnaya*, 114–119 and Chakraborty, "Gender, Caste, and Marriage," 48.
80. For more on the seventy-two Potential (*sadhya*) castes, see Inden, *Marriage and Rank*, 66–67.
81. It is tempting to translate *adharmika* as "immoral" here, but since Vidyasagar stresses that the loss of Second Marriage poses no threat to Dharma, it is best to keep our eyes on the notion of Dharma as enshrining a host of values around religious trust, dutiful ritual performance, and socially beneficial behavior.
82. Readers will recall Vidyasagar's dissent from the 1866 committee report prepared for Lieutenant Governor Beadon, as discussed in the Introduction. For more details, see Ghosh, *Vidyasagar o Bangali Samaj*, 533–35.
83. Vidyasagar employs a neologism, *navya sampradaya*, wherein an older concept of initiatory community (often guru-led) is translated into the logic of a loosely defined social group. He has in mind both the emerging educated reading public and certain distinguished figures who spoke out against his proposal, figures like Bankimchandra Chatterjee and Bhudeb Mukherjee. Bankim's opposition to Vidyasagar's views apparently so upset the latter that Bankim held off republishing his remarks until after the pundit's death in 1891; see Sen, *Vidyasagar*, 180.
84. Vidyasagar's language becomes colloquial here. I take his words, *e dike candra o dike gele-o*, as equivalent to the English idiom "to cry for the moon." The phrase seems to echoe a Bengali proverb that pokes fun at futile gestures: *akash phand pele chand dhara*; see S. K. De *Banglar Pravad*, #217.
85. Gooroodass Banerjee writes that "while the *kulins* generally obtained a plurality of wives, the *vansajas* necessarily found it difficult to obtain wives, and were driven to the reprehensible practice of buying girls for marriage"; see *Hindu Law of Marriage and Stridhan*, 44.
86. I have not been able to locate these two verses attributed to the *Atri Samhita*, though they are cited by Nanda Pandita; see *The Dattaka-Mimansa and Dattaka-Chandrika, Two Original Treatises on the Hindu Law of Adoption*, translated by J. C. C. Sutherland, 70.
87. For more context, see *Padmapurana*, 152–53.
88. Vidyasagar reworks the proverb, *karo poush mash, karo sarvanash* ("for some it is a time of celebration, for some a disaster") to become, *yar kanya, tar sarvanash; yar putra, tar poush mash*; on the proverb, see De, *Banglar Pravad*, #1761.
89. Vidyasagar had four daughters, the eldest of whom was married in 1865, just as these issues were consuming a great deal of his attention.

90. Here the *navya-sampraday* is styled the *navya-pramanika*, implying either "those who take the new to be authoritative" or "those who draw upon new authorities."
91. While I have hitherto translated *samshodhana* as the "eradication" of social evil (*dosha*), here Vidyasagar speaks of *samajer samshodhana*, which makes sense as the "reform" of society.
92. It is worth noting that in answering this objection Vidyasagar repeatedly invokes the idea of "liberation" (*vimochana*) from social evil. His language hovers constructively between established Indic idioms that emphasize freedom from the bonds of error and modern liberal notions of emancipation, just as his appeal to the government rests equally on traditional notions of a king's duty (*raja-dharma*) to his subjects and modern conceptions of government as responsible for promoting public welfare.
93. Vidyasagar paraphrases the sentiments of William Bentinck as expressed in his famous Minute from 1829. For the original text, see "Bentinck's Minute on Sati, 8 November 1892," in B. Harlow and M. Carter, eds., *Archives of Empire*, vol. 1, 350–61.
94. Vidyasagar quotes a Sanskrit phrase, *te ko 'pi divasa gatah*, from Bhavabhuti's *Uttararamacharita*, a text he had both edited in Sanskrit and re-created in Bengali as *Sitar Vanavas* (1860). My thanks to Milinda Banerjee for catching the reference. With these words Vidyasagar gives redoubled force to his longing for the reformist zeal of a bygone era.
95. Chandicharan Bandyopadhyay reports having heard from Vidyasagar's son that Vidyasagar once expressed a desire to travel to England so that his text could be placed before Queen Victoria; *Vidyasagar*, 286. Vidyasagar's younger brother says the claim is baseless; see Vidyaratna, *Bhramnirash. Arthat Shriyukta Chandicharan Bandyopadhyay pranita 'Vidyasagar' namak nutan jivanchariter bhramnirakarana*, 29–30.
96. Vidyasagar throws out a series of cases that seem to turn on the ways "selfish fathers and mothers" (as he will put it) could seek to preserve their prerogative to arrange marriages for their sons just as they see fit. After quickly running through these scenarios, he will claim they do not merit further discussion. It seems he merely hopes to rule out in advance the most selfish kinds of resistance to legislation.
97. On these gifts (*tattva*), see Ronald B. Inden and Ralph Nicholas, *Kinship in Bengali Culture*, p. 19.
98. The reference is to the 1855 petition discussed in the opening Notice.
99. In support of Vidyasagar's point, an editorial in the *Friend of India* (17 July 1856) had pointed out that one signatory of the petition was the Maharaja of Burdwan, "who as the solitary member of a caste which has ceased to exist in these provinces, has no personal interest in the question." His point was that the Maharaja hailed from the Panjabi Khatri caste, a group not implicated in the practice of Kulin polygamy; see Ghose, *Selections from English Periodicals*, vol. 3, 93.
100. Here we notice that Vidyasagar speaks of reform using the combined idioms of "emancipation" and "purification": *duravasthavimochana* and *doshasamshodhana*.
101. In other words, in 1866.

102. Henceforth, for the sake of simplicity, I refer to the author of this text as Smritiratna, even though Vidyasagar consistently refers to "Smritiratna, Vedaratna, and the others." Kshetrapal Smritiratna is one of five pandits singled out by Vidyasagar in Book Two of *Bahuvivaha* for explicit refutation. There he gives Smritiratna credit for not being as arrogant as some!
103. See *The Madana Parijata on Inheritance*, translated by S. Sitarama Sastri, 20; also Trevelyan, *Hindu Family Law*, 30. On this issue Raghunandana follows Yajnavalkya; see *Dayatattvam: The Text along with English Translation*, 5.
104. Surprisingly, Vidyasagar does not pursue the distinction that can be made between general and specific injunctions. This might have been used to argue that Manu's injunctions take precedence over texts like that from the *Madanparijata*. Elsewhere he had adopted this commentarial strategy; see Vidyasagar, *Hindu Widow Marriage*, 77.
105. Vidyasagar does not provide a specific injunction, but the so-called *kalivarjya* duties are enumerated in texts like *Brihannaradiya Purana* (22.13-16), which had been cited with approval by the premodern digest-writer Raghunandana. Vidyasagar referred to this passage when making his case for widow marriage; see Vidyasagar, *Hindu Widow Marriage*, 64.
106. It is worth noting that Vidyasagar cites this verse when addressing the First Objection, but provides there a slightly different Bengali translation.
107. I have taken the liberty of numbering the points adumbrated by Vidyasagar in this paragraph, in order to help the reader make sense of an otherwise unwieldly passage. I also introduce at this point a paragraph break to further clarify the flow of the argument.
108. Vidyasagar knew Taranath well and in Supplement Two, below, he will train his critical attention on his former colleague and sometime friend.
109. As Vidyasagar notes, Tarkavachaspati's comments were published in the influential journal *Somaprakasha* in 1871.
110. See Supplement One of the present work.
111. This would have been around 1866. Taranath seems to refer to the Maharaja of Burdwan's petition, and appears to quote from it directly. As the following sentence reveals, Vidyasagar is bemused that in the space of just five short years Taranath can detect a clear decline in the prevalence of polygamy.
112. This is the same passage from *Madanparijata* cited at the opening of Supplement One.
113. The citation provided by Vidyasagar does not correspond to what is found in other editions; see Patrick Olivelle, *Dharmasutras: The Law Codes of Ancient India*, where the passage occurs at 2.13.7-9.
114. In what follows, Vidyasagar addresses the concept of *shishtachara*, or the "conduct of the learned," which I sometimes translate as "learned conduct" in order to simplify syntax. In classical Dharmashastra, this constitutes one of the valid sources for knowing Dharma. As this passage shows, Vidyasagar hopes to defuse arguments that since the Brahmins of Bengal practice Kulinism, it must be "conduct of the learned" and would therefore qualify as permissible. Just as he did when promoting widow marriage, Vidyasagar treats "local conduct" (*deshachara*) as a less binding source of

Dharma than the Shastras. In that earlier context, he quoted a minor legal digest to the effect that if custom contradicts Smriti, it is the latter that must be followed; see Vidyasagar, *Hindu Widow Marriage*, 201.

115. Vidyasagar takes this example directly from Madhavacharya, who he has previously cited; see *Jaiminiya-nyaya-mala-vistara of Madhavacharya*, edited by Theodor Goldstücker, 27. It is quite likely he was able to consult the Goldstücker edition, which had been published only six years previously.
116. Vidyasagar alludes to—but does not elaborate on—striking mythic characters and episodes be knows can be found in the Epics and Puranas.
117. This would have been around 1866.
118. Dwarkanath expressed his views in *Somaprakasha*, No. 39 (30 Shravana, 1278), where he "suggested that instead of statutory abolition, a penal tax of Rs. 500/- should be imposed on each case of polygamy without sanction in the shastras"; see Sen, *Vidyasagar and his Elusive Milestones*, 65.
119. Vidyasagar does not provide Bengali translations for these Sanskrit passages, so I provide either my own English renderings or those of others as noted.
120. Rocher, *Jimūtavāhana's Dāyabhāga*, 163.
121. There is a slight variant: "My co-wife is a tigress, my mother-in-law irascible, and my sister-in-law a venomous snake"; see Bhattacharya *In Praise of Annada*, vol. 2, 36-37.
122. In the Conclusion to Book Two of *Bahuvivaha*, Vidyasagar will say that to twist the meaning of the shastras, to bend them to one's own purposes, or to make up imaginary claims about their creators are all heinous sins; see Haldar, *Vidyasagar-rachanasamgraha*, vol. 2, 414.
123. On the norms of domesticity in relation to treatment and conduct of women of the lineage (*kulastri*), see Dipesh Chakrabarty, "The Difference-Deferral of a Colonial Modernity," 379 and passim.
124. For this passage, see *Smritichandrika by Devana-Bhatta*, edited by Srinivas Acharya, 573.
125. See *Nirnaya Sindhu of Kamalakara Bhatta*, edited by Jwala Prasad Mishra, 484.
126. It is interesting to note that while discussing Vidyabhushan's sources, Vidyasagar uses the words "caste" (*jati*) and "class" (*varna*) seemingly interchangeably, with no comment or further explanation.
127. The following paragraphs constitute Vidyasagar's refutation of the various proof texts provided by Vidyabhushan mentioned earlier in this section. I take the liberty of numbering them as independent paragraphs to aid the reader in connecting them with the quotations provided above.
128. Here the reference is to the tethering of a victim to the *yupa* during a sacrificial session as outlined in the ancient Vedic ritual manuals.
129. Notice that while Vidyasagar views Manu as a sage (*rishi*), he uses the term "modern" (*abhinava*) to describe the late medieval commentator Achyutananda.
130. *Vidyasundara* is the name of a lengthy narrative within Bharatchandra's *Annadamangal*, which given its popularity was often published in the colonial era as an independent work. Indeed, the publication of an edition of this text launched

Vidyasagar's own printing establishment, the Sanskrit Press, in 1847, which would later publish the present work.

131. While Manu speaks of "class" (*varna*), Vidyasagar uses the word "caste" (*jati*).

132. For more context, refer to the discussion of Exclusionary injunctions (*parisamkhya vidhi*) in Vidyasagar's treatment of the First Objection.

Supporting Evidence

1. *bandyaḥ kusumo dīrghāṅgī ghoṣālī, batbyālakaḥ |*
pārī kulī kuṣāriś ca kulabhiḥ seyako gaṛaḥ |
ākāśaḥ keśārī māṣo vasuyāriḥ karālakaḥ |
bhaṭṭavaṃśodbhavā ete śāṇḍilye ṣoḍaśa smṛtāḥ ||
2. *chaṭṭo 'mbulī tailavāṭī poḍārir haṛaguṛakau |*
bhuriś ca pāladhiś caiva parkaṭiḥ puṣalī tathā |
mulagrāmī koyārī ca palasāyī ca pītakaḥ |
simalāyī tathā bhaṭṭa ime kāśyapasaṃjñakāḥ ||
3. *ādau mukhuṭī diṇḍī ca sāharī rāikas tathā |*
bhāradvājā ime jātāḥ śrīharṣasya tanūdbhavāḥ ||
4. *gangulịḥ puṃsiko nandī ghaṇṭā kunda siyārikāḥ*
sāṭo dāyī tathā nāyī pārī bālī ca siddhalaḥ |
vedagarbhodbhavā ete sāvarṇe dvādaśa smṛtāḥ ||
5. *kāñjivillī mahintā ca putituṇḍaś ca pippalī |*
ghoṣālo bāpuliś caiva kāñjārī ca tathaiva ca |
simalālaś ca vijñeyā ime vātsyakasaṃjñakāḥ ||

Sources not given for notes 21–25.

[It may be that the material in notes 21–25 had been collected by Vidyasagar from the genealogist, Ishvarchandra Tarkabhushan, whom he mentions in the first of his Appendices.]

6. *bahurūpaḥ suco nāmnā arabindo halāyudhaḥ |*
bāṅgālaś ca samākhyātāḥ pañcaite caṭṭavaṃśajāḥ ||
putir govardhanācāryaḥ śiro ghoṣālasambhavaḥ |
gāṅgulīyaḥ śiśo nāmnā kundo roṣākaro 'pica
jāhlanākhyas tathā bandyo maheśvara udāradhīḥ |
devalo vāmanaś caiva īśāno makarandakaḥ ||
utsāhagaruḍakhyātau mukhavaṃśamudbhavau ||
kānukutūhalāvatau kāñjikulapratiṣṭhitau |
ūnaviṃśatisaṃkhyātā mahārājena pūjitāḥ ||

—Source not given [Dhruvānanda Miśra, cited in Vidyanidhi, *Sambandhanirnaya*, 163]

7. *pāladhiḥ parkaṭiś caiva simalāyī ca vāpuliḥ |*
bhuriḥ kulī batabyālaḥ kuśāriḥ seyakas tathā |
kusumo ghoṣālī māṣo vasuyāriḥ karālakaḥ |
ambulī tailavāṭī ca mūlagrāmī ca puṣalī |

ākāśaḥ palasāyī ca koyārī sāharis tathā |
bhaṭṭaḥ sāṭaś ca nāyerī dāyī pārī siyārikaḥ |
siddhalaḥ puṃsiko nandī kāñjārī simalālakaḥ |
bālī ceti catustriṃśad vallālanṛpapūjitāḥ ||
—Source not given [cited in Vidyanidhi, *Sambandhanirṇaya*, 225]

8. *dīrghāṅgī pāriḥ kulabhī poḍārī rāi keśārī |*
ghaṇṭā ḍiṇḍī pītamuṇḍī mahintā gūṛaḥ pippalī |
haṛaś ca gaṛagaṛiś ca ime gauṇāḥ prakīrttitāḥ ||
Source not given [cited in Vidyanidhi, *Sambandhanirṇaya*, 225]

Glossary: English to Sanskrit/Bengali

Note: I avoid the use of diacritical marks and transliterate in terms of Sanskrit orthography rather than Bengali pronunciation (e.g., nivarana *and not* nibarana*), on the assumption this will accommodate the widest range of readers. In some instances I provide translation equivalents as found in Ronald Inden,* Marriage and Rank in Bengali Culture *(see Bibliography).*

abolished	rahita
accomplished (Kulin)	siddha (Kulin)
agency	kartritva
assemblage	mela; *Inden uses* union
attribute	guna
authorized by scripture	vaidha
ban, banning	nivarana
behavior	vyavahara
broken (Kulin)	bhanga (Kulin); *Inden uses* fallen (Kulin)
business	vyavasaya (as in the "business of marriage")
caste	jati; *Inden uses* subcaste
category	shreni; *Inden uses* subcaste
celebrated actions	pratishtha; *Inden uses* famous acts
clan	kula; *Inden uses* coded substance, clan, and generic collectivity
class	varna; *Inden uses* caste
community	sampradaya
conduct	achara
conduct of the learned	shishtachara; *also* learned conduct
contingent (act)	naimittika (karma)
creator (God)	vidhata
custom	pratha
daughter	kanya; *literally* an unwed virgin
decree	shasana
desired	kamya

enacted	vidhivat
entitlement	adhikara
eradication	samshodhana
exchange	avritti; *Inden uses* reciprocal exchange
evil (social)	dosha; *see also* sin; fault
examination, investigation, opinion	vichara
exchange or exchange series	paryaya; same as avritti; *Inden uses* reciprocity
exclusionary (injunction)	parisamkhya (vidhi)
family line	vamsha; *Inden uses* continuing succession of males
fault	dosha
forced	kashta (as in Forced Shrotriya); *Inden uses* troublesome
foreign	yavana (used for Muslims)
framework	pranali
genealogist	ghataka
genealogy	vamshavali
home	ghar; in sense of "family"; also *griha*
ill	klesha
immoral	adharmika
implication	upalakshana
inclination	pravritti
India (Indian)	Bharata (bharatavarshiya)
injunction	vidhi
injustice	anyaya
Kulin rank	kaulinya; *Inden uses* superior generic rank
lady	mahila (refers to a married woman)
last rites	pindadana
law	niyama *also* Restrictive (injunction)
learned conduct	shishtachara; *also* conduct of the learned
Legislative Council	Vyavasthapaka Samaj
lesser (Kulin)	gauna (Kulin); *Inden uses* secondary (Kulin)
life-stage	ashrama
lineage	gotra
marriage	vivaha; *also* kanya-dana and kula-karma
mutual (marriage)	sarvadvari (vivaha)
objection	apatti
originary (injunction)	apurva (vidhi); *same as* utpatti (vidhi)
outcaste	patita
passage	vachana

petition	avedana
polygamy	bahuvivaha
potential (Kulin)	sadhya (Kulin)
prohibited	nishiddha, *occ.* pratishiddha
prohibition	nishedha
proof or proof-text	pramana
public	sarvasadharana
pure	shuddha; *as in* Pure Shrotriya
purport	tatparya
rank	maryada
rejected by the community	samajchyuta
remarriage	punarvivaha
required (act)	nitya (karma)
restrictive (injunction)	niyama (vidhi)
right path	nyaya-patha
rite	kriya
ruling	vyavastha
second marriage	adyarasa; *practiced among Kayasthas*
secondhand (groom)	dupurushiya
Self-Broken (Kulin)	svakrita-bhanga (Kulin)
self-willed	yadriccha; *same as* yadeccha; *also* voluntary
sin	dosha, pratyavaya
son	putra
strength	kshamata
supersession	adhivedana
surname	gai; *same as* paddhati
treatise on clan duty	kulashastra; *Inden uses* code of the family
unsanctioned	avaidha
voluntary	icchadhina, yadriccha, yadeccha
wife	patni
willful	svecchachari

Glossary: Sanskrit/Bengali to English

Note: I avoid the use of diacritical marks and transliterate in terms of Sanskrit orthography rather than Bengali pronunciation (e.g., nivarana *and not* nibarana*), on the assumption this will accommodate the widest range of readers. In some instances I provide translation equivalents as found in Ronald Inden,* Marriage and Rank in Bengali Culture *(see Bibliography).*

achara	conduct
adharmika	immoral
adhikara	entitlement
adhivedana	supersession
adyarasa	Second Marriage; *practiced among Kayasthas*
anyaya	injustice
apatti	objection
apurva	(vidhi) originary (injunction); *same as* utpatti (vidhi)
ashrama	life-stage
avaidha	unsanctioned
avedana	petition
avritti	exchange; *Inden uses* reciprocal exchange
bahuvivaha	polygamy
bhanga (Kulin)	broken (Kulin); *Inden uses* fallen (Kulin)
bharata (bharatavarshiya)	India (Indian)
dosha	evil (social); *also* sin, fault
dupurushiya	secondhand (groom)
dvesha	hatred
gai	surname; *same as* paddhati
gauna	lesser [as in Lesser Kulin]; *Inden uses* secondary (Kulin)
ghar	home (in sense of "family"); *see also* griha
ghataka	genealogist
gotra	lineage
griha	home (in the sense of "family"); *see also* ghar

guna	attribute, quality, virtue; *Inden uses* attribute
icchadhina	voluntary
jati	caste; *Inden uses* subcaste
jatipata	loss of caste
kamya	(karma) desired (act)
kanya	daughter; *literally* an unwed virgin
kartritva	agency
kashta	forced (as in Forced Shrotriya); *Inden uses* troublesome
kaulinya	Kulin rank; *Inden uses* superior generic rank
klesha	ill
kriya	rite
kshamata	strength
kula	clan; *Inden uses* coded substance, clan, or generic collectivity
kulashastra	treatise on clan duty; *Inden uses* code of the family
mahila	lady (refers to a married woman)
maryada	rank
mela	assemblage; *Inden uses* union
naimittika (karma)	contingent (act)
nishedha	prohibition
nishiddha	prohibited
nitya (karma)	required (act)
nivarana	ban, banning
niyama	law, regulation; *also* restrictive (injunction)
nyaya-patha	right path
parisamkhya (vidhi)	exclusionary (injunction)
paryaya	exchange or exchange series; *same as* avritti; *Inden uses* reciprocity
patni	wife
patita	outcaste
pindadana	last rites
pramana	proof or proof-text
pranali	framework
pratha	custom
pratishtha	celebrated actions; *Inden uses* famous acts
pratyavaya	sin; *also* dosha
pravritti	inclination

punarvivaha	remarriage
putra	son
rahita	abolished
sadhya (Kulin)	potential (Kulin)
samajchyuta	rejected by the community
sampradaya	community
samshodhana	eradication
sarvadvari	mutual (marriage)
sarvasadharana	public
shasana	decree
shishtachara	conduct of the learned; *also* learned conduct
shreni	category; *Inden uses* subcaste
shuddha	pure (as in Pure Shrotriya)
siddha (Kulin)	accomplished (Kulin)
svakrita-bhanga (Kulin)	Self-Broken (Kulin)
svecchachari	willful
tatparya	purport
upalakshana	implication
vachana	passage
vaidha	authorized by scripture
vamsha	family line; *Inden uses* continuing succession of males
vamshavali	genealogy
varna	class; *Inden uses* caste
vichara	examination, investigation, opinion
vidhata	creator (God)
vidhi	injunction
vidhivat	enacted
vivaha	marriage; *synonymous with* kanya-dana *and* kula-karma
vyavasaya	business (as in the "business of marriage")
vyavahara	behavior; practice
vyavastha	ruling
Vyavasthapaka Samaj	Legislative Council
yadriccha	self-willed, voluntary; *same as* yadeccha
yavana	foreign (used for Muslims)

Bibliography

Abstract of Letters Received from India, 1859–1867. London, 1867.

Agnes, Flavia. *Law and Gender Inequality: The Politics of Women's Rights in India.* Delhi: Oxford University Press, 2001.

Agnes, Flavia. *Women and Law in India: An Omnibus.* New Delhi: Oxford University Press, 2004.

Aquil, Raziuddin, and Partha Chatterjee. *History in the Vernacular.* Ranikhet: Permanent Black, 2008.

Asad, Talal. "Ethnographic Representation, Statistics and Modern Power." *Social Research* 61, no. 1 (1994): 55–88.

Atwal, Jyoti. *Real and Imagined Widows: Gender Relations in Colonial North India.* New Delhi: Primus Books, 2016.

Bandyopadhyay, Brajendranath. *Sambad patre sekaler katha.* Vol. 2: *1830–1840.* Calcutta: Bangiya Sahitya Parishad, 1970.

Bandyopadhyay, Chandicharan. *Vidyasagar.* Calcutta: De's Book Store, 1987.

Bandyopadhyay, Hemchandra. *Granthavali.* Vol. 1, Part 1. Calcutta: Canning Library, 1884.

Bandyopadhyay, Sekhar. *Caste, Culture and Hegemony: Social Domination in Colonial Bengal.* New Delhi: Sage, 2004.

Bandyopadhyay, Sekhar. "Caste, Widow Marriage and the Reform of Popular Culture in Colonial Bengal." In *From the Seams of History:Essays on Indian Women*, edited by Bharati Ray, 8–36. New Delhi: Oxford University Press, 1995.

Bandyopadhyaya, Asitkumar. *Bangla Sahitye Vidyasagar.* New revised edition. Calcutta: De's Publishing, 1991.

Banerjee, Gooroodass. *Hindu Law of Marriage and Stridhan.* Calcutta: Thacker and Spink, 1879.

Basu, Monmayee. *Hindu Women and Marriage Law: From Sacrament to Contract.* New Delhi: Oxford University Press, 2001.

Basu, N. N. *Banger Jatiya Itihas: The Castes and Sects of Bengal.* Vol. 1, Part 1: *Brahmankanda.* 2nd ed. Calcutta, 1911.

Basu, Swapan. "The Development of Journalism and Public Opinion in Bengal 1818–1910." In *A Comprehensive History of Modern Bengal, 1700_1950*, vol. 2, edited by Sabyasachi Bhattacharya, 737–803. New Delhi: Primus, 2020.

Bhattacharya, France. *Pandit Isvaracandra Vidyasagara (Iswarchandra Vidyasagar) (1820–1891): la tradition au Service d'un humanism modern.* Paris: EHESS, 2014.

Bhattacharya, J. N. *Hindu Castes and Sects: An Exposition of the Origin of the Hindu Caste System and the Bearing of the Sects towards each other and towards other Religious Systems.* Calcutta: Thacker and Spink, 1896.

Bhattacharya, Malini, and Abhijit Sen, eds. *Talking of Power: Early Writings of Bengali Women from the Mid-Nineteenth Cnetury to the Beginning of the Twentieth Century.* Kolkata: Stree, 2003.

Brihannaradiyapuranam. Edited by Pandit Hrishikesh Shastri. 2nd ed. Varanasi: Chowkhamba Amarabharati Prakashan, 1975.

Buckland, C. E. *Dictionary of Indian Biography*. London: Swan Sonnenschein, 1901.

Chakravarti, Chintaharana. *Hindur achara-anushthana*. Calcutta: Papyrus, 2001.

Cassels, Nancy Gardner. *Social Legislation of the East India Company: Public Justice versus Public Instruction*. New Delhi: Sage, 2010.

Catalogue of Bengali Printed Books in the Library of the British Museum. Edited by J. F. Blumhardt. London: Trustees of the British Museum, 1886.

Catalogue of the Library of the India Office. Vol. II. Part IV. Bengali, Oriya, and Assamese Books. Edited by J. F. Blumhardt. London: Eyre and Spottiswoode, 1905.

Chakrabarty, Dipesh. "The Difference-Deferral of a Colonial Modernity: Public Debates on Domesticity in Colonial Bengal." In *Tensions of Empire: Colonial Cultures in a Bourgeois World*, edited by Frederick Cooper and Ann Laura Stoler, 373–405. Berkeley: University of California Press, 1997.

Chakraborty, Aishika, "Gender, Caste, and Marriage: Kulinism in Nineteenth-Century Bengal." In *Intimate Others: Marriage and Sexualities in India*, edited by Samita Sen, Ranjit Biswas, and Nandita Dhawan, 35–65. Kolkata: Stree Publications, 2011.

Chakravartty, S. C. "Kulinism in Bengal." *Indian Culture* 14, no. 4 (1948): 173–82.

Chanda, R. P. *Gaudarajamala*. Rajshahi: Varendra Research Society, 1912.

Chatterjee, Bankimchandra. *Bankim rachanavali*. 2 vols. Edited by Jogeshchandra Bagal. Calcutta: Sahitya Samsad, 1986.

Chatterjee, Heramba Nath. *Studies in the Social Background of the Forms of Marriage in Ancient India*. Calcutta: Sanskrit Pustak Bhandar, 1974.

Chatterjee, Kumkum. "Communities, Kings and Chronicles: The *Kulagranthas* of Bengal." *Studies in History* 21, no. 2 (2005): 173-213.

Chatterjee, Kumkum. "The King of Controversy: History and Nation-Making in Late Colonial India." *American Historical Review* 110, no. 5 (2005): 1454–75.

Chatterjee, Nandini. "English Law, Brahmo Marriage, and the Problem of Religious Difference: Civil Marriage Laws in Britain and India." *Comparative Studies in Society and History* 52, no. 3 (2010): 524–52.

Chatterjee, Partha. "Introduction: History in the Vernacular." In *History in the Vernacular*, edited by R. Aquil and P. Chatterjee, 1–24. Delhi: Permanent Black, 2008.

Chatterjee, Partha. "The Nationalist Resolution of the Women's Question." In *Recasting Women: Essays in Indian Colonial History*, edited by Kumkum Sangari and Sudesh Vaid, 233–53. New Brunswick, NJ: Rutgers University Press, 1990.

Chatterjee, Partha. *The Nation and its Fragments: Colonial and Postcolonial Histories*. Princeton: Princeton University Press, 1993.

Collet, Sophia Dobson. *The Life and Letters of Raja Rammohun Roy*. Edited by D. K. Biswas and P. C. Ganguli. Calcutta: Sadharan Brahmo Samaj, 1988.

Dasgupta, Shuvatri. "A History of Conjugality: On Care, and Capital, in the British Empire c.1872–1947." DPhil Thesis. University of Cambridge. Unpublished.

Datta, Akshay Kumar. "Bahuvivaha." In *Samayikpatre Banglar Samajchitra*, vol. 3, edited by Benoy Ghosh, 5–8. Calcutta: Prakash Bhavan, 1980.

Datta, Swati. *Migrant Brahmanas in Northern India: Their Settlement and General Impact c. 475 to 1030*. Delhi: Motilal Banarsidass, 1989.

The Dattaka-Mimansa, and Dattaka-Chandrika. *Two Original Treatises on the Hindu Law of Adoption*. Translated by J. C. C. Sutherland. Reprint ed. Madras: College Press, 1825.

Davis, Donald R., and Timothy Lubin. "Hinduism and Colonial Law." In *Hinduism in the Modern World*, edited by Brian A. Hatcher, 96–110. New York: Routledge, 2016.

Dayatattvam: The Text along with English Translation. Edited by Heramba Chatterji Sastri. Calcutta: Sanskrit College, 1990.

De, Barun. "The Colonial Context of the Bengal Renaissance." In *Indian Society and the Beginnings of Modernization c. 1830–1850*, edited by C. H. Philips and M. D. Wainwright, 119–126. London: School of Oriental and African Studies, 1976.

De, Barun. "A Historiographical Critique of Renaissance Analogues for Nineteenth-Century India." In *Perspectives in Social Sciences, I*, edited by Barun De, 178–218. Calcutta: Oxford UniversityPress, 1977.

De, Rohit, and Robert Travers. "Petitions and Political Cultures in South Asia." *Modern Asian Studies* 53, no. 1 (2019): 1–20.

Derrett, J. Duncan M. *Religion, Law and the State in India*. London: Faber, 1968.

Dharmasutras: The Law Codes of Ancient India. Translated by Patrick Olivelle. New York: Oxford University Press, 1999.

Dutt, Nripendra Kumar. *The Origin and Growth of Caste in India*. 2 vols. Calcutta: Firma KLM, 1960.

Forbes, Geraldine. "Jogendro Chandra Ghosh and Hindu Postivism: A Case Study in Cultural Adaptation." *Contributions to Indian Sociology* 8 (1974): 1–9.

Forbes, Geraldine. *Women in Modern India*. New Cambridge History of India, vol. IV.2. New York: Cambridge University Press, 1996.

Fraser, Nancy. "Recognition without Ethics?" *Theory, Culture and Society* 18, nos. 2–3 (2001): 21–42.

Fruzzetti, Lina. *The Gift of a Virgin: Women, Marriage, and Ritual in Bengali Society*. Delhi: Oxford University Press, 1990.

Ghosh, Benoy. *Iswar Chandra Vidyasagar*. Builders of Modern India. New Delhi: Govt. of India Publications Division, 1965.

Ghosh, Benoy. *Samayik-patre banglar samaj-chitra*. 5 vols. Calcutta: Praksash Bhavan, 1980 [1960].

Ghosh, Benoy. *Selections from English Periodicals of 19th Century Bengal*. Vol. 3: *1849–56*. Calcutta: Papyrus, 1980.

Ghosh, Benoy. *Vidyasagar o Bangali Samaj*. Reprint. Calcutta: Orient Longman, 1984.

Ghosh, Shrabani. "'Birds in a Cage': Changes in Bengali Social Life as Recorded in Autobiographies of Women." In *Images, Ideals and Real Lives: Women in Literature and History*, edited by Alice Thorner and Maithreyi Krishnaraj, 37–67. Hyderabad: Orient Longman, 2000.

Grihastharatnakara: A Treatise on Smriti by Candeshvara Thakkura. Edited by Kamalakrishna Smrititirtha. Calcutta: Asiatic Society, 1928.

Gupta, Jogendranath. *Vikrampurer Itihas*. Calcutta: Bhattacharya and Sons, 1909.

Harlow, Barbara, and Mia Carter, eds. *Archives of Empire*. Volume 1: *From The East India Company to the Suez Canal*. Durham, NC: Duke University Press, 2003.

Hatcher, Brian A. *Bourgeois Hinduism, or the Faith of the Modern Vedantists: Rare Discourses from Early Colonial Bengal*. New York: Oxford University Press, 2008.

Hatcher, Brian A. "The Era of Vidyasagar." In *A Comprehensive History of Modern Bengal, 1700–1950*, vol. 2, edited by Sabyasachi Bhattacharya, 150–84. New Delhi: Primus, 2020.

Hatcher, Brian A. "Great Men Waking: Paradigms in the Historiography of the Bengal Renaissance." In *Bengal: Rethinking History. Essays in Historiography*, edited by

Sekhar Bandyopadhyay, 135–63. International Centre for Bengal Studies, no. 29. New Delhi: Manohar, 2001.

Hatcher, Brian A. *Idioms of Improvement: Vidyasagar and Cultural Encounter in Bengal.* Reprint edition. New Delhi: Primus Books, 2020 [1996].

Hatcher, Brian A. *A Less Familiar Vidyasagar: Pioneer of Social Research.* Kolkata: Institute of Language Studies and Research, 2023.

Hatcher, Brian A. "Pandits at Work: The Modern Sastric Imaginary in Early Colonial Bengal." In *Trans-Colonial Modernities in South Asia*, edited by Michael S. Dodson and Brian A. Hatcher, 45–67. New York: Routledge, 2012.

Hatcher, Brian A. "Samajvijnani Vidyasagar." *Anandabazar Patrika* (June 4, 2022). https://www.anandabazar.com/editorial/essays/bengali-essay-on-ishwar-chandra-vidyasagar-who-was-also-a-sociologist/cid/1348394.

Hatcher, Brian A. "Sastric Modernity: Mediating Sanskrit Knowledge in Colonial Bengal." In *Modernities in Asian Perspective: Polity, Society, Culture, Economy*, edited by Kausik Bandyopadhyay, 117–51. Kolkata: Setu Prakashani, 2010.

Hatcher, Brian A. "The Shakuntala Paradigm: Vidyasagar, Widow Marriage and the Morality of Recognition." *Journal of Hindu Studies* 6, no. 3 (2013): 363–83.

Hatcher, Brian A. *Vidyasagar: The Life and After-life of an Eminent Indian.* New Delhi: Routledge, 2014.

Heimsath, Charles H. 1964. *Indian Nationalism and Hindu Social Reform.* Princeton: Princeton University Press.

Hennesey, Rosemary. Review of *Justice Interruptus: Critical Reflections on the "Postsocialist" Condition. Hypatia* 14, no. 1 (1999): 126–32.

Hunter, W. W. 1876. *A Statistical Account of Bengal.* London: Trübner and Co.

In Praise of Annada: Bharatchandra Ray. 2 vols. Translated by France Bhattacharya. Cambridge, MA: Harvard University Press, 2017 and 2020.

Inden, Ronald B. *Imagining India.* New York: Basil Blackwell, 1990.

Inden, Ronald B. *Marriage and Rank in Bengali Culture: A History of Caste and Clan in Middle-Period Bengal.* Berkeley: University of California Press, 1976.

Inden, Ronald B., and Ralph Nicholas. *Kinship in Bengali Culture.* Chicago: University of Chicago Press, 1977.

Institutes of the Hindoo Religion by Rughoo Nundun, vol. 2. Serampore, 1835.

Jaiminiya-nyaya-mala-vistara of Madhavacharya. Edited by Theodor Goldstücker. Sanskrit Text Society. London: Trübner, 1865.

Jamison, Stephanie. "Rhinoceros Toes, Manu V17–18, and the Development of the Dharma System." *Journal of the American Oriental Society* 118, no. 2 (1998): 249–56.

Jimutavahana's Dayabhaga: *The Hindu Law of Inheritance in Bengal.* Translated by Ludo Rocher. New York: Oxford University Press, 2002.

Kane, P. V. *History of Dharmasastra (Ancient and Medieval Religious and Civil Law).* 4 vols. Government Oriental Series, Class B, No. 6. Poona: Bhandarkar Oriental Research Institute, 1930.

Karlekar, Malavika. "Reflections on Kulin Polygamy: Nistarini Debi's Sekeley Katha." *Contributions to Indian Sociology* 29, nos. 1–2 (1995): 135–155.

Karlekar, Malavika. *Voices from Within: Early Personal Narratives of Bengali Women.* Delhi: Oxford University Press, 1991.

Kaviraj, Sudipta. *The Imaginary Institution of India: Politics and Ideas.* New York: Columbia University Press, 2010.

Kaviraj, Sudipta. *The Unhappy Consciousness: Bankimchandra Chattopadhyay and the Formation of Nationalist Discourse in India*. Delhi: Oxford University Press, 1998.

Krishnayajurvediyataittiriyasamhita. Anandasrama Sanskrit Series, no. 52. Edited by Kashinath Shastri and Hari Narayan Apte. Poona: Anandasrama Press, 1908.

Kshitishavamshavalicharita. A Chronicle of the Family of Raja Krishnachandra of Navadvipa, Bengal. Edited and translated by W. Pertsch. Berlin: Ferd. Dümmler, 1852.

Kundu, Narottam. "Caste and Class in Pre-Muslim Bengal." PhD Thesis. School of Oriental and African Studies, London, 1963.

The Law Code of Manu. Translated by Patrick Olivelle. New York: Oxford University Press, 2005.

The Madana Parijata on Inheritance. Translated by S. Sitarama Sastri. Madras: Lawrence Asylum Steam Press, 1899.

The Madana-parijata. A System of Hindu Law by Madanapala. Edited by Pandit Madhusudan Smritiratna. Calcutta: Asiatic Society of Bengal, 1893.

Manu's Code of Law: A Critical Edition and Translation of Manava-dharmashastra. Translated by Patrick Olivelle, with the editorial assistance of Suman Olivelle. New York: Oxford University Press, 2005.

Manusmriti. With the Sanskrit commentary *Manvarthamuktavali* of Kulluka Bhatta. Edited by J. L. Shastri. Delhi: Motilal Banarsidass, 1990.

Maine, Henry Sumner. *Ancient Law*. London: John Murray, 1861.

Majumdar, R. C., ed. *History of Bengal*. Vol. 1: *Hindu Period*. Dacca: University of Dacca, 1943.

Majumdar, R. C. "Sanskrita Rajabali Grantha." *Sahitya Parishat Patrika* 4 (1346 B.S. [1939]): 233–39.

Majumdar, Beman Behari. *History of Indian Social and Political Ideas (From Rammohan to Dayananda)*. Calcutta: Firma KLM, 1996 [1934].

Majumdar, Rochona. "A Conceptual History of the Social: Some Reflections out of Colonial Bengal." In *Trans-Colonial Modernities in South Asia*, edited by M. S. Dodson and B. A. Hatcher, 165–88. New York: Routledge, 2012.

Majumdar, Rochona. "Looking for Brides and Grooms: *Ghataks*, Matrimonials and the Marriage Market in Colonial Calcutta, circa 1875–1940." *Journal of Asian Studies* 63, no. 4 (2004): 911–35.

Majumdar, Rochona. *Marriage and Modernity: Family Values in Colonial Bengal*. Durham: Duke University Press, 2009.

Mallampalli, Chandra. (2010): "Escaping the Grip of Personal Law in Colonial India: Proving Custom, Negotiating Hinduness," *Law and History Review* 28, no. 4: 1043–1066.

Mani, Lata. "Contentious Traditions: The Debate on *Sati* in Colonial India." In *Recasting Women: Essays in Indian Colonial History*, edited by Kumkum Sangari and Sudesh Vaid, 88–126. New Brunswick, NJ: Rutgers University Press, 1990.

Mani, Lata. "Production of an Official Discourse on Sati in Early-Nineteenth-Century Bengal." *Economic and Political Weekly* 21, no. 17 (1986): 32–40.

McLane, J. R. *Land and Local Kingship in eighteenth-century Bengal*. New York: Cambridge University Press, 1993.

Menski, Werner F. *Hindu Law: Beyond Tradition and Modernity*. New Delhi: Oxford University Press, 2003.

Metcalf, Thomas J. *The Aftermath of Revolt: India, 1857–1870*. Princeton: Princeton University Press, 1964.

Mitra, Durba. *Indian Sex Life: Sexuality and the Colonial Origins of Modern Social Thought*. Princeton: Princeton University Press, 2020.

Mitra, Indra. *Karunasagara Vidyasagar*. Calcutta: Ananda Publishers, 2000.

Mitra, Subal Chandra. *Isvar Chandra Vidyasagar: A Story of His Life and Work*. Reprint. Delhi: Ashis Publishing, 1975 [1902].

Mitra, Sudhir Kumar. *Hugli Jelar Itihas o Bangasamaj*. 2 vols. Calcutta: De's Publishing, 2013.

Mogey, J. M. "The Contribution of Frédéric Le Play to Family Research." *Marriage and Family Living* 17, no. 4 (1955): 310–15.

Mukherjee, Mandar. *Krishnakumari: Jiban o Dushprapya Sangraha*. Kolkata: Gangchil, 2015.

Mukherjee, S. N. 1977. *Calcutta: Myths and History*. Calcutta: Subarnarekha.

Narada-Smriti. Edited by Heramba Chatterjee Shastri. Calcutta Sanskrit College Research Series, nos. 133 and 135. Calcutta: Sanskrit College, 1988.

Nirnaya Sindhu of Kamalakara Bhatta. Edited by Jwala Prasad Mishra. Mumbai: Khemraj Press, 1905.

O'Malley, L. S. S. *Hooghly: Bengal District Gazetteers*. Calcutta: Bengal Secretariat, 1912.

Padmapurana: Kriyayogasara panchavimshati adhyaya sampurna. Translated into Bengali by Bhagavanchandra Mukhopadhyay. Calcutta: Vishvambhar Laha, 1877.

Pather Panchali, by Bibhutibhushan Bandyopadhyay. Calcutta: Mitra and Ghosh, 1985.

Phipps, Kelly Elizabeth. "Marriage and Redemption: Mormon Polygamy in the Congressional Imagination, 1862–1887." *Virginia Law Review* 95, no. 2 (2009): 435–88.

Raghunandanakrita Udvahatattvam. Edited by Manabendu Bandyopadhyay Shastri. Translated by Hrishikesh Shastri. Kolkata: Sanskrit Pustak Bhandar, 1996.

Ray, Shubha. "Kailashbashini Debi's Janaika Grihabadhur Diary: A Woman 'Constructing' her 'Self' in Nineteenth-Century Bengal?" In *Speaking of the Self: Gender, Performance, and Autobiography in South Asia*, edited by Anshu Malhotra and Siobhan Lambert-Hurley, 95–120. Durham, NC: Duke University Press, 2015.

Raychaudhuri, Tarak Ch., and Bikash Raychaudhuri, *The Brahmans of Bengal: A Textual Study in Social History*. Calcutta: Archaeological Survey of India, 1981.

Report on the Census of Bengal 1872. Edited by H. Beverley. Calcutta: Bengal Secretariat Press, 1872.

Risley, H. H. *The Tribes and Castes of Bengal: Ethnographic Glossary*. Volume 1. Calcutta, 1892.

Roy, Rammohun. *The English Works of Raja Rammohun Roy*. Allahabad: Panini Office, 1906.

Roy, Rammohun. *Rammohun-rachanavali*. Edited by Ajitkumar Ghosh. Kolkata: Haraph Prakashani, 1973.

Roy Chowdhuri, Parvatisankar. *Adisura o Vallalasena: Ambasthajatiya Nripatidiger Aitihasika Vivarana*. Calcutta: Gupta Press, 1881.

Sarkar, Biharilal. *Vidyasagar: Ishvarchandra Vidyasagarer jivani*. Edited and Annotated after the 4th ed. by Prahladakumara Pramanika. Calcutta: Orient Book Co., 1986.

Sarkar, Sumit, and Tanika Sarkar, eds. *Women and Social Reform in Modern India: A Reader*. Bloomington: Indiana University Press, 2008.

Sarkar, Tanika. "Conjugality and Hindu Nationalism: Resisting Colonial Reason and the Death of a Child-Wife." In Tanika Sarkar, *Hindu Wife, Hindu Nation: Community, Religion, and Cultural Nationalism*, 191–225. Bloomington: Indiana University Press, 2001.

Sarkar, Tanika. "Wicked Widows: Law and Faith in Nineteenth-Century Public Sphere Debates." In *Behind the Veil: Resistance, Women and the Everyday in Colonial South Asia*, edited by Anindita Ghosh, 83–115. New York: Palgrave Macmillan, 2008.

Sen, Amiya P. *Vidyasagar: Reflections on a Notable Life*. Hyderabad: Orient Blackswan, 2021.

Sen, Asok. *Vidyasagar and his Elusive Milestones*. Calcutta: Rddhi India, 1977.

Shastri, Shivnath. *History of the Brahmo Samaj*. Two vols. Calcutta: R. Chatterji, 1911.

Singh, Sarva Daman. *Polyandry in Ancient India*. Delhi: Vikas, 1978.

Sinha, Mrinalini. "Gender in the Critiques of Colonialism and Nationalism: Locating the 'Indian Woman.'" *Women and Social Reform in Modern India: A Reader*, edited by Sumit Sarkar and Tanika Sarkar, 452–72. Bloomington: Indiana University Press, 2008.

Sircar, D. C. *Studies in the Society and Administration of Ancient and Mediaeval India*. Vol. 1. Calcutta: Firma KLM, 1959.

Smritichandrika by Devana-Bhatta. Edited by Srinivas Acharya. Government Oriental Library Series. Volume 1: Samskara Kanda. Mysore: Government Branch Press, 1911.

Stephens, Julia. *Governing Islam: Law, Empire, and Secularism in South Asia*. New York: Cambridge University Press, 2018.

Sturman, Rachel, "Marriage and Family in Colonial Hindu Law." In *Hinduism and Law: An Introduction*, edited by Timonty Lubin, Timothy, Donald R. Davis, Jr., and Jayanth Krishnan, 89–104. Cambridge: Cambridge University Press, 2010.

Tantravarttika: A Commentary on Sabara's Bhasya on the Purvamimamsa Sutras of Jaimini. Vol. 1. Edited by Ganganatha Jha. Calcutta: Asiatic Society, 1924.

Tarkaratna, Ramnarayan. *Ramnarayan Tarkaratna Rachanavali*. Edited by Sandhya Bakshi. Calcutta: Sahityalok, 1991.

Tarkavachaspati, Taranatha. *Bahuvivaha-vada*. Calcutta: Kavyaprakasha Press, 1872.

Trautmann, Thomas R. Review of *Marriage and Rank in Bengali Culture*. *Journal of Asian Studies* 39, no. 3 (1980): 519–24.

Trevelyan, Ernst John. *Hindu Family Law as Administered in British India*. London: Thacker and Spink, 1908.

Tripathi, Amales. *Vidyasagar: The Traditional Moderniser*. Delhi: Orient Longman, 1974.

Uberoi, Patricia. *Social Reform, Sexuality and the State*. New Delhi; Thousand Oaks, CA: Sage Publications, 1996.

Udvahatattva of Raghunandan. Edited by H. N. Chatterjee. Calcutta Sanskrit College Research Series, no. 24. Calcutta: Sanskrit College, 1963.

Unavimshati Samhita. Edited and translated by Panchanan Tarkaratna. Kolkata: Sanskrit Pustak Bhandar, 2000.

Vaidya, Narayan Keshav. *A Collection Containing Proceedings which Led to the Passing of Act XV of 1856*. Bombay, 1885.

Vidhiswarup Vichar. Edited by Pandit Jadavendra Nath Roy. Calcutta: Asiatic Society, 1973.

Vidyanidhi, Lalmohan. *Sambandhanirnaya: A Social History of the Principal Hindu Castes in Bengal*. Calcutta: New School Book Press, 1874.

Vidyaratna, Shambhuchandra. *Bhramnirash. Arthat Shriyukta Chandicharan Bandyopadhyay pranita 'Vidyasagar' namak nutan jivanchariter bhramnirakarana*. Calcutta, 1895.

Vidyaratna, Shambhuchandra. *Panditakulatilaka Mahatma Taranath Tarkavachaspatir jivancharita*. Calcutta, 1893.

Vidyaratna, Shambhuchandra. *Vidyasagar jivancharita*. Calcutta. English-Sanskrit Press, 1891.

Vidyasagar, Ishvarchandra. *Bahuvivaha rahita haoya uchita ki na etadvishayaka vichara*. Calcutta: Sanskrit Press, 1871.

Vidyasagar, Ishvarchandra. "The Evils of Child Marriage: Ishvarchandra Vidyasagar." Translated by Brian A. Hatcher. *Critical Asian Studies* 35, no. 3 (2003): 476–84.

Vidyasagar, Ishvarchandra. *Hindu Widow Marriage: An Epochal Work on Social Reform from Colonial India*. A complete translation with introduction and critical notes by Brian A. Hatcher. New York: Columbia University Press, 2011.

Vidyasagar, Ishvarchandra. *The Marriage of Hindu Widows*. Ishvarchandra Vidyasagar. Reprint. Calcutta: K. P. Bagchi, 1976 [1855].

Vidyasagar, Ishvarchandra. *Vidhavavivaha prachalita haoya uchita ki na etadvishayaka prastava*. Calcutta: Sanskrit Press, 1855.

Vidyasagar-granthavali. 3 vols. Edited by Sunitikumar Cattopadhyay, Brajendranath Bandyopadhyay, and Sajanikanta Das. Calcutta: Ranjan Publishing, 1937–39.

Vidyasagar-rachanasamgraha. 3 vols. Edited by Gopal Haldar. Calcutta: Pashcim Banga niraksharata durikarana samiti, 1972.

Wise, James. *Notes on the Races, Castes and Trades of Eastern Bengal*. London: Harrison and Sons, 1883.

Yajnavalkya-smriti. With the commentary Mitakshara of Vijnaneshvara. Edited by Narayan Rama Acarya Kavyatirtha. Delhi: Nag Publishers, 1985.

Zastoupil, Lynn, and Martin Moir, eds. *The Great Indian Education Debate: Documents Relating to the Orientalist-Anglicist Controversy, 1781–1843*. Richmond, Surrey: Curzon, 1999.

Index

For the benefit of digital users, indexed terms that span two pages (e.g., 52–53) may, on occasion, appear on only one of those pages.

Abalabandhabh, 129n.22
Abhijnanashakuntalam by Kalidasa, 105, 110. *See also* Shakuntala
Abhijnana-Shakuntalam by Vidyasagar, 131n.62, 135n.121
abortion, 18, 35, 105. *See also* foeticide
Achyutananda, 104, 109, 147n.129
Act XV. *See* Hindu Widow's Remarriage Act (Act XV)
adhivedana, 21–22. *See also* supersession
Adisura, 12–13, 56, 58–59, 114, 115, 129–30n.32
adultery, 65–66, 84–85, 91, 142n.64
Against High-Caste Polygamy
  Appendices to, xi, 24, 39–40, 47, 138n.9
  audience for, 29–30, 37–38, 143n.69
  citations or quotations in, xii, 7–8, 113, 127n.5, 138n.12
  compilation of, 7–8
  Conclusion to, xi, 7–8
  editions of, xi, 7–8, 127n.3
  empirical data in, xiii, 5–6, 28, 29, 38–41, 119–23, 128n.14, 136n.138, 136–37nn.139–40
  as examination (*vichara*), xiii–xiv
  language of, 135n.113, 138n.6, 138n.8, 139n.21, 144n.84
  lists in, xiii–xiv, 32, 33, 59–60, 76
  narrow focus of, 9
  Objections in (*see* objections)
  petition co-signatory lists in, xiii, 88, 125
  sections or structure of, xii–xiii, 29
  as shastric exegesis, 28–31, 42
  significance of, xii, 20–21, 27–28, 44
  storytelling or narration in, 28, 34–35, 36–38
  Supplements to, xi, 7–8, 27, 41–42
  title of, xi
  translations of, xi–xii
agency, 87, 142n.62
andolan, 22, 23
Anglo-Indian law, xii
Annadamangal. *See* Ray, Bharatchandra
anti-polygamy campaign, 3–5, 20–21
Apastamba, 100, 101–2, 107
Asad, Talal, 41
assemblages, 15, 33, 60–61, 62–63, 65, 75, 118. *See also* Khadaha Assemblage; Phuliya Assemblage
Atri, 82, 141n.50, 144n.86
avritti. *See* exchange

Bahuvivaha rahita haoya uchita ki na etadvishayaka vichara, Book One. *See* Against High-Caste Polygamy
Bahuvivaha rahita haoya uchita ki na etadvishayaka vichara, Book Two, xii, 9–10, 134n.101, 134n.111, 135n.113, 146n.102
Baidyas, 129n.31
Bandhuvargasamavaya Sabha, 23, 45, 137n.1
Bandya (surname), 12, 15
Bandyopadhyay, Bibhutibhushan, 130n.39
Bandyopadhyay, Chandicharan, 131n.66, 135n.124, 137n.140, 145n.95
Bandyopadhyay, Hemchandra, 1, 131n.55
Bandyopadhyay, Sekhar, 129n.24, 129n.25
Bandyopadhyay, Sripati, 61–62
Banerjee, Gooroodass, 135n.117, 137n.147, 139n.17, 142n.62, 144n.85
Bangalar Itihasa, 32, 135n.121
Bankim. *See* Chatterjee, Bankimchandra

Barendra Brahmins, 127n.7
Barishal, 76
Baruihati (fault), 61–62
Basu, N. N., 11
Batgram (village name), 57–58
Beadon, Cecil, 24–25, 27, 46, 138n.5, *See also* Kulinism: Beadon committee on
Bentham, Jeremy, 135n.117
Bentinck, William, Governor-General, 4–5, 86, 145n.93, 145n.94
Beverley, Henry, 128n.15
Bhagavad-Gita, 11–12
Bhagavata Purana, 105, 109–10
Bhattacharya, France, xi–xii
Bhattanarayana (Kulin forebear), 56, 58
Bhrantivilasa, 19
Birsingha, 19, 36, 143n.71
Brahmanda Purana, 93, 94–95
Brahmanical norms, 9, 13–14
Brahmins
  in Achyutananda, 109
  Bengali, xiii–xiv, 8
  in Daksha, 49
  degraded, 56, 57, 64–65
  five from Kanyakubja, 12–13, 56–59, 60, 62, 114, 140n.29
  Kulin (*see* Kulin Brahmins)
  life-stages for, 49
  in Manu, 26–27, 81, 107–8, 110–11
  non-Bengali, 12
  "Seven Hundred," 12, 58, 60, 61–62, 141n.46
Brahmo Marriage Act (Act III of 1872), 5
Brahmo Samaj, 5, 132n.69
Brihannaradiya Purana, 146n.105
British Crown, 5
Broken Kulins, 15, 67–75, 87, 89–90, 97–98, 102, 103, 142n.67
  anecdotes about, 71–75
  marriage as business for, 17, 35, 68, 75, 89–90
  Second-hand, 87, 143n.73
  Vidyasagar's schoolteacher, 8, 17, 37, 143n.71
Buddhists, 5, 129–30n.32
Burdwan, 76, 143n.69
Burdwan, Maharaja of, 23, 45, 46, 145n.99, 146n.111
Calcutta, 6, 77–78, 140n.34, *See also* Kolkata
Calcutta Government Sanskrit College, 4, 6, 32, 96, 97–98
Carroll, Lucy, 129n.23
Cassels, Nancy Gardner, 133n.96
casteism, 8
census, 5–6, 40–41, 128n.15
Chakrabarty, Dipesh, 147n.123
Chakraborty, Aishika, 17
Chanda, R. P., 136n.127
Chandara(Kulin forebear), 56, 58
Chatta (surname), 12, 15
Chatterjee, Bankimchandra [Bankim], 31–32, 34, 135n.120, 136n.130, 137n.143, 144n.83
Chatterjee, Partha, 42, 128n.12
Chattopadhyay, Kalikanta, 37, 143n.71
Chattopadhyay, Madhu, 62
child marriage, 1–2, 4, 5, 10, 133n.97
  Vidyasagar's tract on, 29, 30–31, 34
Christians, 1, 5
Chudamani, Tarakchandra, 132n.81
civilization, 2–3, 21–22
civil marriage, 5
clan goddesses, 65–67, 142n.59
conduct of the learned, 100–1, 102, 103–4, 146–47n.114
contingent duties, 26
courtesans, 65–66, 70. *See also* prostitution

Daksha (Kulin forebear), 56, 58
Daksha Prajapati, 98
Daksha Samhita, 49
Dasgupta, Shuvatri, 131n.65
Dasharatha, 55, 98
Datta, Akshay Kumar, 21–22, 135n.123, 137n.1
Dattaka Mimamsa, 82
daughters
  Broken or Self-Broken, 68, 87
  gifts or *douceur* from families of, 36, 83–84, 88
  giving or receiving, 58–59, 60–61, 76–77, 140n.35, 142n.62
  of good or refined homes, 14, 74–75
  harsh fate of, 70–71, 87

Kayastha, 78–80, 83–84
Lesser Kulin, 59, 60, 62
of maternal family, 100–1
rituals for, 69–70, 71–72
sale of, 82–84, 105
Seven Hundred, 62
Shrotriya, 13, 59, 60
unmarried, 63–64, 65–66, 83–84, 100–1
Vamshaja, 60, 61–62, 67–68, 82
wives bearing only, 50, 107
Dayabhaga, 19–20, 104, 109
Deb, Raja Radhakanta, 24, 133n.92
Debi, Bamasundari, 128n.7
Debi, Kailashbashini, 128n.7, 137n.1, 137n.144
deshachara, 132n.73, 146–47n.114, *See also* Shastras: local or widespread practices vs.
Devala, 108
Devivara Ghataka Visharada, 15, 27–28, 60–62, 63, 64–65, 115, 130n.45, 130n.49, 141n.47, 141n.55
damned, 70–71
Dhaka, 76
Dhandha (fault), 61–62, 118
Dharma (custom), 2–4, 27, 29, 33, 46–47, 56, 80, 99–100, 144n.81
conduct of the learned and, 100–1, 146–47n.114
highest, 99–100
householders', 26
in Kali Yuga, 27
Dharma (god), 98, 100
Dharma Sabha, 133n.92
dharmashastra, 20–21, 55, 101–2, 108
marriages forbidden in, 130–31n.50
scholars of, xii, 46 (*see also* Shastras)
Dighapati, Raja of, 45
Dinajpur, Raja of, 45
district courts or judges, 92
douceur, 36
dramas, 1–2
Dutt, N. K., 130n.49

East India Company, 3–4, 5
education, 10, 22, 25, 41–42, 43, 77–78, 133n.96
English, 77–78, 86
Epics, 147n.116
"Evils of Child Marriage," 29, 30–31, 34
exchange, 13–14, 58–59, 63, 68, 140n.34

faults, 15, 59–62, 130–31n.50, 141n.46
foeticide, 54, 63, 64, 65–66, 84–85, 142n.64, *See also* abortion
Foreign Fault, 61–62
Fraser, Nancy, 20
Friend of India, 136n.139, 137n.142, 145n.99
Friends Harmony Association, 23, 45, 137n.1

gai, 140n.33, 140n.41, *See also* Kulin Brahmins: surnames of
Ganguli (surname), 12
Ganguly, Dwarkanath, 129n.22
Gauda, 57, 58–59
Gautama, 101–2
genealogies, 11, 14, 33–34, 59–60, 130n.48, 136n.127, *See also* Against High-Caste Polygamy: genealogical lists in
genealogists, 58–59, 61–62, 89, 116, 130n.48
ghatak or *ghataka*, 14–15, 32–33, 140n.34, 142n.58
Kulin status of, 59–60, 117
unscrupulous, 142n.60
Ghosh, Benoy, 128n.6, 137n.140
Ghosh, Shrabani, 143n.68
Ghoshal (surname), 12
Grant, J. P., 23
Grihastha-ratnakara, 54

Haldar, Gopal, xi
Harisharma, 82
Hennesey, Rosemary, 19
Hindoo Patriot, 24–25
Hinduism, 5, 9, 132n.73
Hindu law, 2–3, 19–22, 26, 29, 90, 92, 138n.6, *See also* dharmashastra; Shastras
Hindu Widow Marriage (*Vidhava-vivaha*), xiv, 18, 20–21, 23, 28–29, 37, 43, 127n.8, 146n.105, 146–47n.114

Hindu Widow's Remarriage Act (Act XV), 3–4, 128n.16, 132n.73
inheritance rights in, 9–10, 19–20
Hirakoti (village name), 57–58
historiography, 28, 31–33
honor, 14, 17, 106–7
Hooghly District, 16, 38, 40, 76, 119–23, 143n.76, *See also* Janai
householders, 26, 49, 50, 51–52, 53, 93–94, 108
husbands
ages of, 89–90
competition for, 14
duties of, 82–83
finances of, 14, 17, 36, 71–72, 143n.68
heartless, 1, 131n.55
homes of, 16–17, 89–90
list keepers, 38, 143n.68
property of deceased, 9–10, 19–20
of a Vrishali, 63
hypergamy, 8, 13–14, 15, 17, 130n.44

Ibbetson, Denzil, 130n.44
imaginative sociology, 34–38
Inden, Ronald, 11, 129n.20, 129n.30, 130n.44
inference, 100–1
injunctions, 52–53, 93–95, 98–100, 107, 108, 111, 139n.18, 146n.104
In Praise of Annada. *See* Ray, Bharatchandra
intellectuals, 3–4, 31–32, 33–34, 41
Itihasa, 55

Jaiminiya-nyaya-mala-vistara, 100, 147n.115
Jains, 5, 129–30n.32
Jamison, Stephanie, 139n.18
Janai (Hooghly District), 76, 123, 136n.137, 143n.76
Jessore, 76
Jews, 5
Jimutavahana. *See* Dayabhaga

Kali Yuga, 27, 53, 95, 131n.65, 134n.104
Kamakoti (village name), 57–58
Kanauj (Kanyakubja), 12, 56. *See also* Brahmins: five from Kanyakubja
Kanjilal (surname), 12
Kankagram (village name), 57–58
kanya, 140n.35, *See also* daughters
Karlekar, Malavika, 16–17, 128n.14, 129n.22, 132n.69
Kashipur (Cossipore), 6
Kashyapa, 63, 141n.50
kaulinya, 12–13, 14–15. *See also* Kulin rank
Kaviraj, Sudipta, 31–32, 34
Kaviratna, Gangadhara, 134n.111
Kavya, 104
Kayasthas, xiii–xiv, 8, 11–12, 78–80. *See also* Kulin Kayasthas; Maulik Kayasthas
sale of sons by, 82, 83–84
Khardaha Assemblage, 60–61, 62
kings, 14–15, 55–56, 58–59, 98, 99, 100–1, 134n.104
Kolkata, 66–67, 83–84, 143n.69, *See also* Calcutta
Kriya-yoga-sara, 82
Kshatriyas
in Daksha, 49
life-stages for, 49
in Manu, 26–27, 81–51, 107–8, 110–11
in *varna* system, 11–12
Kshitishvamshavalicharita, 139–40n.28
Kulatattvarnava, 116
Kulin Brahmins
Dharma of, 56, 62–63, 65
history of, 11–12
marriage exchanges of, 59, 60–61, 63
surnames of, 12, 59, 115, 116–17, 140n.31, 140n.38
Kulinism, 8, 9, 58–59, 65, 134n.105
apologists for, 33, 65
attributes of, 58–59
Beadon committee on, 25–26, 27, 30, 144n.82
essence or defining feature of, 130n.44, 140n.34
financial aspects of, 14, 16–17
history of, 11–18, 30, 32–33, 56
prevalence of, 134n.105, 137n.147
Kulin Kayasthas, 78–80, 144n.79
Kulin Kulasarvasva, 22–23
Kulinmahilavilap, 1, 131n.55

Kulin rank, 15, 17, 27–28, 33, 37, 75, 130n.42
  attributes of, 13, 58–61, 116
  Creator and, 64–65
  established, 12–13, 33, 56, 58–60
  illusory, lost, or vitiated, 27–28, 33, 62–63, 65, 75
  myth of, 13, 59, 141n.47
  as shared "coded substance," 129n.20
Kundagrami (surname), 12

Lakshman Sena, 13–14
law. *See* Anglo-Indian law; *dharmashastra*; Hindu law; Shastras
learned conduct. *See* conduct of the learned
Legislative Council, 24, 46, 97–98
  Draft Bill before, 24, 26, 90–92
  members of, 24, 46, 133n.88
  petitions to, 23, 24, 45
Le Play, Frédéric, 137n.141
Lesser Kulins, 59, 60, 62
liberation, 70–71, 85–86, 88–89, 145n.92, 145n.100
life stages, 49, 50, 51–52, 93–94, 108
Lilavati Nataka, 132n.81
lineage histories, 32. *See also* genealogies
local committees. *See* punchayets
local conduct, 132n.73, 146–47n.114, *See also* Shastras: local or widespread practices vs.

Madanparijata, 93, 94–95, 98–99, 101–2, 146n.104, 146n.112
Madhavacharya, 100, 147n.115
Mahabharata, 11–12, 131n.62
Majumdar, R. C., 139–40n.28
Mani, Lata, 20–21
Manu
  first marriage in, 50, 107
  highest Dharma in, 99
  injunctions of, 146n.104
  kings in, 55
  rites prescribed by, 143n.70
  as sage, 109, 147n.129
  subsequent marriages in, 25, 26–27, 50–51, 53, 54, 94–95, 98–99, 102, 106, 107–8, 109, 110–11, 139n.19, 148n.131
  on treatment of wives, 106, 142n.66
  Vidyasagar quotes, xii
  Vidyasagar refers to, xii–xiii, 94–95, 101–2
marriages
  adyarasa, 144n.79
  as business, 17–18, 35–36, 75
  contingent, 26, 51, 93–94
  desired or voluntary, 26–27, 51–53, 93–95, 98–99
  male agency in, 142n.62
  mixed-caste or mixed-class, 11–12, 26–27, 52–53, 94–95, 108, 109, 110–11
  required, 26, 51, 93–94
Marshman, John Clark, 135n.121
Matsya Purana, 108
Maulik Kayasthas, 78–80, 144n.79
mela. *See* assemblages
Metcalf, Thomas, 127–28n.4
missionaries, 22
Mitakshara, 21–22, 139n.16
Mitra, Dinabandhu, 132n.81
Mitra, Kishorichand, 23, 45, 137n.1, 137n.144
Mitter, Dwarkanath, 24–25
mixed-caste or mixed-class marriages. *See* marriages: mixed-caste or mixed-class
Mormons, 1
Morrill Anti-Bigamy Act, 1
Mukhaiti (surname), 12, 15
Mukherjee, Bhudeb, 144n.83
Mukherjee, Joykrishna, 25–26, 133n.99
Mukhopadhyay, Gangananda, 61–62, 141n.46
Mukhopadhyay, Hari, 62
Mukhopadhyay, Rashbehari, 131n.61
Mukhya Kulins, 13
Mulukjuri (fault), 61–62
Muslims, 5, 14, 61–62, 85–86, 130–31n.50, 141n.46

Nadha (fault), 61–62
Nadia, 143n.69
Nanda Pandita, 144n.86
Narada-Smriti, 143n.70
Natore, Raja of, 45
Navadwip, 76

Navadwip, Raja of, 45, 46
"new community," 81–82, 144n.83, 145n.90
new ruling (*nutan vyavastha*), 27–28, 65
Nirnaya Sindhu, 108
Nistarini Debi, 16, 17
Nitibodha, 10
nutan vyavastha, 27–28, 65
Nyayaratna, Ramakumara, 134n.111

objections, 29, 87–88, 138n.10
First, 134n.101, 148n.132
Second, 134n.106
Third, 35, 36, 129n.21
Fourth, 38, 40
Fifth, 144n.79
Sixth, 138n.8
Seventh, 37, 128n.8
Olivelle, Patrick, 139n.24, 146n.113

Paithanasi, 63–64
Pal, Kristodas, 24–25
Panchkoti (village name), 57–58
Parashara, 101–2, 106–7
Parsis, 5
Pather Panchali, 130n.39
patriarchy, 9–10, 20–21, 30–31, 129n.25, 129n.27
pedagogy, 10
petitions
Brahmo Marriage Act–related, 5
as method, 70–71, 84–86, 88–89
post-Rebellion, 23, 24–25, 46–48, 138n.4, 138n.5
pre-Rebellion, 23, 45, 125, 133n.84, 137n.2
pro-polygamy, 23, 24, 45, 93
signatories to, 88–89, 125
Tarkavacaspati and, 96, 97–98, 103–4
Phuliya Assemblage, 60–61, 62, 141n.44
poetry, 108
polygamy
abolishing vs. banning of, 138n.6
general vs. Kulin, xiii–xiv, 8
high-caste (*see* Kulinism)
outside Bengal, 85–86
prevalence of, 38, 39–40, 41–42, 68, 75–78, 104, 105, 133n.97, 137n.142, 137n.147, 146n.111
supporters or protectors of, 45, 76, 78, 95–96
terms for, 139n.21
in United States, 1, 2–3
Positivist School, 34
pride, 14, 62, 64–66
Prithu, 11–12
progress, 2–3, 41
property rights, 9–10, 19–20, 132n.71
prostitution, 34–35, 37, 72–73, 74–75, 136n.131, 142n.60, *See also* courtesans
public sphere, 2–3, 5, 9, 22–23, 41–42, 136n.139
punchayets (local committees), 26, 91–92
Puranas, 49, 55, 93, 94–95, 98, 99–100, 104, 105, 108, 109–10, 111, 146n.105, 147n.116
Putitunda (surname), 12

racism, 5
Radhi Brahmins, 130n.38
Radhi Kayasthas, 130n.38
Raghunandana, 141n.50, 146n.103, 146n.105
Ramayana, 55
Rarh, 33, 40, 62–63
Rarhi Brahmins, 33, 127n.7
Ray, Bharatchandra, 105, 110, 111, 143n.68, 143n.70, 147–48n.130
Raychaudhuri, B., 129–30n.32, 130n.36
Raychaudhuri, Tarak Ch., 129–30n.32, 130n.36
Rebellion of 1857, 3–4, 23, 24, 45, 128n.6
recognition, 10, 16–17, 18, 19–20, 30, 37–38
reform, 3–4, 9–10, 20–21, 65, 138n.8, 142n.57
Risley, H. H., 14, 15, 129–30n.32, 130n.44
rites or ritual, 8, 21–22, 82, 93–94, 106, 107, 144n.81
enjoined by Veda, 56, 147n.128
faults, 15
last, 6, 26, 50, 53, 69–70, 82–83, 107
marriage or remarriage, 67, 71–72, 143n.70

performed by Brahmins, 13, 57, 59
of return, 50, 107
Thread Ceremony, 69–70
wife as co-performer of, 82–83
Rohini, 105, 109–10
Roy, Ramaprasad, 23, 45, 133n.88
Roy, Rammohun, 4–5, 10, 20–21, 23, 130n.42, 132n.71, 132n.76, 134n.102, 138n.11, 142n.63

sahamarana. See widow immolation
Said, Edward, 20–21
Samashrami, Satyavrati, 134n.111
Sambandhanirnaya, 33–34, 114, 115, 116, 117, 129–30n.32, 130nn.48–49, 136n.126, 139–40nn.27–28, 140n.41, 141n.44, 144n.79
Sapatni Nataka, 132n.81
Sarkar, Benoy Kumar, 34
Sarvadarshana Samgraha, 135n.121
Second Marriage (*adyarasa*), 78–80
Second-hand Kulins, 68–70, 72, 87, 143n.73
defined, 142n.61
Self-Broken Kulins. *See* Broken Kulins
Sen, Amiya, 131n.61, 141n.48
Sen, Asok, 20–21, 29, 128n.10, 138n.3
Sena dynasty, 12–14, 58–59
Seven Hundred, the, 12, 58, 60, 61–62, 141n.46
sex trafficking, 8–9
Shakespeare, 19
Shakuntala by Kalidasa. *See* Abhijnanashakuntalam by Kalidasa
Shakuntala by Vidyasagar, 18, 131n.62
Shakuntala, 18, 34–35, 36, 105, 110, 111, 131n.62, See also *Abhijnanashakuntalam* by Kalidasa
Shankha-Likhita, 104, 109
Shastras, 45, 46, 99–100
creators of, 48–49, 51–52, 53, 54, 55–56, 93–94, 95, 99–101, 104, 106, 107, 108–10
Dharma rooted in, 48–49
interpretation of, 97–98, 102
kings in, 55–56
life-stages in, 49, 51–52
local or widespread practices vs., 104, 105, 132n.73, 146–47n.114
marriage in, 48–51, 100, 102, 107–8, 109–10
polygamy in, 48–49, 53–55, 56, 93–94, 95–96, 97–100, 101–2, 103, 104, 105, 110, 111
sale of daughters in, 82
shishtachara. See conduct of the learned
Shriharsha (Kulin forebear), 56, 58
Shrotriyas, 13, 17, 59, 60, 61–62, 130–31n.50
sale of daughters by, 82
Shudras, 11–12, 26–27, 49, 138n.13
life stages for, 49
in Manu, 81–51, 107–8, 110–11
Sikhs, 5
Singh, Devnarayan, Raja of Varanasi, 24, 26, 46, 47, 90–92, 138n.4
Sircar, D. C., 139–40n.28
Sita, 34–35, 36
Smriti, 93, 94–95, 98–101, 104, 108, 111, 146–47n.114
Smritichandrika, 108
Smritiratna, Kshetrapal, 93, 94–96, 134n.111, 146n.102
social research, 29
Society for the Protection of the Eternal Dharma, 46–47, 95–96, 97–98, 102, 103–4
sociology, 5–6, 34. *See also* imaginative sociology
Somaprakasha, 102, 146n.109, 147n.118
state intervention, xiii–xiv, 3–5, 23, 25, 41–43, 45, 81–82, 84–85, 128n.6, 128n.8, 145n.94
statistics, xiii, 5–6, 40–41, 128n.15, 137n.140, *See also* Against High-Caste Polygamy: empirical data in
status, 13, 14, 76–77
Stephens, Julia, 128n.11
suicide, 8–9, 134n.102
supersession, 21–22, 50, 54, 95, 107, 139n.16
Suttee. *See* widow immolation

Taittiriya Samhita, 104
Tarkabhushan, Ishvarchandra, 89

Tarkaratna, Ramnarayan, 22–23
Tarkavacaspati, Taranath, xi, 27, 41–42, 96–99, 101–4, 105, 134n.105, 134n.111, 146n.108, 146n.109
Trautmann, Thomas, 129n.30
Tripathi, Amalesh, 128n.9
twice-born classes, 26–27, 49, 50, 82, 107–8, 110–11, 138n.13

Uberoi, Patricia, 137n.143
Udvahatattva, xii–xiii, 49, 54, 63, 114, 139n.26

Vacaspati Mishra, 114, 116
Vaidya, 127n.7
Vaishyas, 11–12, 26–27
  in Daksha, 49
  life stages for, 49
  in Manu, 81–51, 107–8, 110–11
Vallala Sena, 12–14, 22–23, 27–28, 32–33, 58–59, 65, 70–71, 115, 116, 130n.39, 135n.123, 140n.33
Vamana Purana, 49
Vamshajas, 13, 15, 17, 33, 60, 75, 117, 130n.40, 130–31n.50, 141n.46, 141n.47
  daughters of, 60, 62, 67–68, 82
  Kulins as or become, 33, 59, 61–62
  origin of, 60
  types of, 60
  wealthy, 17, 67–68, 69–70
  wives purchased by, 82, 144n.85
vamshavali, 32. *See also* genealogies
Varanasi, 6, 16
Varanasi, Raja of. *See* Singh, Devnarayan
Varendra Brahmins, 130n.38
Varnaparichay, 10
Vashishtha, 101–2
Vasudeva, 105, 109–10
Vedagarbha (Kulin forebear), 56, 58
Vedaratna, Narayan, 93, 146n.102
Vedas, 12, 49, 50, 56, 98, 99–100, 104, 108–9, 111, 147n.128
Vedavyasa, 101–2
Vena, 11–12
Victoria, Queen, 37–38, 86–87, 145n.95
Vidhava-vivaha. *See* Hindu Widow Marriage (*Vidhava-vivaha*)
Vidhisvarupa Vichara, 113
Vidyabhushan, Dwarkanath, xi, 27, 96, 104, 105–6, 108–9, 147n.118, 147n.127
Vidyadarshan, 21–22
Vidyanidhi, Lalmohan, 33–34, 114, 115, 116, 117, 129–30n.32, 130nn.48–49, 136n.126, 139–40nn.27–28, 140n.41, 141n.44, 144n.79
Vidyasagar, Ishvarchandra
  authority of, 2–3
  autobiography of, 19
  biographical details for, 1–2, 6
  as Brahmin or Kulin, 2–3, 8, 9–10, 12, 142n.65
  as committee member, 25–26, 27, 30, 134n.100, 144n.82
  daughters of, 144n.89
  Declaratory Law supported by, 143n.75
  education of, 4, 32
  as Hindu lawmaker or pundit, 27–28, 135n.113
  moral vision of, 18, 30–31
  opposition to, 2–3, 144n.83
  post-orientalist critiques of, 20–21, 132n.73
  as reformer, 8, 9–10, 20–21, 29
  reputation of, 1–2, 10, 24–25, 42–43
  translations by, 19, 32
  travel by, 143n.69
  views on respectability of, 143n.74
  works by, xii, 18, 29, 32, 135n.121
Vidyasundara. *See* Ray, Bharatchandra
Vikrampur, 32–33, 57, 89
virgins, 140n.35, *See also* daughters
Vishnu Samhita, 53, 54, 101–2
voluntary duties, 26–27
Vrishali, 63
Vyasa, 64

widow immolation, 4, 21, 22, 86, 133n.92
widow marriage, 4, 5, 6, 9–10, 43, 146–47n.114
widow marriage campaign, 129n.23, 134n.103
widows, 1–2
  child or young, 8
  high-caste, 129n.22

inheritance rights of, 9–10, 19–20
polygamous, 8
in Varanasi, 16
Wilson, Horace Hayman, 4
Wise, James, 141n.49, 141n.55, 142n.58
wives
adulterous or wanton, 72, 91, 107
barren, 26, 50, 51–52, 53, 54–55, 91, 93–94, 107, 108, 139n.24
diseased, 91, 93–94
lunatic, 91
in name only, 8–9, 68–69, 79
outcaste, 91
reside with husband's family, 70–71
reside with natal relatives, 16–18, 35, 68–69, 70, 79
ritual duties of, 26, 82
as symbolic and material assets, 17–18
women
American, 1
authors, 128n.7
Kulin, 1–2, 8–9, 10, 13–14, 16–18, 28, 70–71, 86–87
Shastras on, 106–7
unmarried, 63–64, 65–66, 83–84
as victims, 1–2, 48
"weaker than men," 45
"women's question," 4, 42, 128n.12, 137n.144

Yajnavalkya, 53, 98, 100, 101–2, 146n.103
Yama, 63
Yogeshvara Pandit, 62, 141n.47
Yudhishthira, 98, 100
yugas, 27, 110, 134nn.103–4, *See also* Kali Yuga